Representing Public Credit

T0270745

Public credit was controversial in seventeenth- and eighteenth-century England. It entailed new ways of thinking about the individual in relation to the State and was for many reasons a site of cultural negotiation and debate. At the same time, it required commitment from participants in order to function. Some of the debates relating to public credit, whose success was tied up in the way it was represented, find their way into contemporary fiction – in particular the eighteenth-century novel.

This book reads eighteenth-century fiction alongside works of political economy in order to offer a new perspective on credible commitment and the rise of a credit economy facilitated by public credit. Works by authors such as Daniel Defoe, Samuel Richardson, and Frances Burney are explored alongside lesser-known fictional texts, including some early it-narratives and novels of sensibility, to give a fully rounded view of the perception of public credit within England and its wider cultural and social implications. Strategies for representing public credit, the book argues, can be seen as contributing to the development of the English novel, a type of fiction whose emphasis on the individual can also be read as helping to produce a certain type of person, the modern financial subject.

This interdisciplinary book draws from economic history and literary/cultural studies in order to make connections between the development of finance and an important facet of modern Western culture, the novel.

Natalie Roxburgh is a research fellow at the University of Oldenburg, Germany.

Routledge Frontiers of Political Economy

Representing Public Credit

Credible commitment, fiction, and the rise of the financial subject

Natalie Roxburgh

Routledge
Taylor & Francis Group

LONDON AND NEW YORK

First published 2016
by Routledge

2 Park Square, Milton Park, Abingdon, Oxfordshire OX14 4RN
52 Vanderbilt Avenue, New York, NY 10017

Routledge is an imprint of the Taylor & Francis Group, an informa business

First issued in paperback 2020

British Library Cataloguing in Publication Data
A catalogue record for this book is available from the British Library

Library of Congress Cataloging-in-Publication Data
Roxburgh, Natalie, author.
Representing public credit : credible commitment, fiction, and the rise of
the financial subject / Natalie Roxburgh.
    pages cm
    Includes bibliographical references and index.
    1. Finance, Public–Great Britain–History–18th century. 2. Credit–
Great Britain–History–18th century. 3. Finance–Great Britain–History–
18th century. 4. Finance in literature–History–18th century. I. Title.
    HJ1013.R69 2016
    336.4109'033–dc23   2015029372

ISBN: 978-1-138-18254-7 (hbk)
ISBN: 978-0-367-59724-5 (pbk)

Typeset in Times New Roman
by Wearset Ltd, Boldon, Tyne and Wear

Contents

Figures

Acknowledgments

I am both lucky and privileged to have met so many wonderful interlocutors in the process of researching and writing *Representing Public Credit*. It takes a village to write a book.

This book started as a dissertation, and therefore I would first of all like to thank my dissertation committee (my generous advisor, Michael McKeon, and insightful readers, Lynn Festa and Richard Dienst) as well as fellow students in the Graduate Program of Literatures in English at Rutgers University in New Brunswick. As a graduate student, I was fortunate enough to take part in the "Problems in Historical Interpretation" Dissertation Writing Seminar in 2010 held at Rutgers (sponsored by the Mellon Foundation) as well as the "Changing Conceptions of Property" Seminar at the Folger Shakespeare Library in Washington, DC, in 2009. Colleagues in both of these seminars had a big influence on the development of this project. I would also like to thank my parents for being supportive of me during the dissertation-writing process, especially during my final year.

Representing Public Credit evolved into its book form with the help of colleagues and friends in my European network. In particular, thanks go to Riccardo Capoferro for leading me through the daunting dissertation-to-book process and being an engaged critical reader. Anna Auguscik has been a diligent and patient reader and also a supportive friend. I am indebted to colleagues at the Money, Power, and Print colloquium held in Leuven in 2014 – especially to Anne Murphy, who has supported this project since its dissertation form, Charles Larkin, for keeping me connected to present-day questions and discussions, and Christine Desan, whose generous sharing of insights was instrumental. I am also grateful to friends and colleagues from the annual Critical Finance Studies conferences, especially to Emily Rosamond, Helen Paul, and Joyce Goggin. Completion of this book would not have been possible without the institutional support from the Fiction Meets Science research group (sponsored by the Volkswagen Stiftung) and the University of Oldenburg. I would especially like to thank Anton Kirchhofer and Susan M. Gaines, who made it possible. Finally, thanks go to Martin Ritter as well as friends in Oldenburg for being understanding and compassionate while I finished this book.

Another version of Chapter 3 appeared in *Eighteenth-Century Fiction* in 2012 with the title, "Rethinking Female Virtue through Richardson's Domestic Accounting." I thank the journal for allowing me to reprint a revised version of that article.

Introduction

There are few things, that are incapable of being represented by fiction.
Thomas Hobbes, *Leviathan* (1651)

This book was conceived in order to make sense of a concept that many eighteenth-century writers found difficult: *public credit*. Public credit, in its most familiar definition, is the debt owed by a central government, or the debt issued by a central government for purchase by interested parties backed by promise-to-pay coupons. What made the English version of public credit so unique was a set of technologies that were unprecedented at the time. The Crown, needing to borrow money to finance imperial wars, contracted with private businesses that consolidated private creditors – financial actors – looking to benefit. Public credit was seen as a threat to those not already participating in the world of finance and was therefore routinely subject to debate and critique. These eighteenth-century debates will likely resonate with readers today, as they reflect fears that finance is ultimately a rigged game designed to enrich a few at the expense of the many. There was, therefore, also a social dimension to these financial innovations, which this book explores by examining eighteenth-century fiction.

When one imagines credit today, one perhaps thinks of a fair system mediated by accounting and other proto-scientific practices backed by institutions.[1] However, this is very much a modern mindset. Early public credit required a feedback loop in order to function: As long as there was commitment from the public, it worked; and as long as it worked, there was commitment. Because many saw this new form of credit as serving particular political and financial interests – of the City, the Bank of England, the stock market, etc. – there were many detractors whose writings suggested that 'monied interests' posed a threat to traditional social values, which tended to be based in landed interests. The premise of this book is that the discursive terrain of fiction – and especially the novel – is one place where the epistemological, social, and economic consequences of public credit are explored and where the 'public' of public credit is both simulated and promoted.

The development of public credit had already been underway in the seventeenth century,[2] but many scholars point to the establishment of the Bank of

England in 1694 as a significant turning point.[3] The Bank was established as a short-term solution for both increasing the money supply by issuing paper credit instruments and also financing wars that protected and promoted commerce. Public credit facilitated through the Bank may have been a non-permanent solution, but it became increasingly stable as the century progressed. By the nineteenth century, when the Bank gained its monopoly, it even facilitated the predominant form of capital, as Bank of England notes – partly owing to their unique combining of the government bond with the bill of exchange – rose very quickly in the hierarchy of monetary forms, becoming the unit of account for all transactions.[4] Public credit allowed for paper money to proliferate as a trustworthy medium of exchange, resolving problems inherent to both coined money, which was often clipped and therefore subject to doubt, and private credit, which meant evaluating a person's reputation.[5] The rise of public credit – which implies trust in government institutions – allowed modern money to be defined as an impersonal mechanism that serves as a store of value, a medium of exchange, a standard of deferred payment, a measurement of value, and the unit of account.

While there is evidence that public credit had begun to function in the 1660s, there was still much resistance throughout the eighteenth century, partly because of older social value systems and partly because there was little incentive for non-investors to think of their worlds in financial terms: in terms of risk and uncertainty, in terms of accounting and credit, and in terms of practices of consumption. Eighteenth-century fiction, especially the novel, accommodates financial ways of thinking to those not already attuned to the world of finance. Fiction, I am suggesting, plays a role in what historians have identified as credible commitment.

Credible commitment, a term used to describe the way in which people come to trust their institutions, was made more pertinent within scholarly discourse through the publication of Douglass C. North and Barry R. Weingast's seminal article "Constitutions and Commitment: The Evolution of Institutions Governing Public Choice in Seventeenth-Century England" in 1989 in *The Journal of Economic History*. North and Weingast's paper discusses the consequences of the political changes that occurred around the time of the Glorious Revolution in 1688–9, and it argues that this period ushered in a new ideological climate favorable to capitalism and hostile to State intervention in the economy.[6] The argument in this article associated credible commitment with the legal protection of creditors and taxpayers, a commitment to servicing the National Debt, and an idea of public credit that emerged around 1688.[7] The notion is important because what is at stake is that citizens trust government institutions enough to invest in them. But this comes with a caveat that institutions, at the same time, "limit economic intervention and allow private rights and markets to prevail in large segments of the economy."[8] The credible commitment thesis is, therefore, tied up with important questions about the relationship between the State and participants in the economy at large.

What discussions of this thesis have not yet accounted for is the way in which those who would have had no reason or incentive to see themselves as tied together as economic players became interested in financial matters. What is at stake has to do with the separation out of the public and private spheres and a need for finance to penetrate the latter. Fictional texts allow the outskirt segments – the intimate recesses of the domestic household – to become part of the economy at large insofar as they acclimate the reader to a new world of finance. Randy Martin calls this process "financialization," and he argues this is a product of the late twentieth century, describing techniques by which "personal finance becomes a way in which ordinary people are invited to participate in that larger abstraction called the economy."[9] This invitation to participate, exacerbated in recent times by mobile phone banking apps and day trading, was a long time coming, which is why I refer to the individual characters featured in novels (as well as the implied readers) as emergent 'financial subjects.'

Representing Public Credit attempts to contribute to the scholarly discussion of the credible commitment thesis, which so far mainly takes place in the disciplines of history and the social sciences, by examining fictional literary texts in the eighteenth century through a literary-historicist analytical framework. As scholars have already been keen to point out, credible commitment does not merely happen 'from above' through changes in political or legal institutions[10] but also 'from below,' insofar as terminologies, ideologies, and ways of thinking transform themselves. By attempting an interdisciplinary method in which I weave together historical accounts of the institutional changes as well as the intellectual or imaginative factors that contributed to credible commitment, this project provides a clearer sense of a larger transformation – what historians often describe as a transition from feudalism to capitalism.[11] In so doing, I hope to further contribute to the scholarly discussion on the eighteenth-century novel, a new genre that emerges in tandem with the rise of public credit during what P.G.M. Dickson calls "the Financial Revolution in England."[12]

Analyzing discursive exchanges pertaining to the concept of *public credit* from a literary-historicist perspective serves as an important complement to histories of institutions and the ideologies that accompanied them. Public credit "was not only linked to representative politics – credit fluctuated with political power – but it was itself a representative system, based in part on paper money, exchequer bills, and stocks that had representative rather than intrinsic value."[13] Rather than using terms that are legible to us today from the perspective of a more fully-fledged financial capitalism and democracy with very different stakes, eighteenth-century understandings of what was entailed by the term *public credit* provides a sharper picture of what is at stake in the credible commitment thesis. The debate about credible commitment can also enrich our understanding of literary history insofar as it became necessary to get individuals with economic interests to hold a government to account,[14] and an economically defined sort of individual is what gives rise to the novel.[15] Literary history also helps to provide a historical context for Charles Taylor's "economic model," a social order in which people see themselves as mutually benefiting each other, which he associates with modernity.[16]

A key virtue of *Representing Public Credit* is that it helps to historicize the rise of the 'economic individual' identified by Ian Watt and others, which I have called the 'financial subject' since it is finance (the rules of credit and debt) and not merely basic economics (household economy, barter, or exchange) that is engendered by this radically new form of credit. While at the beginning of the century, commitment is between the State and the individual investor, by the latter half of the century – especially in the wake of the Seven Years War – commitment works differently. As Peter de Bolla points out, supporting public credit during and after the war also means supporting a healthy, wealthy nation.[17] In effect, individuals gradually came to be seen as representatives of public credit. But this did not eradicate social concern. Indeed, many novels express a worry about the social implications of public credit even while they reflect acceptance of change. Using the evolution of public credit in particular (and not only 'credit' or the 'credit economy') as a site of contemporary discourse sheds new light on the various genres of fiction, both canonical texts as well as lesser-known ones, that emerge in the eighteenth century.

A key rhetorical strategy for eighteenth-century writers advocating in favor of public credit was to argue that it serves the public good and is not merely in the service of private financial or political interests. This book emphasizes one institution in particular, the Bank of England, in order to describe the process by which people came to imagine that the State's interaction with public creditors served the public good. One consequence of this sort of imaginary work, which I argue is woven into the early development of the novel, was that people were, by the end of the eighteenth century, able to take on the role of what James Macdonald calls the "citizen creditor."[18] The Bank's way of presenting itself as being for the public good was to represent itself as being disinterested, which it went to great lengths to achieve. Following both Marieke de Goede's and Mary Poovey's respective assertions that finance is an interpretive and textual practice[19] whose contractual, rule-governed practices "tended to *create* what [they purport] to describe,"[20] I read the Bank as a central text whose function is to represent disinterestedness. This makes it a very modern institution.

Central banking, which is in its de jure form a twentieth-century innovation, tends to be important de facto at critical points in history when States or monarchs require an entity to finance activity beyond the ability of the Treasury. Central banking's role in credible commitment is particularly applicable in the wake of the global financial crisis of 2007–8, which was to a large degree a product of policies enacted in the 1980s that downplayed the necessity of regulation and the participation of the State in the economy, with the assumption that economics is a neutral science and not subject to political influence. For some commentators, this crisis was a long time coming and occurred due to the way economic theory in the United States purged itself of institutionalism over the course of the twentieth century.[21] In this recent case, the United States Federal Reserve was required to serve as a political entity rather than as a freestanding agent in an economy: It had to serve as a regulator to the economic institutions that had proven themselves to be not at all self-sufficient.[22] The Fed bailed out Wall Street rather than Main Street, a decision that would have not been possible through democratic political processes alone. Indeed, if this had been done through political mechanisms, it might be difficult to imagine that constituents would have believed the government was acting for the public good.

There is a historical precedent for this, which is important for this book's central argument. In the political aftermath of the English Civil War, the Crown, feeling itself approaching crisis, was in no position to employ a fiscal-political solution (i.e., taxation) for funding the Nine Years War in 1694. The solution was to use a bank, a chartered private company that would act as a partner to the Crown. In so doing, the Crown could solve financial problems without having to make disadvantageous political decisions. In contrast to modern central banks, however, many people in the eighteenth century did not see banks as politically neutral institutions.

The notion that public credit was fair and trustworthy, subject to no particular political authority, was not apparent to many contemporaries, but it can be seen as part of a general process of what Michael McKeon calls the "devolution of absolutism."[23] When one examines contemporary debates, a question that arises is whether the 'public' of public credit was really built up of individual interests (as the liberal tradition argues) or whether a government's capacity to revolutionize (and regulate) finance was ultimately the mechanism that drove the development of the economy by producing individuals with interests. The answer to this question, like the division between economics and politics in general, might be somewhat murky. But what does emerge quite clearly is a notion that, whatever it was before the Financial Revolution, the 'individual' comes out of the period as a financial subject whose interests are aligned with and secured by a State.

To grapple with what is at stake in the credible commitment thesis, one must consider several histories simultaneously. A complete or totalizing exegesis is probably not possible within the scope of a single scholarly monograph.[24] The key questions that inform this study are the following: How did William III's initial loan to finance war transform itself into a permanent system of credit that implicated (at least in theory) all members of the public (turning people into citizen-creditors) by the end of the century? How did the Bank of England, a scheme that was initially set up to be temporary, transform the way the public perceived it from a private company with particular ties to the Whig party to a public entity that served all interests and therefore the public good? And what is the relationship between the public sphere, in which the various fictional genres – especially the novel – evolve and establish themselves, and public credit? This last, most important, question requires elaboration, for it entails a link between the ideals and practices of the public sphere and a new experience of credit. Both the public sphere and public credit are contractual, rationally and empirically oriented, envision a super-individual system, and require an experience of temporality that is not natural but conditioned by printed communication. Fiction does not merely reflect upon, embrace, or rail against contemporary finance: It also assists it by transforming what it means to be an individual subject whose interests are tied to the State.

Literature review

Admittedly, *Representing Public Credit* enters a crowded field. Throughout the latter half of the twentieth century, scholars working in literary studies have read the development of eighteenth-century fiction alongside the Financial Revolution. Many critics – following Watt's *The Rise of the Novel* (1957) – argue that the novel came into being with the rise of individualism, an ideology that emphasizes the moral value and worth of the individual. At the same time, scholars note that eighteenth-century fiction often reveals a sort of cultural wonder – or dread – regarding the radical economic transformation that took place around contemporaries as they lived their lives.[25] Part of this has to do with a clash of cultures. The novel, in effect, emerges during a time when financial capitalism (and its supporting ideologies) was becoming more important to cultural practice even while older cultural hierarchies (and their respective ideologies) persisted, which is related to a key argument McKeon makes in *The Origins of the English Novel* (1987). Studying finance and fiction in the eighteenth-century is somewhat difficult because, without going fairly deep into the historical moment, one often feels oneself to be swimming in a sea of discursive contradiction. McKeon's work, often cited in this project, helps one wade through this murkiness by showing how older and newer ways of thinking – ideologies – confront each other in fiction by relating "questions of truth" to "questions of virtue," giving rise to the new genre of the novel.

Critics and literary historians have made headway in honing more specific questions that arise when newer forms of credit come up against traditional modes of social trust. More broadly, quantitative or economic credit is differentiated from qualitative credit (or, to put it simply, trust that obtains in traditional social relations such as the family). I will provide a brief overview of these works here but will return to most of them in more detail. Laura Brown's *Ends of Empire* (1993) examines female writers in the context of mercantile capitalist ideology. Colin Nicholson's *Writing and the Rise of Finance* (1994), mostly focusing on Jonathan Swift and Alexander Pope, deals with the cultural opposition to the type of cultural changes entailed by the inauguration of the permanent National Debt. Sandra Sherman's *Finance and Fictionality* (1996) provides a reading of Daniel Defoe's oeuvre that suggests his writings reflect a new economic environment in which credit was as fungible as – and also determined by – fiction. James Thompson's *Models of Value* (1996) argues that the early novel explores values emphasized by political economy when the crucial instruments of public credit (such as paper money) in England first were created. Deidre Shauna Lynch's *The Economy of Character* (1998) discusses the emergence of characters in fiction as having come into being alongside new forms of finance, such as credit and currency, and argues that debates about character allow for social distinction in a new commercial culture. Catherine Ingrassia's *Authorship, Commerce, and Gender* (1998) explores narrative fiction in the context of paper credit (and the changing conception of property entailed by it) especially insofar as it led to the emergence of authorial personae of women in the marketplace.

Martha Woodmansee and Mark Osteen's edited collection, titled *The New Economic Criticism* (1999), similarly argues that "the science of political economy emerged concurrently with the rise of the quintessentially bourgeois literary form, the novel" and that "[l]iterary texts, and particularly novels ... both produce and respond to reformulations of the nature and representation of credit."[26] Finally, Margot C. Finn's *The Character of Credit* (2003) provides a truly interdisciplinary reading of financial and emergent fictional texts to argue that personal character prevailed as a way of ascertaining someone's creditworthiness despite conflicting legal and social structures in the wake of the Financial Revolution. These works form an important basis for the present study, which asks similar questions by examining discourses on public credit in particular rather than credit in general.

Given the impact of the newer forms of credit illuminated by these studies in finance and fiction, one begins to see how a new vocabulary of terms emerges in the wake of the Financial Revolution: credit versus trust, public credit versus private credit, reputation, character, paper money, accounting, and so on. An analysis of public credit in particular rather than credit in general allows for new readings of canonical texts because it invites one to acknowledge the process of negotiation required, as public credit in the early eighteenth century was vigorously debated and not a stable entity. Therefore, while this book enters a crowded field, it also sheds new light on the particular texts that have been covered by this field as well as explores texts that have not yet received much critical attention.

That being said, literature scholars have also already examined eighteenth-century fiction in relation to public credit in particular. Patrick Brantlinger's *Fictions of State* (1996) argues that public credit required a new notion of State, one that was produced through writing. He says that

> [p]ublic credit ... is an ideological, economic corollary of nationalism, patriotism, public opinion, and kindred terms. Public credit is not a concept that stands alone; it is relational, comparative, and thoroughly, reciprocally interwoven in other social and ideological processes such as imperialism, capitalist development or modernization, and the postmodern mushrooming of the global debt crisis.[27]

Brantlinger's work draws an important connection between fiction (including the fictions inherent in political economy) and the State, from the eighteenth century to the 1990s. His study is a great influence on this book, which seeks to develop more specifically a way of understanding how public credit, which is ultimately ideological, comes to be a stabilized and stabilizing entity.

Mary Poovey's *Genres of the Credit Economy* (2008) also examines public credit in particular. Credit is a form of contractual writing, and it also functions as money through the way it becomes "naturalized" over time.[28] Her interdisciplinary project exposes the long process by which credit instruments came to be part of everyday life, transforming social values in the eighteenth and nineteenth centuries. Poovey's study shows how the fictive work of credit instruments has an important relationship to the rise of literary value, and she calls on critics to reflect on what it means to study *literature*, a concept which comes from insisting on a separation of economic and literary writing. Poovey's project helps one to register the various forms of writing that emerge through and alongside public credit, arguing (as in her *History of the Modern Fact* [1998]) that double-entry bookkeeping is fundamental.

In his *The Secret History of Domesticity* (2005), which uses the concepts of *public* and *private* to analyze eighteenth-century culture more generally, McKeon identifies a fundamental component of credit when he argues that

> what made credit so mysterious was that its objective possession depended on its subjective perception: the public is to the private as objective capital is to subjective credit. The problem of credit – the fact that its highly consequential actuality is grounded in an insubstantial virtuality – therefore makes it ideally suited to narrative virtualization.[29]

McKeon's understanding of credit as an "insubstantial virtuality" that renders itself suitable for narrative forms suggests a link to other virtual entities, such as the public sphere where these narratives – fictions – are read and discussed by the reading public. In both the public sphere and public credit, there is a contractual background, an assumption that if one behaves well, the whole system will thrive and thus others will behave well in return. What behaving well actually entails – for which there was by no means a cultural consensus – is what works of fiction, especially those that came to be designated as novels, explore.

The public sphere and public credit share common roots, both institutional and ideological. Public credit is an important vector for the creation of a polity insofar as it implies the creation of a State – through a structured network of owners, domestic and international – as separate from a sovereign ruler. To discuss public credit *represented* in texts in order to suggest that each person is also a *representative* of public credit also implies the emergence of a social imaginary that allows individuals to believe that by acting on their own interests they are participating for the sake of the public good. I would like to emphasize here that this type of thinking emerges in the eighteenth century after certain ideologies prevail over others.

This project will attempt to link these insights to what Taylor, borrowing from Michael Warner's *Letters of the Republic* (1990), has identified as the "modern social imaginary," meaning that people develop a self-understanding through the modern economy, the public sphere, and the practices and outlooks of democratic self-rule.[30] Public credit seems central to the "economic model" Taylor discusses, for it is an entity that requires individual efforts and commitments that presuppose beneficial interdependence. But it is also a model that comes into being with a struggle.

Emphasizing public credit – as opposed to credit in general or private credit in particular – sheds new light on the way novels engage in, adjust to, and produce a financially literate public sphere. The broader thesis, one that likely had a great influence on Taylor's *Modern Social Imaginaries* (2004), is by now familiar. Jürgen Habermas' *The Structural Transformation of the Public Sphere* (published in 1962 but only translated into English in 1989) might be said to have opened this mode of inquiry with its investigation of what he calls the "bourgeois public sphere," which

> may be conceived above all as the sphere of private people come together as a public; they soon claimed the public sphere regulated from above against the public authorities themselves, to engage them in a debate over the general rules governing relations in the basically privatized but publicly relevant sphere of commodity exchange and social labor.[31]

The imagination of individuals united as a public through print, the argument goes, meant that people began to envision a public in which they participated. Habermas makes a connection between print and an imagination of a community whose political authority no longer resides in an absolute monarch, but rather in a democracy fueled by rational-critical debate in a public sphere. Benedict Anderson's *Imagined Communities* (1983) is similar in its overall thesis, but it argues that the origins of nationalism can be accounted for through a concept of an imagined community: "It is *imagined* because the members of even the smallest nation will never know most of their fellow-members, meet them, or even hear of them, yet in the minds of each lives the image of their communication."[32] More explicitly than Habermas, who has also been taken to task for his belief that the public sphere is somehow inherently democratic, Anderson provides an important connection between print and the rise of the State. It requires people to know one another by proxy – through new print media, which, as Christian Thorne argues, is hardly intrinsically democratic, but wrought with advantages for some and disadvantages for others.[33]

To some degree, Taylor's category of the "social imaginary" also assumes a level playing field, as it describes the way people conceive of social surroundings, a "common understanding that makes possible common practices and a widely shared sense of legitimacy."[34] This comes with a different attitude toward society, as "the new understanding of the individual has as its inevitable flip side a new understanding of sociality, the society of mutual benefit, whose functional differentiations are ultimately contingent on whose members are fundamentally equal."[35] When one accounts for this model by examining the rise of public credit, the more recent, modern notion of individualism seems quite different. That is to say, when we read works such as Bernard de Mandeville's *The Fable of the Bees* (1705/14), the idea of the individual implicit in "private vices, public benefits" is one that both benefits from and is a benefit to others partly because of the virtuous operations of the State, which is very different from the view of individualism that minimizes the role of political actors. The early eighteenth-century individual is a precursor to the later notion that is considered by nineteenth- and twentieth-century political economists to be the independent agent or 'invisible hand' of the marketplace. For this type of interested, politically detached, individual to emerge, credible commitment had to happen, which implies not only trust in the State but also a notion that one's interests are tied to it.

Because traditional social hierarchies are often effaced in the more modern understanding of the individual, studying finance and fiction requires one to historicize the process by which the individual emerges alongside the State. This has implications for critics seeking to understand individualism through the rise of the novel, as those following Watt do, as well as for scholars working on finance and fiction in the eighteenth century. A newer economic model provides a new model of order, but because it has to do with how individuals engage with each other in an imagined collective, the transition from credit as trust to credit as a number calculated through a proto-scientific method needs further elaboration.

This leaves one with the need to elaborate what the term *proto-scientific* means. In different ways, both Joyce Appleby's *Economic Thought and Ideology in Seventeenth-Century England* (1978) and Mary Poovey's *A History of the Modern Fact* (1998) emphasize the way emergent political economy came to provide the public with a notion that every interest was being served through the perceived neutrality and objectivity of emergent scientific method. Appleby argues that the "scientific mode of observation and analysis, once adopted, created its own demands, and economic reasoning became integral to the modern transformation of England."[36] For Poovey, the descriptive nature of political economy, grounded in double-entry bookkeeping that serves as a prototype for the modern "fact," ensured that people believed the workings of the economy were politically neutral.[37] Political economy served as a written discourse with a neutral and descriptive form that stemmed from systematic accounting practices, presenting itself in such a way that people could believe that the State's role in organizing economic activity was disinterested, thereby suggesting that it overcame problems of competing political interests that helped fuel civil wars in the seventeenth century. Jacob Soll argues that accounting is central to the modern State to the degree that, when the mechanics of accounting break down, social and political crises ensue.[38] This book suggests that accounting's role in creating and maintaining the modern State is important but not to be overemphasized, namely because there is a difference between accounting and the public perception of accounting. Representational strategies for conveying disinterestedness go beyond the ledger.

Following de Goede's call to read finance as a set of discursive practices rather than following an "uncritical acceptance of the categories and containers of value offered by the financial industry,"[39] this study challenges the exclusive centrality of bookkeeping in the Financial Revolution while at the same time acknowledging that it was an important factor. Given the complicated attitudes toward accounting in this period, it is difficult to assume that contemporaries would have been able to take on today's attitudes toward quantification or systems of bookkeeping as a shorthand for truth and virtue. Poovey tells an important story about what came after the Financial Revolution – namely, the way accounting began to serve as an origin of conjectural theory and statistics. But the way that we moderns understand accounting's application to earlier eighteenth-century cultural outlooks requires a bit of revision. People in the eighteenth century, especially those who had nothing to do with commerce, had to be trained to align accounting with truth and virtue. From the perspective of today's science-driven society, it is perhaps tempting to conclude that this proto-scientific thinking, grounded in a politically neutral system of double-entry bookkeeping, self-sufficiently and unproblematically ensured a transition to the modern economy and the theories that accompany it. A short historical overview of some of the problems entailed by public credit – as a system of finance and not one of basic exchange – puts pressure on this notion. I provide this overview in the first chapter.

In order to address what I perceive to be a critical gap in accommodating previous scholarship on finance and fiction to the problem of credible commitment, I have chosen a set of texts that have not yet been read together. In one sense, many of the texts I have chosen serve as the ideological inverse of the first study I cited, Nicholson's *Writing and the Rise of Finance*. Whereas Nicholson analyses what he calls "Opposition writers" who struggle with the "task of resisting forces apparently moving beyond any civic control," the texts I have chosen accommodate themselves to these forces even while attempting to preserve an ethos of traditional culture.[40] This decision was made because key to my overall thesis is the notion that the proto-scientific thinking we now associate with a credit system had to be accommodated to traditional value systems. That is to say, public credit had to be made personal even while it had to proclaim itself as an impersonal, politically neutral system of linking strangers together. In addition, writers had to find a way of resolving a contradiction arising from the presence of competing and contradictory ideologies.

This study is organized in three main parts. The introduction provides a way for understanding public credit as having emerged out of a general transformation to economically constituted property, giving way to an "economic model." This required a notion that a State's function is to serve the 'public good.' Part I examines the way the 'public good' gets taken up in writings supporting public credit. Public credit is not only configured through accounting, for it also requires fictions – representational strategies – that convey disinterestedness. Part II examines various types of fiction that take on some of the cultural conflicts resulting from the rise of public credit. I compare their formal strategies to get a sense of how the novel differentiates itself from other forms of fiction in the later eighteenth century, arguing that the virtualization of trust, new to contemporaries, puts additional pressure on the novel's generic concerns, which can be seen as an extension of the representational questions I discuss in Part I.

Selection of texts

As a literary scholar, I see my task as studying literary representation and the means by which representation is achieved. Fiction trains individuals to embrace the virtuality of public credit by the way it represents character, probabilistic thinking, and the development of narrative suspense, producing new values that accommodate readers to a virtual economy in the making. I employ textual analysis to substantiate this claim, since it is important to the overall argument that the language and discourses of the time are taken on their own terms.

Writers in the early decades of the late seventeenth and early eighteenth centuries engaged in debates over whether public credit served the public good or whether it served particular political interests. I provide a background for this debate by discussing factors that allow for emergence of an "economic model," or an economy of mutual benefit, which had yet to become a cultural consensus in this period. I identify five distinct but overlapping historical contexts:

1   the emergence of economically constructed property in relation to new theories of the State;
2   the ascendancy of individual interest as a new organizing principle;
3   the development of credit money as a contract between the individual and the State;
4   questions of credible commitment with regard to the Bank of England; and
5   the functions of public opinion and disinterestedness in garnering support for public credit.

These contexts provide a framework for understanding controversies surrounding public credit as well as offer insights on how writers saw it best to represent it.

Part I deals with the feedback loop between commitment from public creditors and the State. I discuss writings in the period between 1710 and just after the South Sea Bubble in 1720 in order to examine the way public credit was a posed as a political question rather than a self-sufficiently functional machine of State. The second chapter emphasizes the representational techniques used to create support – commitment – for public credit. I begin by examining a period when public credit was particularly threatened owing to a change of political power from the Whigs to the Tories in 1710, and I focus on the economic pamphlets of Daniel Defoe, who was commissioned by Robert Harley to advocate for public credit. The chapter compares the way Defoe attempts to produce commitment in these pamphlets to his treatment of social and economic issues in his fictions. I use the term *credible framing* to describe Defoe's representational strategies because an outside authority governs the way an inside account is to be read. I discuss the South Sea Bubble to account for Defoe's rhetorical techniques in *The Compleat English Tradesman* (1726), in which Defoe insists that the way public credit is managed has nothing to do with the whims of stockjobbers. He distinguishes between virtuous accounting and using the ledger at the expense of the public good. Public credit, like private credit, is sustained though virtuous management, an idea that finds its way into his novels.

In the third chapter, I turn to two canonical works of the eighteenth century, providing a close reading of Samuel Richardson's *Pamela* (1740) and *Clarissa*

(1747–8) in order to discuss the way the internalization of the new form of credit works within a cultural context. Richardson, like Defoe before him, domesticates double-entry bookkeeping in an attempt to represent the virtue of his protagonists. But, as is the case in the Bank of England, the accounting ledger always requires a supplement – a fiction that comes from another type of authority – in order to be trusted, which is evidenced by what has been called "the *Pamela* controversy" which led to a debate about fictional aesthetics. I read *Pamela* and *Clarissa* next to some of the problems the Bank of England had to confront in order to reflect on the way questions about credibility become formally internalized in fiction. *Virtue*, the operative term in this debate, shifts in meaning. This has an impact on the development of the novel, for virtue becomes virtual through representational strategies.

Part II deals with a second feedback loop, namely what Christine Desan calls a "fiat loop," referring to the fact that Bank of England notes were from early on accepted as payment for taxes.[41] Here, the textual analysis highlights an intellectual and ideological shift in understanding money and credit, one which renders trust virtual. This section's contribution has to do with the transformation required for moving from traditional social obligation to imagining an economy in which individual abstract players come to trust one another, an important step for revisiting the credible commitment thesis as well as for accounting for the rise of public credit in particular.

The fourth chapter addresses the fact that the general attitude toward public credit changed after the Seven Years War. As a functional system, it was no longer in crisis. However, writers expressed concern that it was radically transforming social life. Credit began to mediate between people who did not know each other and, in so doing, virtualized trust. I provide a close reading of two financial 'it-narratives' published around the time of the Seven Years War (1754–63) that explicitly link money (specie and credit, respectively) to print circulation. What one observes when comparing two very popular examples – Charles Johnstone's *Adventures of a Guinea* (1760–5) and Thomas Bridges' *Adventures of a Bank-note* (1770–1) – is two distinct but nonetheless related notions of money, which means that these texts also implicitly (and sometimes explicitly) ask the question of how public credit functions. Bridges' and Johnstone's respective it-narratives mark a transition in the wake of the Financial Revolution, helping an emergent reading public to understand how money (both coined and paper) circulates as well as commenting on some of the consequences of this transition. These two literary texts reflect the debate between the earlier notion that money is a corrupting force and the idea that Bank-authorized paper money is a positive development for a healthy, wealthy State. While it is tempting to suppose that these fictions merely reflect the contemporary debate, I will suggest that by simulating a public through fictional narrative strategies, these two narratives – within a then hugely popular but now practically extinct genre that dates back to *The Tatler* in 1709 – help to produce a unified public that is also essential for public credit. Indeed, a comparison between these two texts reveals that money and credit have merged insofar as they both circulate as currency – at this point without question – within a public.

The fifth and final chapter of *Representing Public Credit* examines the English cultural tradition of sensibility as an implicit cultural critique of public credit. The novels I analyze distinguish between older forms of social obligation and the new forms of credit made possible by public credit. I trace the way credit works in two novels in order to discuss what critics have said about novels of sensibility (and quixotism, as well) in this period. What several novels of sensibility share is nostalgia for older forms of social obligation. At the same time, they are concerned with the effects of luxury and the social impact of credit (which critics have already pointed out). This chapter connects previous discussions of two novels – Sarah Fielding's *David Simple* (1744) and Frances Burney's *Cecilia* (1782) – to my work on public credit. One can see that these novels, much like Swift and other opponents earlier in the century, are critical of the new social life of credit. As with my other primary sources, this framework produces new readings. These later novels of sensibility capture the ambivalence of public credit's mediating function by registering new rules of social engagement predicated on abstraction while still seeking to imagine a world in which social mediation – and the virtualization of social relationships – played a much smaller role.

While critics such as Janet Todd have already linked sensibility to economics, I use the epistemology of public credit to suggest that part of what is at stake in sensibility as a literary trend is a concern with the way abstractions came to mediate social relations and virtualize trust. The novels I analyze feature characters who are problematically indebted to others, and I use the framework developed for understanding public credit as a means for reading these passages. Despite their critical outlooks, these conservative novels offer ways of accommodating traditional social values to newer concerns emanating from public credit. Burney's *Cecilia*, which shares several ideological concerns with *David Simple* and its sequel, utilizes more realist narrative strategies in order to interrogate the protagonist's coming into contact with the newer form of credit dominating social life. I compare the representational strategies in the two novels in order to rethink literary realism through the rise of public credit.

I offer these readings of eighteenth-century texts as a way of piecing together a hitherto unexamined aspect of finance and fiction. While no single study on such a complicated topic can 'nail it all down,' what I hope to show in the following is that public credit was and is elusive for a reason. It is an insubstantial virtuality that contemporaries could not help but narrativize in order to feel it as part of their lives. And this narrative production was important for the emergent financial subject's increasing need to hold the State to account. Indeed, it is public credit's ultimately mysterious and unintelligible nature, coupled with the fact that its mystery helped to transform cultural, social, political, and economic life, that makes it worth reassessing through the language and the stories of the past by way of the questions we might be asking ourselves in the present.

Notes

1 See Jacob Soll, *The Reckoning*, xiv.
2 See D'Maris Coffman, *Excise Taxation and the Origins of Public Debt*.
3 See P.G.M. Dickson, *The Financial Revolution in England*.
4 See Christine Desan, *Making Money*, 15.
5 See Deborah Valenze, *The Social Life of Money in the English Past*, 2; see also Craig Muldrew, *The Economy of Obligation*, 17.
6 See Steve Pincus, *1688*, 368.
7 See D'Maris Coffman, "Credibility, Transparency, Accountability, and the Public Credit under the Long Parliament and Commonwealth, 1643–1653," 78.
8 Douglass C. North and Barry R. Weingast, "Constitutions and Commitment," 808.
9 Randy Martin, *Financialization of Daily Life*, 17.
10 See North and Weingast, 803.
11 See Robert Brenner, *Merchants and Revolution*, 651.
12 Dickson, 57.
13 Mark Knights, *Representation and Misrepresentation in Later Stuart Britain*, 15.
14 See Anne L. Murphy, "Demanding 'Credible Commitment,'" 178.
15 See Ian Watt, *The Rise of the Novel*, 60.
16 See Charles Taylor, *A Secular Age*, 12.
17 See Peter de Bolla, *The Discourse of the Sublime*, 114.
18 See James Macdonald, *A Free Nation Deep in Debt*, 8.
19 Marieke de Goede, *Virtue, Fortune, and Faith*, 5.
20 Mary Poovey, *Genres of the Credit Economy*, 56.
21 See Norbert Häring and Niall Douglas, *Economists and the Powerful*, 8.
22 See Charles James Larkin, "Monetary Policy and Central Banking."
23 See Michael McKeon, *The Secret History of Domesticity*, 16–17.
24 Indeed, this is true of the Financial Revolution in general. One must pay attention to various historical threads, such as the coin shortage and the need for paper money, traditional relations between private creditors, the rise of the permanent standing army, colonies, and slavery, religious influences, post-Civil War political concerns, new taxation methods, and so on.
25 See Sandra Sherman, *Finance and Fictionality in the Early Eighteenth Century*, 7.
26 Mark Osteen and Martha Woodmansee, "Taking Account of the New Economic Criticism," 5–6.
27 Patrick Brantlinger, *Fictions of State*, 29.
28 Poovey, *Genres of the Credit Economy*, 59.
29 McKeon, 444.
30 Charles Taylor, *Modern Social Imaginaries*, 69.
31 Jürgen Habermas, *The Structural Transformation of the Public Sphere*, 27.
32 Benedict Anderson, *Imagined Communities*, 15.
33 Christian Thorne, "Thumbing Our Nose at the Public Sphere," 531.
34 Taylor, *Modern Social Imaginaries*, 23.
35 Ibid., 18.
36 Joyce Oldham Appleby, *Economic Thought and Ideology in Seventeenth-Century England*, 128.
37 Mary Poovey, *A History of the Modern Fact*, 243.
38 Soll, xiv.
39 De Goede, xvi.
40 Colin Nicholson, *Writing and the Rise of Finance*, 9.
41 Desan, 311–12.

Works cited

Anderson, Benedict. *Imagined Communities: Reflections on the Origin and Spread of Nationalism*. London: Verso, 1983.

Appleby, Joyce Oldham. *Economic Thought and Ideology in Seventeenth-Century England*. Princeton: Princeton University Press, 1978.

Brantlinger, Patrick. *Fictions of State: Culture and Credit in Britain, 1694–1994*. Ithaca: Cornell University Press, 1996.

Brenner, Robert. *Merchants and Revolution: Commercial Change, Political Conflict, and London's Overseas Traders, 1550–1653*. Cambridge: Cambridge University Press, 1993.

Coffman, D'Maris. *Excise Taxation and the Origins of Public Debt*. Houndmills: Palgrave Macmillan, 2012.

Coffman, D'Maris. "Credibility, Transparency, Accountability, and the Public Credit under the Long Parliament and Commonwealth, 1643–1653," in *Questioning Credible Commitment: Perspectives on the Rise of Financial Capitalism*, edited by D'Maris Coffman, Adrian Leonard, and Larry Neal, 76–103. Cambridge: Cambridge University Press, 2013.

De Bolla, Peter. *The Discourse of the Sublime: Readings in History, Aesthetics and the Subject*. Oxford: Basil Blackwell, 1989.

De Goede, Marieke. *Virtue, Fortune, and Faith: A Genealogy of Finance*. Minneapolis: University of Minnesota Press, 2005.

Desan, Christine. *Making Money: Coin, Currency, and the Coming of Capitalism*. Oxford: Oxford University Press, 2014.

Dickson, P.G.M. *The Financial Revolution in England: A Study in the Development of Public Credit, 1688–1756*. London: Macmillan, 1967.

Habermas, Jürgen. *The Structural Transformation of the Public Sphere: An Inquiry into a Category of Bourgeois Society*, translated by Thomas Burger. Cambridge, MA: The MIT Press, 1991.

Häring, Norbert and Niall Douglas. *Economists and the Powerful: Convenient Theories, Distorted Facts, Ample Rewards*. London: Anthem Press, 2012.

Hobbes, Thomas. *Leviathan*. 1651. Cambridge: Cambridge University Press, 1991.

Knights, Mark. *Representation and Misrepresentation in Later Stuart Britain: Partisanship and Political Culture*. Oxford: Oxford University Press, 2005.

Larkin, Charles James. "Monetary Policy and Central Banking: The Relevance of the Financial Revolution Today." *SSRN* (June 12, 2014). http://dx.doi.org/10.2139/ssrn.2588446. Accessed July 15, 2015.

Macdonald, James. *A Free Nation Deep in Debt: The Financial Roots of Democracy*. Princeton: Princeton University Press, 2003.

McKeon, Michael. *The Secret History of Domesticity: Public, Private, and the Division of Knowledge*. Baltimore: Johns Hopkins University Press, 2005.

Martin, Randy. *Financialization of Daily Life*. Philadelphia: Temple University Press, 2002.

Muldrew, Craig. *The Economy of Obligation: The Culture of Credit and Social Relations in Early Modern England*. Houndmills: Palgrave Macmillan, 1998.

Murphy, Anne L. "Demanding 'Credible Commitment': Public Reactions to the Failures to the Early Financial Revolution." *The Economic History Review* 66.1 (2013): 178–97.

Nicholson, Colin. *Writing and the Rise of Finance*. Cambridge: Cambridge University Press, 1994.

North, Douglass C. and Barry R. Weingast. "Constitutions and Commitment: The Evolution of Institutions Governing Public Choice in Seventeenth-Century England." *The Journal of Economic History* 49.4 (1989): 803–32.

Osteen, Mark and Martha Woodmansee, editors. "Taking Account of the New Economic Criticism: An Historical Introduction," in *The New Economic Criticism: Studies at the Intersection of Literature and Economics*, 3–50. London: Routledge, 1999.

Pincus, Steve. *1688: The First Modern Revolution.* New Haven: Yale University Press, 2009.

Poovey, Mary. *A History of the Modern Fact: Problems of Knowledge in the Sciences of Wealth and Society.* Chicago: University of Chicago Press, 1998.

Poovey, Mary. *Genres of the Credit Economy: Mediating Value in Eighteenth- and Nineteenth-Century Britain.* Chicago: University of Chicago Press, 2008.

Sherman, Sandra. *Finance and Fictionality in the Early Eighteenth Century: Accounting for Defoe.* Cambridge: Cambridge University Press, 1996.

Soll, Jacob. *The Reckoning: Financial Accountability and the Rise and Fall of Nations.* New York: Basic Books, 2014.

Taylor, Charles. *Modern Social Imaginaries.* Durham, NC: Duke University Press, 2004.

Taylor, Charles. *A Secular Age.* Cambridge, MA: Harvard University Press, 2007.

Thorne, Christian. "Thumbing Our Nose at the Public Sphere: Satire, the Market, and the Invention of Literature." *PMLA* 116.3 (2001): 531–44.

Valenze, Deborah. *The Social Life of Money in the English Past.* Cambridge: Cambridge University Press, 2006.

Watt, Ian. *The Rise of the Novel: Studies in Defoe, Richardson and Fielding.* London: Hogarth, 1957.

1 Historical contexts for the "economic model"

This book is about a development of empire, from the inside outwards. It is, however, admittedly problematic to study literature's relationship to emergent financial capitalism without also examining the global forces at play in the seventeenth and eighteenth centuries, especially with regard to Europe's gradual process of accruing colonial territories, its trading in human slaves, and its many experiments with banking and other financial schemes that served both domestic and international trade. This book focuses on England despite the need to acknowledge that doing so means that this study will have to leave out an account of greater Europe as well as the developing world of global trade. There are two reasons for such a focus. The first is historical: What took place in the last decades of the seventeenth century was somewhat of an anomaly, when England's "economy diverged from the European pattern," in part owing to the new way the State began to use finance and to develop financial engineering in order to handle its revenues.[1] The second reason is discursive: Because of the way public credit was structured, there is a strong tie to particularly English problems and discussions. The world of fiction that I will be examining in the chapters to follow engages with these particular issues and their social implications.

In the first decades of the eighteenth century, contemporaries often found themselves at a loss to describe or define public credit, let alone to defend it. Jonathan Swift refers to it in *The Examiner* as "such a Complication of Knavery and Couzenage, such a Mystery of Iniquity, and such an unintelligible *Jargon* of Terms ... as were never known in any other Age or Country of the World."[2] Swift's insistence that public credit is unintelligible, coupled with strong political disapproval, has to do with a notion that "the Wealth of the Nation, that used to be reckoned by the Value of Land, is now computed by the Rise and Fall of Stocks."[3] In the same year, Daniel Defoe writes in a pro-government pamphlet titled *An Essay upon Publick Credit* that public credit is "what all People are busie about, but not one in Forty understands: Every Man has a Concern in it, few know what it is, nor is it easy to define or describe it."[4] From both of these perspectives, which differ very much in their political orientations but which are both by authors who would also go on to write fiction, public credit seems abstruse and unintelligible. It is discussed as a set of practices that potentially operate too much like stock-jobbing,[5] which was a pejorative term used to describe those who play the markets, seen by most Georgians as a form of immoral gambling and not enough like a permanent solution to a nation's financial problems.[6]

In this sense, commitment was very much a problem in the early eighteenth century.

By the middle to late eighteenth century, a more systematic approach to the management of national wealth was taken up by writers we now call political economists, in works such as Sir James Steuart's *An Inquiry into the Principles of Political Oeconomy* (1767) and Adam Smith's *The Wealth of Nations* (1776). In these, public credit is one component of political economy, subject to description and analysis like other natural mechanisms studied by the emergent social and natural sciences, a mode of thinking that would also be made more prevalent by the physiocrats in France. These works treat the State's management of its wealth like the household, the *oikos* from which the term 'economics' derives, supposing that private credit and public credit work much in the same way.[7] This comes, in part, from a seventeenth-century patriarchalist tradition in which the family was seen as analogous to the State.[8] Clearly, something happened between the beginning of the century when Defoe and Swift were writing and the second half of the century when Steuart and Smith were writing. In the early eighteenth century, there was no consensus that public credit was an intrinsic part of the State's functioning, one that could or should implicate all individuals. Indeed, as one notes through Swift's statement, it was seen as quite onerous to those with inherited property in land. By the end of the century, each individual would come to be seen as a representative of public credit with an investment in the State.[9] The State is no longer conceptualized as that which belongs to the Crown but rather as an aggregate of individuals, an abstraction that nonetheless functions.

What this book explores is a transition whereby people stopped thinking in terms of tangible interpersonal trust and started to think in terms of abstractions – imagining such entities as the nation, the State, the public, the Bank of England, and so on. Through discussions and debates in the seventeenth and early eighteenth centuries, one observes that a society in which people see themselves participating in an economy of mutual benefit was not yet in place as a shared fiction. Taylor's "economic model," articulated in *Modern Social Imaginaries* (2003) and *A Secular Age* (2007), reflects a period when economics and politics are seen as separate from one another.[10] For Taylor, the economy – an objectified reality usually summarized by Smith's metaphor of the "invisible hand" – is one of the forms of social self-understanding crucial to modernity.[11]

Twentieth- and twenty-first-century commentators, speaking from the perspective of the present in which the concept of economics is no longer something to be questioned, tend to emphasize eighteenth-century thought that describes people as mutually benefiting each other by acting out of their interests, summarized most famously in Bernard de Mandeville's "private vices, public benefits" in *The Fable of the Bees: or, Private Vices Publick Benefits*

(1705/14). In his preface, Mandeville promises to "shew that those very Vices of every Particular Person by skilful Management were made subservient to the Grandeur and worldly Happiness of the whole." While it certainly resonates with modern readers insofar as 'human nature' defined in these terms is seen as a key basis for modern society, such a description that imagines self-interest as good for the whole of society was both new and controversial in the early eighteenth century.[12] Examining early eighteenth-century texts prompts one to consider what parts of the *homo economicus* are natural. In this regard, modern commentators often inquire about the conditions under which a human can be seen as "rational individual, who, led by narrowly egotistical motives, sets out to maximize his benefit."[13] Seeing the world in this way was important for credible commitment 'from below,' and it is also pertinent to contemporary discussions surrounding a key public creditor, the Bank of England. I am, therefore, using the "economic model" in order to convey what was different in the past for the purpose of showing how radical public credit actually was in its time but also how it developed out of particular English historical contexts.

In this chapter, I will be painting with broad strokes for the reason that a fairly wide variety of developments in the seventeenth century find their way into the discourses of the following century. In what follows, I identify five distinct but overlapping historical contexts for the development of an economy of mutual benefit:

1   the emergence of economically constructed property in relation to new theories of the State;
2   the ascendancy of individual interest as a new organizing principle;
3   the development of credit money as a contract between the individual and the State;
4   questions of credible commitment with regard to the Bank of England; and
5   the functions of public opinion and disinterestedness in garnering support for public credit.

Discussing these historical contexts together suggests that, sometime in the seventeenth century, there was the beginning of a structural transfer of power from the absolute authority of the monarch to a system that did not require the older hierarchy in order to function. This is part of what Taylor refers to when he discusses a transition to a "horizontal society" and what Michael McKeon refers to in terms of the devolution of absolutism.[14] Public credit both required this transformation of power and also radically exacerbated it. Examining these various historical contexts together provides a map of what was so controversial about public credit in the early decades of the eighteenth century and why credible commitment was still an ongoing problem.[15]

Economically constituted property and the fiction of the modern state

The separation of economics and politics, key to Taylor's notion of the "economic model," can be said to have begun in the seventeenth century. Historians note a shift whereby property, once provided politically by monarchs and lords, gradually became valued and constituted in economic terms. In his *Merchants and Revolution* (2003), Robert Brenner discusses a process by which "politically constituted property" waned with the emergence of "economically constituted property." The merchant class, whose right to trade internationally was legally sanctioned by monopolies protected by the Crown, brought a new form of wealth into the realm whose value was determined by various forms of credit, such as bills of exchange. The Crown had allowed merchants to buy cheap and sell dear by protecting sanctioned monopolies, creating a precarious alliance between merchants and the Crown because the monarch created and maintained these monopolies in exchange for political and financial support, and the financial gradually became more important than the political.[16] Through legal changes, property became something that was protected within the law as an impersonal institution rather than constituted by the king and his agents.

This newer form of wealth had an effect on the landed classes. Landholders

> could refrain from depending on the monarchy to provide alternative opportunities for income through offices and other perquisites. The upshot was that ... English landlords ceased to require forms of state, of political community, either local or national, that had as one of their central functions the economic support of the members of the dominant class by means of the maintenance of *politically constituted forms of private property.*[17]

In other words, protected by the legal system, English landholders began to depend on a market rather than State power for their land and livelihood. By the end of the seventeenth century, this also meant that the English State had a higher level of taxation and more advanced forms of bureaucratic administration than other places in Europe, but this did not proceed unproblematically, of course.[18]

If one follows Brenner's particularly Marxian account, one way of reading the English Civil War is as a power struggle resulting from the more recent prevalence of economically constituted property. The causes of the Civil War, which took place between 1642 and 1651, are debated by historians, although a general consensus seems to be that its grounds were simultaneously economic, political, and religious. Monarchical power had declined under James I, who was seen as recklessly advocating absolutist doctrine, or the divine right of kings, often at the expense of his constituents.[19] This was viewed by many as a betrayal of the legal framework that had been in place since the Magna Carta, which marked the beginning of constitutional law. Charles I, like James before him, shared an absolutist bent and even dismissed parliament when its interests conflicted with his own. Eventually, this meant that he "pinn[ed] himself into a financial corner" and was then forced to raise taxes against the will of many of his constituents.[20] The ensuing political power struggle mapped onto a religious one: Anglicans (supporting the king) were pitted against puritan factions, which tended to be comprised of the 'middling sort.' In three separate wars in this period, royalists supporting the king fought against parliamentarians.

Besides significant religious factors that a purely Marxian account might ignore, the Civil War can also be attributed to the waning of political power through the ascendency of economically constituted property. Without having access to liquidity, the king's ability to govern was undermined. Like James before him, Charles I lacked resources – particularly credit – for financing ongoing wars. City money-lenders refused to help him on the grounds that he would not be able to repay them.[21] The "personal government of Charles I broke down ... because it lost the confidence of the propertied classes. There were no safe investments under the English *ancien régime*."[22] The army resolved to behead Charles I in 1649 because his government was not in tune with the interests of constituents. Rather, the king was perceived to be pursuing his own private – even personal – interests, raising taxes without parliamentary consent and proroguing when it conflicted with his own agenda. This famous crisis of the seventeenth century can be read as a political-economic one insofar as political authority by itself could no longer suffice to keep the State intact because the neglect of the interests of constituents posed a threat.

Reflecting on the execution of the king and the ensuing political and social instability, Civil War discourse often emphasized the role of the State – the commonwealth – in protecting the interests of each individual, and these interests are explicitly defined in terms of property ownership. Besides drawing on legal precedents evoked by the Magna Carta, Civil War discourse emphasizes constituent power by drawing from the Continental tradition of defining the preservation of the State through the cultivation of peace for its subjects. For example, Giovanni Botero's *Reason of State* (1589) proposed the development of a specifically political language.[23] Johannes Althusius' *Politica Methodice Digesta* (1603) defined politics as "the science of linking human beings to each other for a social life."[24] In these theories, politics was described as a sort of system. This is key.

This shows up quite clearly in Thomas Hobbes' *Leviathan* (1651), when he defines the authority heading the commonwealth as a "representative" of each person contained within it:

> A *commonwealth* is said to be *instituted*, when a *multitude* of men do agree, and *covenant, every one, with every one*, that to whatsoever *man*, or *assembly of men*, shall be given the major part, the *right* to *present* the person of them all, (that is to say, to be their *representative*;) every one, as well he that *voted for it*, as he that *voted against it*, shall *authorize* all the actions and judgements, of that man, or assembly of men, in the same manner, as if they were his own, to the end, to live peaceably amongst themselves, and be protected against other men.[25]

A key function of a commonwealth is to protect property, which, because of natural liberties – meaning that men have natural rights to all things – is ultimately the cause of war.[26] Hobbes' model of the state of nature posits an invasion of "each by each." Each individual is naturally inclined to usurp the property of the next. The solution to the problem of the inherent instability in the state of nature is that each subject forms a contract with the Leviathan. Hobbes imagines the role of the State to be an almost systematic complex of social, commercial, political, and religious relationships that unites people, protecting them from a tendency to invade one another, a situation that would upset the balance of the whole. While it stops short of specifying a definition of property, *Leviathan* serves as a prescriptive corrective for what happened during the Civil War. The Leviathan's authority comes from its being designed to protect the interests of each constituent rather than pursuing the interests of the particular actor.

This (for its time) fairly radical model of the State – ultimately a fiction that Hobbes uses to tell the story of how and why absolute political power is legitimate even in spite of recent turbulent events – is famously represented in graphic form (see Figure 1.1). In the frontispiece to the volume, which bears a striking resemblance to King John's royal seal on the Magna Carta, one observes a king holding a sword and a scepter. Covering the king's body are countless individual constituents that imbue him with a sort of protective armor. The figure of the king, symbolized by constituent power through the tiny bodies that make up his own, hovers over other symbols of prosperity, security, and wealth.

While people surrender themselves to the Leviathan in Hobbes' absolutist political theory, the symbolism on the frontispiece is revealing: It is not a surrender to an arbitrary ruler, for the Leviathan figure is already configured as a power constituted by the individuals (and their property) that it is meant to represent.

Hobbes' *Leviathan* tells a story about why constituents need the State and, in so doing, holds the State to account for the protection of property. This work of political theory is, therefore, simultaneously descriptive and prescriptive insofar as it attempts to resolve a real and threatening problem. Tellingly, Hobbes explicitly provides a place for fiction in the construction of political authority, arguing that "[t]here are few things, that are incapable of being represented by Fiction."[27] The Leviathan, or the State, is also a fiction, created by humans rather than nature by pooling together the wealth of the constituents:

> For by art is created that great LEVIATHAN called a COMMONWEALTH, or STATE, (in Latin CIVITAS) which is but an artificial man; though of greater stature and strength than the natural, for whose protection and defence it was intended.... The *wealth* and *riches* of all the particular members, are the *strength*.[28]

Already in *Leviathan*, written in the midst of crisis, there is a notion that the State's strength comes from (or should come from) an aggregate of individuals. Indeed, the political actor serves as the representative of this aggregate. He is a

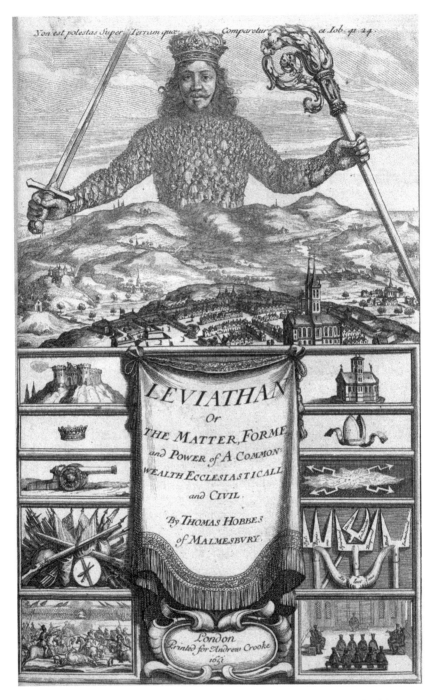

Figure 1.1 Frontispiece to *Leviathan* (© The British Library Board (C.175.n.3)).

synthetic notion insofar as he stands in for – he represents – the interests of an aggregate at the same time as the management of these individual interests are the very definition of the State.

Other Civil War thinkers use similar constellations in articulating the ground for political power. In *A System of Politics* (published posthumously in 1700 but written decades earlier), James Harrington follows a Hobbesian premise when he writes: "All government is interest, and the predominant interest gives the matter or foundation of the government."[29] As its title would suggest, Harrington describes the State as an almost natural mechanism that springs from natural interest. For Henry Ireton, a key contributor to the Putney debates (an ongoing discussion between members of the New Model Army on the topic of the new constitution) and a thinker who had a different political outlook from Hobbes, the future of political stability was tied to an understanding of political power produced by "permanent interest" in the commonwealth. How does one determine who is permanently interested? Through ownership of property.[30] If one owns land in the commonwealth, he or she must be interested in the whole of the commonwealth. Interest becomes even more clearly defined in Ireton's argument: It is through property ownership in the form of land that one can be said to have an interest.

One notes from reading Civil War discourse that 'economics' is not yet part of the conceptual framework. Nonetheless, a relationship of commitment between the State and the individual (with interests in property ownership) is already well-established by the middle of the seventeenth century. Indeed, it is what allows these thinkers to posit the State as a sort of system. Ellen Meiksins Wood summarizes the important implications of Brenner's analysis by pointing to the way economics emerges from this as a distinct category: "Brenner's principal questions, then, were these: how was it that old forms of 'politically constituted property' were replaced in England by an 'economic' form," which then contributed to "a distinctive pattern of self-sustaining economic growth?"[31] Especially after the Civil War, solutions to political problems gradually came to be worked out in economic terms, and this had to do with the strengthening of the marketplace as distinct from political power, which corresponds to a transition from personal relationships between particular people to a virtual economy of impersonally conceptualized actors. The economy comes to be conceptualized as that which is considered to be self-sustaining insofar as individuals, each thought to have an interest, will naturally act upon them – what Christine Desan, in a tradition of scholarship that includes works such as Albert O. Hirschman's *The Passions and the Interests* (1977), calls "the ascendance of interest."[32] The State is the entity that ensures that individual interests are preserved. What was left was to make pursing one's interest a morally acceptable activity – to make it so that interest could be a mechanistic spring from which the State derives its power.

On interest: fictions of the individual and the public good

Interest is a key term in most studies on the emergence of capitalism. David Graeber goes so far as to say that the

> story of capitalism ... is not the story of the gradual destruction of tradi-
> tional communities by the impersonal power of the market. It is, rather, the
> story of how an economy of credit was converted into an economy of
> interest; of the gradual transformation of moral networks by the intrusion of
> the impersonal – and often vindictive – power of the state.[33]

In Graeber's reading, credit has existed for thousands of years, but it is gradually transformed into interest in the early modern period.

The difficulty in reading the seventeenth century through the concept of interest is that a more rational, calculable notion of interest is a product of later eighteenth-century and early nineteenth-century thought. Despite the way the term was instrumentalized in post-Civil War discourse, *interest* was still very much understood to be a pejorative term, one that implied pursuing one's advantage without moral consideration, often at the expense of others. While *interest* eventually became a term that economists use to posit the way indi-viduals within a marketplace get counted in an aggregate, it was not until the nineteenth century that the word was used in this way.[34] E.P. Thompson emphas-izes a gradual retreat of a "moral economy" which became replaced by a "notion of 'economics' as a non-normative object of study, with objective mechanisms independent of moral imperatives," but he also argues that it "was separating itself off from traditionalist theory during the mercantilist period, and with great difficulty."[35] Throughout the seventeenth and eighteenth centuries, local customs with their accompanying moralities often took precedence over the newer 'economy' even while there seems to be a shift in thinking about the individual in relation to society. To historicize interest, and to register what is so different about credit after its ascendency, is also to historicize individualism.

C.B. Macpherson reads Hobbes and Locke together in order to posit "posses-sive individualism" as a root of liberal democratic theory: "Its possessive quality is found in its conception of the individual as essentially the proprietor of his own person or capacities, owing nothing to society for them."[36] This is an important criterion for what he calls the "possessive market society," as "man's energy and skill are his own, yet are regarded not as integral parts of his person-ality, but as possessions, the use and disposal of which he is free to hand over to others for a price."[37] This is very different from a customary or status society, in which owning one's labor does not allow for movement up and down within a social hierarchy. Macpherson's reading of Hobbes and Locke asks the question of how this concept of individual comes into being.

One important outcome of the emergence of economically constructed prop-erty was the concept of the individual who owned his or her labor even when he or she had no landed property to speak of. Wood suggests that English agrarian capitalism came from the necessity for members of the gentry to improve their land in order to compete and survive, thus producing the conditions of possibility for the modern wage laborer.[38] Before the middle of the seventeenth century, peasants lived on the land in customary relationships with a landlord. In 1646, an official ordinance abolished feudal tenures, formalizing what had taken place de facto during the transition to economically constituted property.[39] As feudal tenures were gradually dissolved, peasants who had been allowed to subsist on the land were forced to sell their labor (as their only property) in order to pay rent. People who had no landed property were required out of necessity to work for a wage, for there were fewer and fewer spaces to thrive without land ownership. In this way, economically constituted property began to encompass more than just landholders and merchants, but peasants as well, insofar as they could sell their labor.

For John Locke, in his *Second Treatise of Government* (1690), owning landed property is a natural right, one that is justified by the fact that one mixes it with one's body (now conceptualized as another form of property) in order to improve it through his labor.[40] For this reason, Locke argues that land is something that a government must protect.[41] However, Locke adds another category to this constellation. The political power of civil government, and the property it sustains, comes "only from the Public Good."[42] Locke's approach to government is one of contractual, albeit tacit, consent, and this justifies the ownership of property through the ownership of one's self. Unlike Hobbes, Locke is able to assume that humankind in a state of nature is free and equal, and it is only corrupted by bad governments and arrangements of property not in accordance with a public good.

There seems to be a sea change in political thinking between Hobbes' and Locke's respective social contracts. For Hobbes, the story is that natural rights produce a problem that can only be resolved through the State; Locke tells the story of a State that is always a potential problem, and the "public good" is used as a measure by which to gauge its legitimacy. In the final chapter of the *Two Treatises*, Locke says that the right to rebel is justified, for if natural rights to property are taken from people, they have a natural right to insubordination.[43] A State is only secure if its ruling authorities ensure (or at least persuade citizens) that they are serving a "public good." That is to say, commitment is posed as a problem here more so than in *Leviathan*; through the concept of the "public good," it serves as a structuring principle of political legitimacy. The individual, owning his body as his property and therefore embodying interest, has a natural right to hold the State to account.

In the cases of Hobbes, Harrington, Ireton, and Locke, there is already evidence of a shift, one that had been fomenting under the Stuart monarchy, whereby absolutism starts to wane. Political power is only viable when the monarch heads a commonwealth whose interests he upholds and preserves. Ireton registers this interest explicitly in terms of landed property. Landed property is posited as a natural right in Locke's reading, and the labor of the individual is what justifies it. Brenner's and Wood's respective analyses illuminate the extent to which

landed property was already beginning to become configured not only economically but also financially, meaning that it had a potential to produce profit,
should one decide to mix one's labor (which comes from the natural property
that is one's body) with it or to employ others to do so. The difference is whether
one's interest comes from owning land or from owning one's body (which has
the potential to transform the land), reflecting a changing conception of property
tied to the concept of an individual which is becoming increasingly abstract and
economically configured.[44]

Interest gradually becomes regarded as something that all individuals naturally
possess, and this gives way to an economic way of thinking, what Joyce Appleby
calls *ideology*. *Ideology* is what happens to politics when one comes to believe one
has a natural interest. It is the formation of shared beliefs that do not explicitly
serve particular political interests.[45] While this definition is narrower than the
version often used today, it is relevant to the discussion that follows because of the
way economic activities become naturalized as a means for acting politically. This
is pertinent to Brenner's and Wood's discussions on the transition to economically
constituted property: People act on their own interests without explicitly or con-
sciously serving a political power. The demise of absolutism, then, is not only
about the loss of monarchical power but also a gradual displacement of power onto
economic functions, namely an "economic model."

On money: mediating individual interest

The rise of public credit constitutes a financial and not merely an economic
transition insofar as it meant that people began to see it as morally acceptable to
pursue profit through usury, which was hitherto thought to be un-Christian or
amoral.[46] This change is also tied to a new conception of money. By the end of
the seventeenth century, many English citizens were already implicated in a
network of exchange mediated by money. But money still meant, for the most
part, coin or specie. Bills of exchange and other credit instruments were still
restricted to merchants and bankers, even though these newer credit instruments
were beginning to have an indirect effect on others. Public credit changes this.

As one notes from reading Swift and Defoe, credit at the level of State was not
seen as a natural part of economic practice at the beginning of the eighteenth
century. But with the turn toward economically constituted property and a new
theory of State that posited individual interests adding up to the public good, conditions were set for the rise of public credit. "Public credit did more than suggest a
world in which individual interests aggregated to amount to the common good,"
writes Desan. "[I]t designed that world."[47] In *Making Money* (2014), Desan shows
how the English found a way to monetize the public credit held by the Bank of
England. This was a radical move for its time. After all, the moral economy, in
which pursuing one's interests was seen as detrimental to society, persisted.

When one examines printed discourses about credit and debt in the early
seventeenth century, one is struck by a radically different tone from what one is
likely to find a century-and-a-half later. For example, in *The Debt Book* (1625),

Henry Wilkinson writes vehemently against contracting a debt, arguing that the only debt one should have is loving others. Borrowing money is not only wrong, but dangerously addictive, because

> debt is a consumer of credit and State, of goods and good name, however some men thinke the contrarie, yet there is no question to be made. How ofter [*sic*] do we see, that as after the biting of an Aspe, the man smitten fals asleepe, but the poison dispeareth it selfe through everie member till the whole bodie be poisoned: So after debt contracted, specially upon the hard tearmes of usurie, or ill conditions the debter is lulled a sleepe by the sweetnes of the present supply, but the debt passeth as a poison through every part of a mans substance ... till all be turned into debt.... Yet for all that; as the dropsie-man delighteth in abundance of drink, though most hurtfull in that disease, because it satisfies the present appetite: so men in debt alreadie are willing to continue, yea to multiply the same, (because thereby their present need is served) though it be never so pernicious in the conclusion.[48]

The treatise, cheekily dedicated to Charles I and therefore functioning as a political critique of the Crown, insists that contracting a debt is to transform one's appetite unnaturally. Other seventeenth-century pamphlets reflect similar notions. In *The Worth of a Peny, or, A Caution to Keep Money* (1667), Henry Peacham writes that "[m]isery is ever the Companion of borrowed Money. Hereby a man is made cheap, and undervalued, despised, deferred, mistrusted, and oftentimes flatly destroyed."[49] Debt is not only a moral problem that competes with traditional values such as love: These writers argue that going into debt inevitably entails personal ruin. It is bad, in other words, for one's interests because it implies permanent loss. Here, there is a sharp distinction between debt (which is borrowed from others) and money (which one presumably owns).

But this general attitude, especially with regard to the State's use of credit, gradually began to change after the Civil War. The increased use of money – and the fact that money mediated more relationships than ever before – also meant that it became scarcer. Coin shortages, along with the accompanying problem of coin clipping, abounded. At the level of State, this shortage was felt to be detrimental. The government began to experiment with permanent debt mechanisms in order to remedy its own cash-flow problem. Exactly when the National Debt originates is subject to scholarly controversy, but most argue that it began around or just after the Civil War. D'Maris Coffman's *Excise Taxation and the Origins of the National Debt* (2013) suggests that the public debt and the development in the fiscal State originates in excise taxation methods of the 1640s.[50] Michael Braddick argues that the groundwork for a permanent national public debt and thus the modern tax State lies in the 1650s and 1660s through the expansion of the tax base so that the flow of funds was taken "out of the hands of the monarch by means of appropriation and audit."[51] This was a significant turn of events because, especially during the Interregnum, while the monarch was still not believed to be trustworthy, an evolving system of checks on the Crown through the strengthening of parliament itself became more trustworthy. That is to say, the State had evolved along the lines of the social contract – with a built-in apparatus for commitment – described by Hobbes, Harrington, Ireton, and Locke. Another crisis in the 1690s would lead to a type of financial engineering that transformed the public debt into paper money that circulated freely.

The famous debate between John Locke and William Lowndes (then Secretary to the Treasury) over the value of money in the 1690s reveals a set of strong disagreements as to what gives money its value (the basis for a definition of money as store of value). Specie, seen as intrinsically valuable and measurable by its metal content was very different from a piece of paper promising the bearer an amount of specie of a given content. Locke and Lowndes found themselves in a debate about how to deal with coin clipping, which was an ongoing problem over the course of the seventeenth century. In this debate, Locke took the position that money is valuable because of the quantity of metal contained within it while Lowndes argued that the stamp on the coin held a greater significance. This debate resulted in the "Great Recoinage of 1696," in which Locke's position prevailed. Debased coins were recalled and new, milled coins were minted with the proper amount of metal according to the stamp.

According to Locke, who was also a first subscriber to the Bank of England and whose ideas about money were by no means mainstream, money should consist of the metal it purports to have by stamp because this is the only way to ensure that it is universally valued, for gold and silver have intrinsic value. Locke's *Some Considerations of the Consequences of Lowering of Interest, and Raising the Value of Money* (written in 1691) sparked a fierce debate in parliament. Locke also published *Short Observations on a Printed Paper* (1695), *Further Observations Concerning Raising the Value of Money* (1695) (an essay refuting Lowndes' *A Report Containing an Essay for the Amendment of Silver Coins* [1695]), and *Several Papers Relating to Money, Interest and Trade* (1696) in the ensuing years. In *Short Observations*, Locke writes:

> Money has and will always have its value from the quantity of Silver in it, and not from the stamp and denomination, as has been already proved, and will some time or other be evidenced with a witness in the Clipp'd Money. And if it were not so, that the value of Money were not according to the quantity of Silver in it, *i.e.* that it goes by weight, I see no reason why clipping should be so severely punished.[52]

Locke's concern is that coin clipping violates the laws of civil society and poses a threat to the State.[53] The case of clipped coins provided evidence that money's value originates from a quantity of metal. However, the quantity within a coin is not always self-evident to the beholder. Indeed, it must be secured by the State, whose legitimating function is to guarantee the protection of property and the public good. In "Further Considerations Concerning Raising the Value of Money," Locke writes that

[t]he use and end of the public Stamp is only to be a guard and voucher of the *quantity* of Silver which Men contract for. And the injury done to the publick Faith, in this point, is that which in Clipping and false Coining heightens the Robbery into Treason.[54]

Constantine George Caffentzis, rescuing Locke from commentators who too simply associate Locke with a 'quantity theory of money,' argues that Locke's view "represents a momentous transformation in intellectual perspective and social policy."[55] Locke's view of money is importantly tied to the health of the State. Paper money is ultimately a debt contract that the State secures. A bill is not an equivalent to money; rather, it is a contract that promises cash, and a reliable, solvent State enables this. Any threat to money as a contract is a threat to the State, a conclusion Locke deduces a posteriori from the way the State has seen it necessary to punish coin clipping. Specie may be intrinsically valuable, but the State is what promises to preserve the intrinsic value in coined money that is not tangible to the bearer. This logic will be what allows paper money to circulate as promise-to-pay coupons. Currency represents the value it is purported to have, and the State guarantees this value through representational strategies.

When confronted with the problem of a liquidity crisis earlier in 1682, William Petty recommended the following as an answer for what to do when there is a shortage of money:

We must erect a Bank, which well computed, doth almost double the Effect of our Coined Money: And we have in *England* Materials for a Bank which shall furnish Stock enough to drive the Trade of the Whole Commercial World.[56]

Petty advocates supplementing scarce coinage through the establishment of a separate bank. Petty's scheme, one of the many pamphlets by 'projectors' which will be discussed in the next chapter, reflects an acceptance that credit could supplement cash.

According to the *Oxford English Dictionary*, one early use of the term *paper money* (as opposed to *paper credit*) was by British merchant and early political economist John Pollexfen in 1697.[57] "[I]n Considerations of *Trade* and *Coyn*," he says, "Arguments from Interest ought to be taken for as good Proof as Demonstration."[58] In his *A Discourse of Trade, Coyn, and Paper Credit*, Pollexfen describes a process by which the nation became capable of "making Paper to pass for Money."[59] Attributing the increased use of paper credit to not having enough circulating coin, Pollexfen discusses a shift whereby the government needed to secure paper money because it had become necessary for commerce.

The striking of Tallies for the supply of the Publick hath been long practiced here, and by Authority, but Paper Credit for the carrying on of Commerce is new, and hath been left (till of late) to take its own way, though a matter of great importance, and well worth the care of the Government.[60]

With the use of paper money, writes Pollexfen, "the Interest of the Banks [is] so interwoven with the Government, that the Publick Faith must be their support."[61] While goldsmiths and bankers had issued notes as forms of paper credit since the middle of the seventeenth century, this newer form of paper credit is "grounded on the greatest Authority, and Publick Faith."[62] Through the establishment of the Bank of England and the production of paper money, public credit evolves in order to consolidate all individuals who use money as investors in the State, rendering quite literal the earlier notions:

1   that government is for the protection of property;
2   that all individuals have interests; and
3   that this interest through property is economically configured.

By the end of the seventeenth century, therefore, one observes a notion of money in the form of a credit contract with the State. It is not the intrinsic value within the paper object that ultimately matters but rather trust in a State that will guarantee that it will function. This, according to Desan, was helped along by the fact that the government accepted the notes for tax payment, which by itself indicates a sort of commitment: "The event that catalyzed the growth in public debt and made the property rights of public creditors so compelling was the currency attached for the first time to public credit."[63] One should not underestimate the significance of this innovation: "The Bank notes that eventually became 'money' resulted from an event that was structurally different. That event was the reconfiguration of value at the collective level."[64] A key event in the history of finance is thus the establishment of the Bank of England, an entity that would through financial engineering institutionalize the aggregate of individual interests through a financial means by issuing promise-to-pay contracts, which would create new attitudes about indebtedness. The establishment of the Bank along with the rise of public credit allowed for new financial engineering, in which debt could be made perpetual – and therefore turned into liquidity – with the right management. This would still require the support of investors, who could believe that the State would credibly commit to repaying investments over the long term. For many, however, this understanding of the State was still seen as a sort of utopian way of thinking.

Credible commitment and the Bank of England

Douglass C. North and Barry R. Weingast's 1989 version of the credible commitment thesis asserts that it was the Glorious Revolution in 1688 and the subsequent political settlement that transformed public finances.[65] That is to say, in this reading, commitment was offered 'from above' through the intentional design of government structures such as parliament. More recently, however, the emphasis on institutions being the solitary motor for credible commitment has been put under pressure. For example, James Macdonald argues that credible commitment was still very much a problem in the first few decades of the eighteenth century:

In hindsight, it is temptingly easy to see the Revolution of 1688 as a clean break in English history: before, the struggle against would-be autocrats with limited means and no credit standing; after all, the installation of a Dutch-style representative government (or perhaps, more accurately, a mercantile oligarchy) with the ability to leverage national power through cheap long-term debt. Yet the process was far more complex and hard-fought than this simple paradigm suggests. It would take until after 1720 for a stable form of parliamentary government to be securely established.[66]

The idea that political solutions could by themselves stabilize commitment does not hold up when one examines the problems that many of these new (or redesigned) institutions faced. Anne Murphy, for example, shows that

> before 1720 at least, Parliament in fact proved itself little better than the Stuart monarchs at honouring its financial obligations. Credible commitment, therefore, was not offered from above. It had to be demanded from below by the people who invested in the government's debt.[67]

The problem was one of reconciling the ideal institutional forms with the expectations that the public had of such institutions. If one thinks of credible commitment as a process of coming to hold the State to account, the missing link would be *to what the public decides to hold the State accountable*. And, in the seventeenth century, the public (an abstraction) was only just beginning to hold the State (another abstraction) accountable to an idea of the public good (perhaps the most significant abstraction at the turn of the century).

Whether or not one partially or fully accepts North and Weingast's version of credible commitment, and even if one takes on board Macdonald's critique or Murphy's discussion of the way parliament took decades to learn how to manage the National Debt, most scholars agree that the Glorious Revolution was a turning point in the possibility for establishing a credit system. With the overthrow of James II and the transfer of power to William III and Mary II came major changes in financial policy. By 1688, there was a need to take out long-term loans, and the system had developed to allow for this.[68] Besides general cash-flow problems, the public debt originated to a large degree from the practical need of William III to finance war with France. Prior to the Glorious Revolution, the Crown still had control of the State's purse strings; after the events of 1688, the king's power became more limited, and this allowed parliament to undertake financial innovations.[69] "The fact that Parliament guaranteed all these loans made them 'debts of the nation' or 'national debts,' and both Englishmen and foreigners were quick to realize that this change from merely royal security was extremely important."[70] The new stable regime with its use of financial actors that had hitherto been separate from government partly solved problems faced by earlier regimes. One layer of commitment is governmental; another involves the Bank.

When accounting for the origins of economically constituted property and the ideological questions it presents, one observes that the Bank of England and other institutions were part of a much larger transition. This is not to undermine their importance, but rather to point out that what happened during the Financial Revolution was a long time coming. That being said, the Bank of England institutionalized the aforementioned emergent principles already in play – such as individual interests and the public good – that were merely ideas in the seventeenth century. Indeed, this is how Desan defines capitalism: "'Capitalism' came when government institutionalized interest in material profit as the engine – the pump – that made money as well as debt."[71]

Conceived by William Paterson and Michael Godfrey, the Bank of England was formally established in 1694 through an initial £1,200,000 subscription "upon a fund of Perpetual Interest backed by Parliament charter."[72] When the Bank received its first charter, it was not envisioned as a permanent institution designed for central banking functions in mind, as are modern State banks.[73] After all, it was a private institution required to apply to parliament for renewed charters. Between 1696 and 1781, the Bank applied for six short-term renewals. The spending power of the British government increased by 34 percent in the 1690s and by about 40 percent in the eighteenth century.[74] Historians describe a circular relationship between the Bank (and the City) and particular political interests in the government. Phillip Geddes describes this interrelationship as a "virtuous circle: the Bank's shareholders, City merchants in the main, lent money to the Government to wage wars. These wars increased Britain's commercial influence and opened up new areas for trade, from which these same City merchants profited."[75] The Bank was initially beneficial to the State because the former allowed the latter to wage war, but this meant that the interests in the City came to support this sort of political policy. John Brewer even goes so far as to say that this interrelationship is responsible for the modern "fiscal-military State."[76] J.L. Broz and R.S. Grossman argue that, by contrast to other important modern institutions, the Bank came into being by "contracting under uncertainty" in the beginning, but gradually became a "linchpin of credible public finance."[77] The Bank strengthened the State, allowing it to surmount the economic and political problems it faced in the previous century, and the State strengthened the Bank. However, despite the rebuilding of trust in the government around the time of the Glorious Revolution, the Bank had to produce a trust of its own. There is a temporal factor that should be acknowledged here. While the Bank was not set up as a permanent institution (indeed, legally it only became permanent in 1844), the logic of the credit system implied a future-oriented trajectory.

While the Bank borrowed protocols from other banks of its time, it differed from the banks of Amsterdam, Hamburg, Venice, and Genoa in a fundamental way. Whereas the large Continental banks, which pre-date the existence of the Bank of England, were banks of deposit and exchange, the Bank of England was set up as a bank of note issue from its outset.[78] Early Bank of England historian James E. Thorold Rogers writes:

> Paterson and his associates saw that there was not and could not be a subsidiary currency which was not assured on a basis of the precious metals.

They saw that it was possible to circulate paper currency, and this to an amount which was considerably in excess of the specie on which it was at any moment actually supported, in other words that it is possible and expedient to circulate bills, payable on demand,... [without assuming] that the demand for payment would be an immediate claim, and that this suspended liability might be an addition to the currency, and a source of profit for those whose credit enabled them to float it.[79]

While it was impossible for the Bank to back all of its paper issue on coin (since the shortage of coin was the problem from the outset), Paterson used a principle of "suspended liability." In other words, the Bank issued paper that promised to be redeemed for cash when given notice, but relied on its own credit to ensure that these bills would be trusted. The Bank

purported to give in its bills the equivalent of what it had received, but it never pretended to take the deposit for any purpose than that of trading with it. It never professed to make its issues square exactly with its coin and bullion, though of course it made its liabilities square with its assets, plus the capital of its shareholders, and in time, plus its rest or reserve i.e. its accumulated and undivided profits ... It coined, in short, its own credit into paper money.[80]

This point is crucial. While this private company accounted for its own issuing of coin, it profited not from coin but from investments from extending credit to the State. It used profits from these investments to continue the process of issuing paper, which the State committed to accepting for tax payments.

Early commentators recognized that this sort of paper money was unique. In *A Letter to a Friend Concerning Credit of the Nation* (1694), the anonymous author of a pro-Bank pamphlet writes:

Any Banker's Notes pass currently in all Paiments, and are esteemed equal to Money; and not because Men do generally believe, that a Banker hath always Money lying by him to pay all his Debts, though they should be demanded all at once ... if a Banker should do so, from whence could he get Profit to maintain Tellers, Book-keepers, Porters, pay great Rents, and get something over and above to reward his Care and Pains?[81]

Built into the plans for the Bank was the idea that paper currency could circulate without the exact amount of coin and bullion necessarily backing it. Money defined in terms of what the State accepts for payment was present in this feat of financial engineering from the outset. Herein lies a commitment issue that would need to be resolved. The Bank itself had a private interest, which was to profit and to maintain its assets. However, it also had to represent itself as working for the public good. It was up to the Bank to maintain its public image in order to do so. The assumption that all paper would not be called for redemption was based on a presupposition that investors' trust in it would not compel them to redeem paper for coin. Public opinion, for this reason, needed to be on the side of public credit.

By "coining its credit into paper money," the Bank solved the State's money shortage problem by creating a credit contract that functioned as money insofar as it was endlessly transferable and accepted for State payments. Depositors were allowed three methods of investment, the most significant being the "running cash note," which meant that they were issued a receipt for their deposit. These paper receipts, partially printed, were usually given in exchange for coin. A cashier would write by hand the name of the depositor and the amount, but, from the outset, notes included the words "or bearer" so that they could be circulated from person to person. It was this "running cash note" that developed to become paper money. The notion that there need not be a supply of cash ready at hand (coin by contrast to paper; the two terms are differentiated in the writings of this time) was problematic to varying degrees throughout the century. If the public perceived that the Bank would not be able to pay out in cash, a run on the Bank might ensue, which would inevitably adversely impact the capacity of the State to carry out its political functions. There was, in other words, a risk always already implicit in the institution that solved so many of the State's problems.

The Bank, besides gradually transforming itself into a politically necessary State institution over the course of the century, was a set of systematic internal practices or a "series of devices," to use the term offered by J.G.A. Pocock, that allowed it to issue paper money and to provide a loan to the government.[82] It was also much more than that. While it stood in a rented building until 1734, its permanent move to Threadneedle Street that year meant that its architectural design could ensure that its edifice looked safe to the public. The Bank had a physical embodiment – a concrete, stalwart building located in the City. Geographical and architectural decisions served to galvanize public trust. While its institutional practices were grounded in double-entry bookkeeping and the quantification of credit, the Bank's public 'face' was qualitative, garnering a reputation that members of the public could imagine. By 1760, the Bank serviced approximately 70 percent of the National Debt.[83] Further, depositors (including other banks) had to physically go to the Bank in the City to cash their notes. Even while other banks issued their own notes, therefore, they became increasingly dependent on the Bank of England. By 1781, Lord North would refer to the Bank as "part of the constitution," for it would take on "all the money business of the exchequer."[84] The financial engineering so controversial in the seventeenth century was by the end of the eighteenth century becoming to seem more natural.

Public opinion and the fiction of disinterestedness

One of the paradoxes that emerges in this history has to do with the fact that, if the State is ultimately involved with the Bank, it is difficult to imagine that commitment leads to what North and Weingast describe as the proliferation of private rights and markets.[85] Further, the underlying risk of a bank run meant that what the public thought about the State's management had an impact on the State's ability to function. Public trust in State institutions was important, which contradicts a notion that the markets ran by themselves. Carl Wennerlind writes:

> Public credit thus came to depend on how public opinion perceived the state's current capacity to service the interest payments and its imaginary ability to repay the debt in some distant, theoretical future. In this new culture of credit, public opinion became the arbiter of public credit, dictating everything from England's imperial campaigns, fiscal administration, and legislative decisions to the choice of ministers.[86]

The fact that public opinion could present a threat to public credit also meant that public opinion itself would need to be managed.

The seventeenth century can be characterized as a period of crisis that resolved itself by separating economic discourse from political discourse. Steve Pincus argues that one of the important results of the Glorious Revolution was a "revolution in political economy" in the last decades of the seventeenth century.[87] In this revolution, political economists began to write by using quantitative analysis rather than by using older rhetorical strategies. The story often goes that the new discourse modeled itself on the merchant's handling of double-entry bookkeeping as well as on the emergent practices of a more systematic scientific empiricism, such as that found in the establishment of the Royal Society in 1662. Accounting (or the balancing of credits and debts through a double-entry bookkeeping ledger) was a key facilitator insofar as it is systematic and can be taken as truthful, virtuous, and politically neutral.[88]

To a great degree, this emphasis on accounting is corroborated by documentary evidence from the seventeenth century. In the late 1670s, William Petty, a member of the Royal Society, argues that his method breaks from previous traditions by relying on quantitative measurements as empirical proof. Following traditions of mechanistic philosophy used by his peers at the Royal Society as well as his own *Discourse Concerning the Use of Duplicate Proportions* (1674), which "combined an attempt to bring mechanical principles a wide public with a remarkable and idiosyncratic matter theory,"[89] Petty integrates mechanistic philosophy into his advocacy of using numbers in *Political Arithmetic* (1690). Petty writes:

> The method I take ... is not yet very usual. For (instead of only using comparative and superlative words, and intellectual arguments) I have taken the course (as a specimen of the Political Arithmetic I have long aimed at) to express myself in Terms of Number, Weight, or Measure; to use only arguments of sense, and to consider only such causes as have visible foundations in Nature: leaving those that depend upon the mutable minds, opinions, appetites, and passions of particular men, to the consideration of others. Really professing myself as unable to speak satisfactorily upon these grounds (if they may be called grounds!) as to foretell the cast of a die, to

play well at tennis, billiards, or bowls (without long practice) by virtue of the most elaborate conceptions that ever have been written *de projectilibus et missilibus*, or the angles of incidence and reflection.[90]

Using numbers, Petty argues, helps a nation understand its domestic resources so that it can plan accordingly. At the surface, it may seem that numbers themselves are what carry authority. Mary Poovey, however, complicates this point by showing that it is the process by which one arrives at a balance – the algebra – that renders numbers authoritative. Rather than using persuasive rhetoric to get across this point, political economy utilizes a *disinterested* method, relying on quantification through accounting and description, which implies that the economy has a 'natural' propensity to self-regulate.[91] What we would now call 'objectivity' is key for the progress of political economy as a proto-scientific discourse. Reading Petty's tract in the context of mechanistic philosophy, it seems that disinterestedness has a variety of modes of representation, accounting being one of them.

By examining the role of the State in the production of modern money, it becomes somewhat difficult to compare the emergence of political economy – and economics – with that of the natural sciences, and this is partly for the reason that political economy only becomes possible through the creation of certain fictions about how humans behave, some of which I have outlined above. As long as we act in a predictable way, purging ourselves of irrational inclinations, the system will work and can be analyzed objectively. What double-entry bookkeeping will provide is the proto-scientific function of disinterestedness so important for maintaining the fiction that a private corporation was looking out for the public good. This representation of disinterestedness takes the concept of the State as discussed in Civil War discourse one step further. Principles of the economy that we can now take for granted as part of the economic model were ones made through human innovation to an even greater degree than that which is usually acknowledged to be the case in the natural sciences. Indeed, this is because public opinion is ultimately a key factor, and it required a considerable effort in representing disinterestedness as a way of managing the inherent risk of a bank run.

And yet, these human innovations will nonetheless be called 'natural.' Adam Smith will start with a labor theory of value, opening his *The Wealth of Nations* (1776) with a chapter on maximizing productive powers through the division of labor, a natural division which leads to "natural opulence." The notion that the pursuit of individual interest is beneficial for the whole of society – one that is described through the disinterested methods of political economy – would eventually transmogrify into something like Smith's principle of the disinterested "invisible hand," that leads to natural progress.[92] Boldly, Smith argues: "Had human institutions ... never disturbed the natural course of things, the progressive wealth and increase of the towns would, in every political society, be consequential, and in proportion to the improvement and cultivation of the territory or country."[93] For Smith to be able to say this in his famous critique of mercantilism, a great transformation had to take place, one requiring that individuals, owning their labor, have interests not directly tied to political power in a traditional, vertical social hierarchy that is seen to put these interests together in a disinterested way. It requires, in other words, the horizontal economic model.

The road to laissez-faire was somewhat rocky, as many were not convinced that the institutional changes, methods of financial engineering, and ensuing innovations were a feasible solution. Charles Davenant's worried rumination would set the scene for later eighteenth-century debates. In *A Memoriall Concerning Credit* (1696), Davenant emphasizes the importance of public opinion for the survival of the government and its credit mechanisms:

> [I]f men begin to entertain an ill Opinion of the State of Things, If the Nations Debt is Suffered to Swell beyond all Compass, If they See Private Property is not at all made the common Care ... the People will despaire of the future, and draw their Effects, as soon as possible out of Public hands, into their own Possession, which at once must sink all Sort of Credit, and with its ruine, hazard the very being of the Government.[94]

Davenant, whose analysis reflects the social contract theories of Hobbes and Locke, points to a potential problem in emergent public credit: It is based on a public's perception of the future. If the perception turns negative, individuals will "draw out their effects" from the public fund into their own personal hands.

This prediction about human behavior constructed through a telling metonym exemplifies how the market, increasingly determined by public credit, is intertwined with the other two principle aspects of the modern virtual public: the public sphere and representative government.[95] Because public credit is susceptible to public opinion, a public imaginary is implied, one whose development has been described by Benedict Anderson in his notion of the "imagined community," Jürgen Habermas in his "bourgeois public sphere," and Charles Taylor in his "modern social imaginary."[96] Public credit, because it is governed partly by public opinion, requires individuals to imagine themselves united as a collective: in a nation, a marketplace, a commonwealth, or an economy.

In *Discourses on the Public Revenues and on Trade* (1697), Davenant suggests that credit not only fluctuates based on the irrational whims of people. It also has a more stable ground, and this has to do with the government's producing confidence in its public through a virtuous management of funds. In the *Discourses*, Davenant describes the way in which a government is capable of producing public confidence when he argues that

> when it can be made appear, there is a fund sufficient to satisfy all pretensions, men's minds will become quiet and appeased; mutual convenience will lead them into a desire of helping one another. They will find, that no trading nation ever did subsist, and carry on its business by real stock; that trust and confidence in each other, are as necessary to link and hold a people together as obedience, love, friendship, or the intercourse of speech.[97]

This passage opens up several lines of inquiry that will be important for the next chapter. First, using a "fund" in this way denies a material basis for public credit – it is an intangible entity that individuals of the public cannot see. Since public credit uses accounting mechanisms to keep track of creditors and debtors, this fund exists only if all investors do not pull out at once. The public, as a group, must trust that the fund exists in order for public credit to remain stable even while they acknowledge that one cannot do business on "real stock." Second, Davenant asserts that trust in other citizens of the nation was already part of trade relationships to begin with, for no one has ever been dependent upon "real stock" by itself. Credit may be subject to opinion, but the members of the nation have always already trusted one another through the act of engaging in commerce. We have already tacitly consented, Davenant's writing suggests, why not acknowledge it? Finally, Davenant's use of the word "public" implies that there are multiple individuals that come together to form an aggregate served by this material fund that is nonetheless dependent on opinion.

There seems to be a delicate balance between self-interestedness and disinterestedness, as both contribute to the functioning of the machine. Because of the role of public opinion, it is difficult to uphold the notion that accounting and other proto-scientific practices by themselves ground public credit. Rather, it is the rhetoric of disinterestedness writ large that facilitates the pursuit of individual interest, which will take various forms. This coincides with the representation of political power as more abstract and less dependent on particular people with particular interests. D'Maris Coffman, examining the origins of public credit, writes that the "British state, in a historical and ideological sense, evolved out of the need to develop a political language that abstracted sovereign power so that it was not dependent on a particular type of rule."[98] Indeed, even the term *State* begins to convey this difference:

> During the Civil Wars and Interregnum, Parliament used the abstraction of "the state" to refer to the exercise of powers which, under other circumstances, were the preserve of the sovereign. The result was that contemporaries distinguished the "state" from the "publike" and saw the duty of Parliament to maintain the "publick faith" and the "publike credit."[99]

The separation of *State* and *public* implies that the latter is able to hold the former accountable. This is achieved not only directly through politics, but also indirectly through public opinion, which the Bank and State work very hard to manage. This is the fundamental feedback loop that forms the basis for early public credit.

The Bank of England serves as a sort of text, as a way of mediating between the newer, abstract system of credit and the concrete world of trust through which traditional social relationships were organized. Part of what we see in an attempt to mind this gap is the use of other abstractions, such as the 'public interest,' the 'public faith,' and especially the 'public good,' terms that carry over from the seventeenth century in order to suggest that all interests are being served under the post-Civil War political regime. Discourses in the early eighteenth century demonstrate that representing public credit as a means for acting for the public good invites people to hold the State to account. In this phase of the transition to economically constituted property, property itself becomes more abstract. However, rather than moving from trust to credit (as if they are in competition with one another), one observes a translation of trust *in* tangible people to trust in abstractions meant to *stand in for* people: the Bank, the nation, the State, the public, and so on. This has the effect of turning each individual into a representative of public credit and is key to the shift from vertical to horizontal power that Taylor characterizes as the economic model that is part and parcel of modernity.

The readings that follow ultimately suggest that part of what is at stake in the credible commitment thesis is the process by which commitment could be made applicable to all individuals. That is to say, public credit implies that a contract between people through the virtuous working of the State is tacit – not unlike Locke's model. We are in tacit agreement that we exist together in an economy of mutual benefit. We hold the State to account that this contract, this enforceable promise, might be observed. The Bank of England is the party that authorizes this new contract.

But this new form of contract is still too newfangled for its time. As Roy Kreitner points out, the modern contract requires one to have

> a sense that obligation [that] is the result of voluntary choice, based on rational, calculating decision making, exercised by an individual. It teaches us that other forms of obligation are marginal and exceptional. The road to obligation leads to the market, passing through promise and consideration, that is, contract, which can be distinguished sharply from obligation that arises elsewhere, through gift or status.[100]

The economic model, which is – as I have argued – also a financial one, implies a new social contract with a new financial subject. And this sort of individual, this person who is newly subject to the rules of finance, will feature in and become endemic to the rise of the novel, a form of fiction whose key function is to resolve ideological contradiction.

Notes

1 Steve Pincus, *1688*, 396.
2 Jonathan Swift, *The Examiner and Other Pieces Written in 1710–1711*, 7.
3 Ibid., 6.
4 Daniel Defoe, *An Essay upon Publick Credit*, 6.
5 The term stock-jobbers, referring to market dealers, was made popular by Thomas Shadwell's *The Stock-Jobbers, or The Volunteers*, published posthumously in 1693.
6 See Helen Julia Paul, *The South Sea Bubble*, 16–17.
7 The most obvious difference is that, while private credit was used primarily for trade, what was at stake in public credit was geopolitical success in war.

8 See Michael McKeon, *The Secret History of Domesticity*, 113.
9 Peter de Bolla, *The Discourse of the Sublime*, 115.
10 See Charles Taylor, *Modern Social Imaginaries*, 17–22, 213.
11 Ibid., 176, 183.
12 See Marshall Sahlins, *The Western Illusion of Human Nature*, 84.
13 Tomas Sedlacek, *Economics of Good and Evil*, 14.
14 Taylor, 158; McKeon, *The Secret History of Domesticity*, 16–17.
15 One of the important factors that this book does not have the space to explore is the role foreign investors (especially the Dutch) played in the establishment of English public credit (see Marjolein T. Hurt, " 'The Devil or the Dutch' ").
16 Robert Brenner, *Merchants and Revolution*, 670.
17 Ibid., 651–2.
18 Ibid., 715.
19 Tristram Hunt, *The English Civil War*, 3.
20 Ibid., 18.
21 See Christopher Hill, *The Century of Revolution, 1603–1714*, 106.
22 Ibid.
23 Giovanni Botero, *The Reason of State*, 3, 12.
24 Johannes Althusius, *Politica Methodice Digesta*, lxiii.
25 Thomas Hobbes, *Leviathan*, 115.
26 Ibid., 119.
27 Ibid., 108.
28 Ibid., 9.
29 James Harrington, *The Commonwealth of Oceana and a System of Politics*, 271.
30 See A.S.P. Woodhouse, ed., *Puritanism and Liberty*, 109.
31 Ellen Meiksins Wood, *The Origin of Capitalism*, 50.
32 Christine Desan, *Making Money*, 274.
33 David Graeber, *Debt*, 332.
34 See Albert O. Hirschman, *The Passions and the Interests*, 32; see also J.A.W. Gunn, *Politics and the Public Interest in the Seventeenth Century*, 327.
35 E.P. Thompson, *Customs in Common*, 270.
36 C.B. Macpherson, *The Political Theory of Possessive Individualism*, 3.
37 Ibid., 48.
38 Wood, 70.
39 See Michael McKeon, "Civic Humanism and the Logic of Historical Interpretation," 88.
40 John Locke, *Two Treatises of Government*, 306.
41 Ibid., 310.
42 Ibid., 286.
43 Ibid., 446.
44 Another component of the emergence of individualism is religious. Larry Siedentop defines the West in terms of the decay of moral boundaries defined by domestic spheres and land ownership whose function was to allow for family worship (*Inventing the Individual*, 17). His account discusses the role Christianity plays in promoting a notion of the individual over the family as a secularization narrative (ibid., 349).
45 See Joyce Oldham Appleby, *Economic Thought and Ideology in Seventeenth-Century England*, 6.
46 See Thompson, 70.
47 See Desan, 280.
48 Henry Wilkinson, *The Debt Book*, 67–8.
49 Henry Peacham, *The Worth of a Peny*, 9.
50 See D'Maris Coffman, *Excise Taxation and the Origins of Public Debt*, 201.
51 Michael J. Braddick, *The Nerves of State*, 44.
52 John Locke, "Short Observations on a Printed Paper," 358.

53 See Constantine George Caffentzis, *Clipped Coins, Abused Words, and Civil Government*, 46.

54 John Locke, "Further Considerations Concerning Raising the Value of Money," 415.

55 Caffentzis, 47.

56 William Petty, *Sir William Petty's Quantulumcunque Concerning Money*, 7.

57 *Oxford English Dictionary Online*, s.v. "Paper money."

58 John Pollexfen, *A Discourse of Trade, Coyn, and Paper Credit*, 2.

59 Ibid., 63.

60 Ibid., 64. Exchequer tallies had been used since the medieval period to register the collection of taxes. They were discontinued in the early nineteenth century, as the Bank took on more and more functions of the Exchequer.

61 Ibid.

62 Ibid., 68.

63 Desan, 290.

64 Ibid., 300.

65 Douglass C. North and Barry R. Weingast, "Constitutions and Commitment," 804.

66 James Macdonald, *A Free Nation Deep in Debt*, 168.

67 Anne L. Murphy, "Demanding 'Credible Commitment,'" 180.

68 See P.G.M. Dickson, *The Financial Revolution in England*, 45.

69 See J. Lawrence Broz and Richard S. Grossman, "Paying for Privilege," 54.

70 Dickson, 50.

71 Desan, 296.

72 John Giuseppi, *The Bank of England*, 10.

73 H.V. Bowen, "The Bank of England During the Long Eighteenth Century, 1694–1820," 1.

74 Braddick, 44.

75 Philip Geddes, *Inside the Bank of England*, 15.

76 John Brewer, *The Sinews of Power*, 250.

77 Broz and Grossman, 50.

78 See R.D. Richards, *The Early History of Banking in England*, 136.

79 James E. Thorold Rogers, *The First Nine Years of the Bank of England*, 71–2.

80 Ibid., 9.

81 *A Letter to a Friend*, 1.

82 J.G.A. Pocock, *The Machiavellian Moment*, 425.

83 J.H. Clapham, *The Bank of England*, 103.

84 Quoted in ibid., 174.

85 See North and Weingast, 808.

86 Carl Wennerlind, *Casualties of Credit*, 169.

87 Pincus, 393.

88 See Mary Poovey, *Genres of the Credit Economy*, 55; see also Andrea Finkelstein, *Harmony and the Balance*, 252.

89 Simon Schaffer and Steven Shapin, *Leviathan and the Air-Pump*, 309.

90 William Petty, "Political Arithmetic," 7.

91 See Poovey, 55.

92 Adam Smith, *An Inquiry into the Nature and Causes of the Wealth of Nations*, 1:456.

93 Ibid., 1:378.

94 Charles Davenant, "A Memoriall Concerning Credit," 78.

95 McKeon writes: "The abstraction of the market went hand in hand with the abstraction of the economy, the self-willed activity of private citizens, from the political and public authority of the state" (*The Secret History of Domesticity*, 27).

96 See Benedict Anderson, *Imagined Communities*, 15; Jürgen Habermas, *The Structural Transformation of the Public Sphere*, 27; and Taylor, 23.

97 Davenant, "Discourses on the Public Revenues, and on the Trade of England," 152.

98 Coffman, *Excise Taxation*, 201.
99 D'Maris Coffman, "Credibility, Transparency, Accountability," 98.
100 Roy Kreitner, *Calculating Promises*, 10.

Works cited

Althusius, Johannes. *Politica Methodice Digesta.* 1603. Cambridge, MA: Harvard University Press, 1932.

Anderson, Benedict. *Imagined Communities: Reflections on the Origin and Spread of Nationalism.* London: Verso, 1983.

Appleby, Joyce Oldham. *Economic Thought and Ideology in Seventeenth-Century England.* Princeton: Princeton University Press, 1978.

Botero, Giovanni. *The Reason of State.* 1589. London: Routledge and Kegan Paul, 1956.

Bowen, H.V. "The Bank of England During the Long Eighteenth Century, 1694–1820," in *The Bank of England: Money, Power and Influence, 1694–1994*, edited by Richard Roberts and David Kynaston, 1–18. Oxford: Clarendon Press, 1995.

Braddick, Michael J. *The Nerves of State: Taxation and the Financing of the English State, 1558–1714.* Manchester: Manchester University Press, 1996.

Brenner, Robert. *Merchants and Revolution: Commercial Change, Political Conflict, and London's Overseas Traders, 1550–1653.* Cambridge: Cambridge University Press, 2003.

Brewer, John. *The Sinews of Power: War, Money and the English State, 1688–1783.* New York: Alfred A. Knopf, 1989.

Broz, J. Lawrence and Richard S. Grossman. "Paying for Privilege: The Political Economy of Bank of England Charters, 1694–1844." *Explorations in Economic History* 41 (2004): 48–72.

Caffentzis, Constantine George. *Clipped Coins, Abused Words, and Civil Government: John Locke's Philosophy of Money.* Brooklyn: Autonomedia, 1989.

Clapham, J.H. *The Bank of England: A History*, vol. 1. Cambridge: Cambridge University Press, 1945.

Coffman, D'Maris. *Excise Taxation and the Origins of Public Debt.* Houndmills: Palgrave Macmillan, 2012.

Coffman, D'Maris. "Credibility, Transparency, Accountability, and the Public Credit under the Long Parliament and Commonwealth, 1643–1653," in *Questioning Credible Commitment: Perspectives on the Rise of Financial Capitalism*, edited by D'Maris Coffman, Adrian Leonard, and Larry Neal, 76–103. Cambridge: Cambridge University Press, 2013.

Davenant, Charles. "Discourses on the Public Revenues, and on the Trade of England," in *The Political and Commercial Works of that Celebrated Writer Charles D'Avenant, LL.D.*, vol. 1, edited by Sir Charles Whitworth, 125–459. London: n.p., 1771.

Davenant, Charles. "A Memoriall Concerning Credit," in *Two Manuscripts*. Baltimore: Johns Hopkins Press, 1942.

De Bolla, Peter. *The Discourse of the Sublime: Readings in History, Aesthetics and the Subject.* Oxford: Basil Blackwell, 1989.

Defoe, Daniel. *An Essay upon Publick Credit.* London: n.p., 1710.

Desan, Christine. *Making Money: Coin, Currency, and the Coming of Capitalism.* Oxford: Oxford University Press, 2014.

Dickson, P.G.M. *The Financial Revolution in England: A Study in the Development of Public Credit, 1688–1756.* London: Macmillan, 1967.

Finkelstein, Andrea. *Harmony and the Balance: An Intellectual History of Seventeenth-Century English Economic Thought.* Ann Arbor: University of Michigan Press, 2000.

Geddes, Philip. *Inside the Bank of England.* London: Boxtree Limited, 1987.

Giuseppi, John. *The Bank of England: A History from its Foundation in 1694.* London: Evans Brothers Limited, 1966.

Graeber, David. *Debt: The First 5,000 Years.* Brooklyn: Melville House Publishing, 2011.

Gunn, J.A.W. *Politics and the Public Interest in the Seventeenth Century.* London: Routledge, 1969.

Habermas, Jürgen. *The Structural Transformation of the Public Sphere: An Inquiry into a Category of Bourgeois Society,* translated by Thomas Burger. Cambridge, MA: The MIT Press, 1991.

Harrington, James. *The Commonwealth of Oceana and a System of Politics.* Cambridge: Cambridge University Press, 1992.

Hill, Christopher. *The Century of Revolution, 1603–1714.* London: Routledge, 1980.

Hirschman, Albert O. *The Passions and the Interests: Political Arguments for Capitalism before its Triumph.* Princeton: Princeton University Press, 1977.

Hobbes, Thomas. *Leviathan.* 1651. Cambridge: Cambridge University Press, 1991.

Hunt, Tristram. *The English Civil War: At First Hand.* London: Phoenix, 2002.

Hurt, Marjolein T. "'The Devil or the Dutch': Holland's Impact on the Financial Revolution in England, 1643–1694." *Parliaments, Estates and Representation* 2.1 (1991): 39–52.

Kreitner, Roy. *Calculating Promises: The Emergence of Modern American Contract Doctrine.* Stanford: Stanford University Press, 2006.

A Letter to a Friend, concerning the Credit of the Nation: and with relation to the present Bank of England, as now establish'd by Act of Parliament. London: E. Whitlock, 1697.

Locke, John. *Two Treatises of Government,* 2nd edn, edited by Peter Laslet. Cambridge: Cambridge University Press, 1967.

Locke, John. "Further Considerations Concerning Raising the Value of Money," in *Locke on Money,* vol. 2, edited by Patrick Hyde Kelly, 410–81. Oxford: Clarendon Press, 1991.

Locke, John. "Short Observations on a Printed Paper," in *Locke on Money,* vol. 2, edited by Patrick Hyde Kelly, 345–59. Oxford: Clarendon Press, 1991.

Macdonald, James. *A Free Nation Deep in Debt: The Financial Roots of Democracy.* Princeton: Princeton University Press, 2003.

McKeon, Michael. *The Secret History of Domesticity: Public, Private, and the Division of Knowledge.* Baltimore: Johns Hopkins University Press, 2005.

McKeon, Michael. "Civic Humanism and the Logic of Historical Interpretation," in *The Political Imagination in History: Essays Concerning J.G.A. Pocock,* edited by D.N. DeLuna, 59–99. Dexter: Owlworks, 2006.

Macpherson, C.B. *The Political Theory of Possessive Individualism: Hobbes to Locke.* Oxford: Oxford University Press, 2011.

Mandeville, Bernard de. *The Fable of the Bees: or, Private Vices Publick Benefits.* London: J. Roberts, 1714.

Murphy, Anne L. "Demanding 'Credible Commitment': Public Reactions to the Failures of the Early Financial Revolution." *The Economic History Review* 66.1 (2013): 178–97.

North, Douglass C. and Barry R. Weingast. "Constitutions and Commitment: The Evolution of Institutions Governing Public Choice in Seventeenth-Century England." *The Journal of Economic History* 49.4 (1989): 803–32.

Oxford English Dictionary Online.

Paul, Helen Julia. *The South Sea Bubble: An Economic History of its Origins and Consequences.* Abingdon: Routledge, 2011.

Peacham, Henry. *The Worth of a Peny, or, A Caution to Keep Money. With the causes of the scarcity and misery of the want hereof in these hard and mercilesse times, etc.* London: n.p., 1664.

Petty, William. *Sir William Petty's Quantulumcunque Concerning Money.* London: n.p., 1682.

Petty, William. *The Discourse made before the Royal Society 26 Nov. 1674, concerning the use of Duplicate Proportion … Together with a new hypothesis of springing or elastique motions.* London: n.p., 1764.

Petty, William. "Political Arithmetic" in *Later Stuart Tracts*, edited by George A. Aitken, 1–66. Westminster: Archibald Constable and Co., 1903.

Pincus, Steve. *1688: The First Modern Revolution.* New Haven: Yale University Press, 2009.

Pocock, J.G.A. *The Machiavellian Moment: Florentine Political Thought and the Atlantic Republican Tradition.* Princeton: Princeton University Press, 1975.

Pollexfen, John. *A Discourse of Trade, Coyn, and Paper Credit.* London: Brabazon Aylmer, 1697.

Poovey, Mary. *Genres of the Credit Economy: Mediating Value in Eighteenth- and Nineteenth-Century Britain.* Chicago: University of Chicago Press, 2008.

Richards, R.D. *The Early History of Banking in England.* London: Frank Cass and Company, 1958.

Rogers, James E. Thorold. *The First Nine Years of the Bank of England.* Oxford: Clarendon Press, 1887.

Sahlins, Marshall. *The Western Illusion of Human Nature.* Chicago: Prickly Paradigm Press, 2008.

Schaffer, Simon and Steven Shapin. *Leviathan and the Air-Pump: Hobbes, Boyle, and the Experimental Life.* Princeton: Princeton University Press, 1985.

Sedlacek, Tomas. *Economics of Good and Evil: The Quest for Economic Meaning from Gilgamesh to Wall Street.* Oxford: Oxford University Press, 2011.

Siedentop, Larry. *Inventing the Individual: The Origins of Western Liberalism.* London: Allen Lane, 2014.

Smith, Adam. *An Inquiry into the Nature and Causes of the Wealth of Nations*, 1776, 2 vols. London: Oxford University Press, 1976.

Swift, Jonathan. *The Examiner and Other Pieces Written in 1710–1711*, edited by Herbert John Davis. Oxford: Basil Blackwell, 1957.

Taylor, Charles. *Modern Social Imaginaries.* Durham, NC: Duke University Press, 2004.

Thompson, E.P. *Customs in Common.* London: The Merlin Press, 1991.

Wennerlind, Carl. *Casualties of Credit: The English Financial Revolution, 1620–1720.* Cambridge, MA: Harvard University Press, 2011.

Wilkinson, Henry. *The Debt Book, or a Treatise upon Rom.* London: R.B. and G.M. for R. Bird, 1625.

Wood, Ellen Meiksins. *The Origin of Capitalism.* New York: Monthly Review Press, 1999.

Woodhouse, A.S.P., editor. *Puritanism and Liberty: Being the Army Debates (1647–49).* London: Dent, 1938.

Part I

Framing credible commitment through fiction

2   The public good, credible framing, and Daniel Defoe's fictions

To describe the political and financial changes that ensued after the Civil War and Restoration, J.G.A. Pocock uses the term "the Machiavellian moment," which is when the English republic, traumatized by recent events, begins to confront the problem of its own stability in time. For Pocock, this has a direct tie to the Financial Revolution, for it implies "associating the national prosperity directly with the stability of the regime, the expanding activities of government and – most significant of these – the prosecution of war."[1] The Financial Revolution and the commitment it entailed was accompanied by a radically changing conception of property, from that of land to something moveable and virtual. Those "who own and manage it may own and manage everything – including, it is beginning to appear, the social perceptions and the minds of men."[2] Public credit came with inherent risks that meant that public opinion had to be managed. Pocock regards this as lamentable, but it can also be seen as part of the financial engineering necessary for the success of public credit. Part I of this book discusses the way commitment is framed through fiction.

Pocock's more negative reading of the Financial Revolution is based on his being very well acquainted with the way many felt about the transformation at the beginning of the century. When one pores over texts that explicitly discuss finance in the late seventeenth and eighteenth centuries, one discovers an underlying cultural anxiety. Indeed, Sandra Sherman also comments on this phenomenon through her experience researching for her book on Daniel Defoe. She writes:

> As I encountered these texts on endless reels of microfilm, it seemed as if I were watching unfold the unmediated anxieties of a culture afraid of texts. The authors betray an emerging, chilling self-awareness. They accept credit as inescapable, but articulate the crux at the heart of emergent capitalism: credit necessary to sustain trade exacts the price of diminished apprehension. To engage in a market ... was to accept a phenomenon implicating reading in uncertainty.[3]

Even as one reads on through later eighteenth-century texts, this anxiety never fully disappears. This was clearly a revolutionary time that requires one to revisit some important cultural concepts that emerge in the period.

This chapter rethinks works attributed to Defoe, author and hired political hack, in order to examine some of these cultural concepts, for these works – including economic pamphlets and fictional narratives – articulate an economic theory that accommodates the complexities of public credit to contemporaries. Defoe's central rhetorical move – advocating for the public good as the highest virtue – should be seen as a component of credible commitment, for ultimately it serves the purpose of producing a standard by which the State can be held to account. During two key crises, in 1710–11 and in 1720 after the South Sea Bubble, Defoe's writings provide the public with a notion that all individuals participate in the State, and he models the way these individuals should ideally behave.

In the early eighteenth century, political interest groups were divided on the question of what constituted wealth. Political factionalism emerged from two initially slang, pejorative terms – 'Whig' and 'Tory' – that eventually became accepted labels for two opposing sides. While the Whigs were mainly comprised of commercial interests and tended to support projects overseas, the Tories, who represented traditional landed interests, were more of a mixed crowd, some of whom favored the restoration of the Stuart monarchy while others were more moderate.[4] The Whig-sponsored Bank of England and East India Company, representing the 'monied interests,' posed a threat to the interests of the Tories, who had tried unsuccessfully to establish a Land Bank in 1695 in an attempt to muster some financial power for themselves. The new form of credit emanating from Whig strongholds threatened the landed classes and their value systems so much that writers began to publicly oppose the threat to the traditional order.[5] The Tories saw the new form of credit as both a corruption and a threat to their interests as well as to an older form of social organization.

As both James Macdonald and Carl Wennerlind point out, the period of 1710 and 1711 is an important time for assessing the evolution of credible commitment, perhaps just as important as the Glorious Revolution.[6] The opposition against the 'monied interests' seemed particularly threatening to the survival of public credit in 1710, when a transfer of power from the Whigs under Queen Anne to the Tories was to take place. In 1711, the Tories ended up accepting the necessity of public credit, chartering a national creditor that they could manage, the South Sea Company.[7] In a relatively short period of time, therefore, England (and, by the Act of Union of 1707, Britain) had three main public creditors: the South Sea Company (1711), the East India Company (1707), and, of course, the Bank of England (1694), all of which, along with other individual wealthy private creditors, maintained the National Debt.

Both once active for the Whigs, Defoe and Jonathan Swift were recruited for the Tories when Robert Harley took power in 1710.[8] In a 1710 issue of the *Examiner*, Swift writes of his perception of state of public credit:

> Several Persons who had small or encumbered Estates, sold them, and turned their Money into those Funds to great Advantage: Merchants, as well as other monied Men, finding Trade was dangerous, pursued the same Method:

But the War continuing, and growing more expensive, Taxes were Encreased, and Funds multiplied every Year, 'Till they have arrived at the monstrous Height we now behold them. And that which was first a Corruption, is at last grown necessary, and what every good Subject must now fall in with, although he may be allowed to wish it might soon have an End.... By this means, the Wealth of the Nation, that used to be reckoned by the Value of Land, is now computed by the Rise and Fall of Stocks.[9]

While it may be questionable whether many small estates were actually implicated in public credit in this early period, this passage is interesting for its rhetorical alignment of public credit and corruption, even while it argues that public credit has become necessary. Indeed, if one mostly reads eighteenth-century texts that promote a definition of wealth tied to land, the Pocockian account of the Financial Revolution becomes quite convincing.

The general attack on public credit often likened the public creditors, including the Bank of England, to stock-jobbing, which was seen as morally unwholesome, an activity associated with Jewish people, foreigners, and dissenters with socially destabilizing effects for women and servants.[10] The problem, as Swift himself points out, is that which had been seen by those outside of the 'monied interest' as a corruption, at least by 1710, had become necessary, for the fiscal-military State to which John Brewer refers was already very much up and running.[11] Indeed, Daniel Defoe would acknowledge this explicitly:

> *The Credit of the Nation* is ... *its Politick Life* – Money is the Sinews of the War; Credit is Money – Money is the Life and Soul of all our Opposition to *Popery*; of all our Alliance against *France*, and at this Time, *No Credit, no Money.*[12]

Defoe would spend the next decade writing in order to transform the public perception of public credit from something similar to stock-jobbing to a feasible, necessary, and long-term entity in which both parties participate. Mark Knights calls on scholars to explore the link between opinion, credit, and partisan politics in further depth, for "[p]ublic credit relied on political representations of the parties and their leaders. Public discourse of political affairs was thus an integral part of the evolving financial system, and frequent elections had a place in establishing the state of creditworthiness."[13] In essence, the project was one of getting Tory opposition to come on board with new finance, but this also entailed revising deeper cultural attitudes – ideologies – and, indeed, transforming and managing the "minds of men" since the latter, insofar as public opinion mattered, was tied to public credit's survival.

A critical consensus is that Defoe's fiction and non-fiction are both preoccupied with economic questions, but there is less agreement as to his precise position. Maximilian E. Novak notes that there "was hardly a cause that Defoe espoused which he did not eventually attack."[14] Defoe's personal experience as a merchant (dealing in hosiery, woolen goods, and wine) meant that he took up well-informed discussions on the topic of credit in the radically changing economic climate of the later seventeenth century. He was personally bankrupt in 1692 and again in 1706, and he therefore had a personal investment in writing about private credit.[15] His public life was extraordinary. While a fugitive from debt prosecutors in 1704, he approached the Tory politician Robert Harley for help. From then on, Defoe, officially a Whig, offered Harley his services, acting as a propagandist/journalist and secret agent.[16] Critics estimate his written output to consist of approximately 566 separate works, including substantial writing for 27 periodicals.[17] He is known as the father of a type of fiction – adventure romances – associated with the rise of the novel, and he is the founder of one of the earliest regularly circulating periodicals, *The Review* (1704–13), which established many journalistic techniques found in modern newspapers. Within this massive collection of writing, Defoe's works on public credit are particularly fascinating given his explicit and implicit ties to the State, his role in developing various genres that comprise the emergent public sphere, and the seemingly personal attention he pays to what is required for credit, namely accounting and reputation. Defoe can be called a key financial engineer insofar as he registers the feedback loop between the State (qua government) and the public as a crucial ground for public credit.

The particular political and economic concerns in the first decade of the eighteenth century have significant implications for how scholars comprehend Defoe's understanding of credit. Defoe may be the father of the adventure romance, but he began his career as a pamphleteer – as what might have been called a few decades earlier a 'projector.' To put it simply, 'projectors' were what skeptics and critics called early engineers. The "project was at best a vision of a future society and an audacious plan about realizing this vision through collective action."[18] However, at worst,

> the projector had become something of an established literary stereotype. In the context of political economy, the projector came to stand for the rent-seeker who pretended public service to pursue their self-interest and that of the crown at the expense of people's rights and properties.[19]

The tradition of writing Defoe comes from implies an attempt to transform and improve things – a tradition of 'useful knowledge' that was often seen and condemned as being self-interested. Very conscious of the various critiques of projecting, Defoe does not merely describe what credit is like: He also prescribes what it should be like and calls on people to take action. Further, he tries to separate himself from the types of projectors who have acquired a bad reputation. Therefore, a complete account of Defoe's take on credit would need to consider this tradition of writing and the fact that, while often characterized as descriptive, it also implicitly prescribes a new way of doing things.

Reassessing Defoe's writings on public credit in particular provides a context for a few prominent notions, including Ian Watt's claim that "society must value every individual highly enough to consider him the proper subject of its serious literature" and that Defoe himself embodied this new outlook of individualism and hence can been seen as instrumental for the rise of the novel.[20] Public credit also requires one to historicize Defoe's economic beliefs insofar as they contribute to his shifting political outlooks. Novak describes Defoe as a mercantilist, albeit a complicated one.[21] While mercantilism is not usually associated with economic individualism, Defoe can be said to be for the individual as much as he was for the nation. In Defoe's writings, the individual is not a self-sufficient entity, but rather a productive participant within a community from which all might benefit. Defoe's descriptions of how public credit functions can be read as prescriptions required for sustaining a radically new financial system. His works attempt to convince readers to believe that they are part of a nation of commerce, or, more specifically, a State that manages the interests of all of its individual constituents. This is not quite the economic individualism that forms the groundwork for laissez-faire theory, for it implies a necessary participation of institutions. In this sense, Charles Taylor's notion of the "horizontal society" and the economically driven individualism that would accompany it as part of the modern social imaginary is still nascent rather than already well established in this period.

The reading that follows will differ somewhat in perspective from that of Sherman, who uses Defoe's oeuvre to contest the notion that print media and the discursive encounters it permitted both produced and resulted from a public sphere. Sherman disputes Jürgen Habermas' notion of the rational public sphere directly when she argues that "Defoe's ability to instantiate cultural anxiety; to contribute to epistemological uncertainty which is its cause; and to use such uncertainty to evade interrogation, creates a complex persona 'trapped' in culture but exploiting this trap" and that this "challenges rational debate in the public sphere."[22] While this reading is indeed an apt description of credit in general, public credit is represented a bit differently. Descriptions of public credit have a tendency to stabilize it rather than to contribute to anxiety about it.

The following reading complicates the primary authority some have given to double-entry bookkeeping's connections to the rise of a credit economy. Because the accounting ledger lacks a tie to the real, the combination of the ledger and a regulating authority (e.g., the State) work together to reduce anxiety about credit in Defoe's writings. Defoe's version of public credit is, in effect, a stability-producing machine. Furthermore, rethinking the credible commitment thesis through Defoe's more propagandist writings provides a new way of reading his overtly fictional writings, which will be addressed at the end of this chapter. Techniques of representation for defending public credit will then be used to reassess works that critics have associated with the rise of the novel.

The virtuous projector

One of the most significant texts for getting a sense of Defoe's unique development as a writer is through his first signed work, *An Essay Upon Projects*, first published in 1697 (and later expanded to *Essays Upon Several Projects* [1702], which I will be citing here). This was before Defoe had much of a public reputation: He was at this point in time only known as a failed businessman.[23] Subtitled "[t]he means by which the Subjects in general may be eased and enriched," the collection of proposals resembles the many economic pamphlets published throughout the seventeenth century. A *projector* was a *schemer*, another term with an ambivalent meaning used by critics to describe ideas for banks and other nascent financial institutions. It is somewhat ironic, therefore, that Defoe uses the word "projects" in his title. Despite his being critical of this new type of writing, Defoe actively participates in the "Projecting Age" he describes.[24] Reading through this long document, which covers everything from banking to establishing an academy for women, one gets a sense that a younger Defoe found his niche writing on behalf of a group of people that felt a need to transform things, which was the case for many such 'projectors' in the 1680s and 1690s, such as Charles Davenant, Josiah Child, John Locke, Nicholas Barbon, and, of course, the father of political arithmetic, William Petty.

Essays Upon Several Projects sets the tone for later writings through its pragmatic avowal of moderatism and its down-to-earth demonstration of practical know-how. Always a self-promoter, Defoe (who would have been just over 30 at the time) elevates his own economic project above that of other 'projectors.' The "True-bred Merchant," he says, is "the most Intelligent Man in the World, and consequently the most capable, when urged by Necessity, to Contrive New Ways to live."[25] He carefully distinguishes between *"New Inventions and Projects*, between Improvement of Manufactures of Lands, which tend to the immediate Benefit of the Publick, and Imploying the Poor" and projects which "bring People to run needless and unusual hazards."[26] What is more, Defoe introduces the sections that follow with a further discussion of good and bad projects, and good and bad projecting. In effect, he calibrates his own projecting by anticipating critiques of other projects. Defoe discusses a "New Trade, which we call by a new Name, Stock-Jobbing, which was at first only the simple Occasional Transferring of Interest and Shares from one to another" but has lately become more complex.[27] Indeed, stock-jobbing has even been exacerbated by projecting: "Stock-Jobbing nursed Projecting, and Projecting in return has very diligently pimp'd for its Foster-parent, till both are arrived to be Publick Grievances; and indeed are now almost grown scandalous."[28] Stock-jobbing, which Defoe would do his utmost to disassociate from public credit in the years to follow, is the bugbear that has to be sequestered from more virtuous public projects.

In summary, Defoe sets up the terms he will use for his eventual defense of public credit in the introduction to *Essays Upon Several Projects*:

A meer Projector then is a Contemptible thing, driven by his own desperate fortune to such a Streight that he must be deliver'd by a Miracle, or Starve, and when he has beat his Brains for some such Miracle in vain, he finds no remedy but to paint up some Bauble or other, *as Players make Puppets talk big.*[29]

But the Honest Projector is he, who having by fair and plain principles of Sense, Honesty, and Ingenuity, brought any Contrivance to a suitable Perfection, makes out what he pretends to, picks no body's pocket, puts his Project in Execution, and contents himself with the real Produce, as the profit of his Invention.[30]

It is not for no reason that the first project he defends in the work is a State-managed bank. When managed right, he argues, a bank is a necessary and virtuous project and completely unlike that of the scheming stock-jobber. The difference hinges on whether the project is for the public good or for private interests alone, drawing from seventeenth-century discourse. In the decades to follow, he would elaborate on this. Through his own version of financial engineering, he builds a sort of fictional machine.

Reading Defoe's financial oeuvre, one finds that he envisions a tight (if a bit confusing) relationship between public and private credit, and this is often mediated through a discussion of the relationship between the public good and private interests. Defoe examines both private and public credit in *The Review*, famous for its allegory featuring the figure of Lady Credit. *An Essay upon Publick Credit* (1710) describes in very abstract terms the individual (albeit impersonal) actors that make up government. His *The Compleat English Tradesman* (1726), a manual on how to be an effective merchant, spends pages discussing a necessary literacy in using the instruments of private credit, advertising itself as a way of educating merchants inexperienced in using credit and unaware of the importance of keeping accurate accounts. These core texts allow one to see how Defoe puts public credit together as a simple and semi-coherent mechanism, one whose seeming neutrality – its disinterestedness – is able to undercut political factionalism. His technique, however, is not restricted to the accounting ledger. His machine also works through another form of abstraction: depersonalization.

The Review has received much critical attention owing to Lady Credit, but the historical moment and its pressures made these more famous passages what they are. *The Review* became increasingly preoccupied with questions of credit. Set up to discuss "the matter of our English Trade" in its earliest issues when Defoe was traveling throughout Scotland and Europe for Harley, who served as the Chancellor of the Exchequer from 1710 to 1711, *The Review* also came to examine English politics and war. But Defoe eventually shifted his focus from military strategy to national finance in a period when investors worried about what B.W. Hill calls the "loss of the City" in 1710, resulting from the transfer of power from the Whigs to the Tories.[31] Whig and Tory partisanship was particularly troublesome in 1710, after a high-church Anglican, Dr. Henry Sacheverell, was tried and convicted for preaching a seditious sermon accusing the government of failing to punish non-conformists. Riots ensued, and factions in this violence mapped onto religious and political positions. This event incited a mob composed of Tories who railed against "Whig and immigrant Bank directors" along with dissenting preachers.[32] Defoe's response to this discord was to describe the way public credit and private credit are interdependent in order to show that political factionalism endangers the interests of all individuals.[33] Evoking seventeenth-century discourse, he asks that, no matter which political party has power, public credit must be supported.

In general, Defoe's writings often distinguish between credit that is grounded problematically (or credit that behaves too much like stock-jobbing) and that which is genuinely trustworthy.[34] Defoe also distinguished credit based on visible goods and previous exchange relationships from the more unstable credit that stock-jobbers manipulated for their own ends.[35] He seems to try to produce trust in public credit insofar as it – like private credit – is grounded on past precedents that have proven stable rather than the speculations on an unknown future taken up by stock-jobbers and other bad projectors. For this, he would use a credible commitment thesis of his own. Distinguishing good and bad credit (or true and false credit), then, is one feature of Defoe's writings that remains constant throughout his oeuvre. But there are two aspects of this newfangled credit that need to be accounted for:

1   its basis in systematic accounting, or double-entry bookkeeping; and
2   the fact that for public credit to work, constituents (or, to be more precise in this period, investors) needed to be unified in supporting it.

There is, therefore, simultaneously an epistemological and a moral dimension to this rhetorical work.

There is a good reason that so many critics have read Defoe's texts in order to make sense of eighteenth-century financial history. Defoe has a fundamental role in establishing the "economic model" through his avid defense of public credit. Defoe's economic writings help to establish a society of mutual benefit for promoting new communal or social links through common participation. Defoe describes an institutional apparatus that runs independently of particular players – a system or mechanism – that overcomes the problem of self-interest endemic to the "age of projectors." Further, he refers to a logic of private credit with its means of regulating indebtedness through a system of accounting. Finally, his writings help to put forth the notion that individual constituents of the State relate to one another in a public sphere, which he helps to cultivate in readers by developing narrative suspense around issues of credit and reputation – a way of projecting that is tied not only to economic futures, but also to domestic and private ones.

A disinterested and depersonalized state: *An Essay upon Publick Credit*

In the 1690s, pamphlets in support of the Bank of England used such terms as *the public good* and *the public interest*, words that carry over from Civil War discourse, to justify its existence. William Paterson's scheme for the Bank, published in 1694, uses the language of private and public interest in order to argue that the Bank's private status as the government's creditor is in the interest of all constituents: "Thus a Society of Private Men will be obliged by their Estates and Interests, to strengthen and corroborate the publick Security of this Bank."[36] Individual people looking out for their individual interests serve as Paterson's guarantee that the institution will remain secure and serve both its private investors and the public effectively. *A Letter to a Friend* (1697), a key text supporting the establishment of the Bank, is "Written by a Member of the said Corporation, for the Publick Good of the Kingdom." Those who argued in favor of the Bank, therefore, rhetorically attempted to ensure the public that all interests would be served.

Whether or not the Bank was just another scheme of the 'projectors' (to use the contemporary pejorative terms) was subject to debate. The Bank's private status was controversial from its outset – in part, because it was not perceived as benefitting everyone. Parliament sought to secure the Bank by inserting into its charter a clause that specified that it could only lend to the government with parliamentary consent. This helped the bill pass but did not completely eradicate public concern.[37] A few commentators specifically condemned the way Bank and City interests benefitted directly from government support. For example, *A Short View of the Apparent Dangers and Mischiefs from the Bank of England*, published in 1707, argued that the Bank merely pursued its own private interests rather than acting on behalf of a public good.[38] In effect, through the creation of the Bank, the government supported the existence of a private business that more directly served the interests of the Whigs.

One reason the Bank was argued to be controversial was because a parliament-sponsored project led to the empowerment of a particular political party. The Whigs had been instrumental in enabling William of Orange to take the throne in the Glorious Revolution. Further, Sir John Houblon, the Bank's first director, was a Huguenot merchant and Whig. The political empowerment of City interests through public credit strengthened the political factions empowered after the Glorious Revolution. The personal finances of investors were thus joined to the post-1688 regime and therefore ensured the continuance of it.[39] Charles Davenant's "The True Picture of a Modern Whig" (1701) worries about this, as do many other pamphlets. However, as with Swift's writings, it is important to recognize these statements as 'interested' ones. The Bank was not yet a permanent institution; it was still possible to steer its development.

The year 1710, in which Defoe published *An Essay upon Publick Credit*, was the beginning of the Harley ministry, in which the Tories brought down the Whigs under the reign of Queen Anne.[40] Defoe needed to justify the existence of public credit in order to ensure that the new government acknowledge former debts. What is at a stake in the discussion is provided in the subtitle of the text, "BEING An Enquiry how the PUBLICK CREDIT comes to depend upon the Change of *Ministry*, or the Dissolutions of *Parliaments*; and whether it does so or no." *An Essay upon Publick Credit*, having to grapple with the possibility of political instability that would also entail financial crisis, ultimately asks the new Tory administration to honor the debts of the old Whig government, but in doing so, it provides readers with a well-defined notion of public credit that does the

work of rendering the particular government official an abstraction without particular, individual interests. This part is crucial.

Defoe's writings trouble the notion that accounting alone provides the proto-
scientific, neutral force that ushers the world seamlessly into financial capitalism.
Instead, he helps readers to envision another sort of neutral and disinterested
system. In its description of the State, *An Essay upon Publick Credit* explicitly
describes the financial branches of government as a mechanistic entity that functions without particular human actors.

> In this the Great Officers of the Treasury and Exchequer are, as we may say,
> perfectly Passive; their Business is indeed Active; so the Wheels of a Clock,
> their Business is to go round; but they are subject to the Influence of *their
> Position*, the Operations of the Springs and Wheels that guide *their Motion*,
> by which they act passively, if that may be said, *that is*, of meer Necessity.[41]

This description does the work of removing the active agency of individual
players. The State is a mechanism, and the individuals that make it up are
passive entities subject to natural mechanical motions. While these agents play a
role in the overall business of government, their activity is as systematic as a
clock, regulated by their positioning in a predictable machine.

What is it, then, that springs from such a mechanism? Moving on, Defoe
argues that credit is an extension of this play of active officials who react
passively.

> CREDIT is not the Effect of this or that Wheel in the Government, moving
> regular and just to its proper Work; but of the whole Movement, acting by
> the Force of its true Original Motion, according to the exquisite Design of
> the Director of the whole Frame.[42]

Credit is the cumulative effect of a system of impartial agents regulated by a stabilizing force. Using the words "design" and "director" seems to hearken to religious terminology, as if who or what is in charge is a supernatural, absolute
authority. So far, one imagines a system of impartial agents regulated from
above by an overseer of the whole plan, or the "whole frame" (a term Katherine
Clark explores in her cumulative reading of Defoe).[43]

Using this philosophical-theological argument, Defoe attempts to define
public credit in particular. Tellingly, when he names the various players that
make up a government, these participants are without personal qualities; they are
depersonalized. Public credit renders the individual agents that help to constitute
it as neutral, for

> the Publick Credit is *National*, not *Personal*, so it depends upon No *Thing*
> or *Person*, No *Man* or *Body of Men*, but upon the Government.... Neither
> does our Credit depend upon the Person of the Queen, *as Queen*, or the indi-
> vidual House of Commons, *Identically*; as if *no Queen* but her present

Majesty...: *But* it will remain a Truth, that *every Queen*, or *every King*, and *every Parliament*, succeeding the present ... shall keep up *the same* Character.[44]

This passage is particularly striking, as it suggests that the depersonalization of each participant means that public credit ends up having, in the end, a unified and stable character. Public credit has integrity as long as its component parts work as a machine. This passage entices readers to stop imagining Queen Anne or Harley, for example, and instead envision a mechanism with faceless administrators at the helm. What is interesting in this formulation is that it is also an abstraction – it is precisely *not* the particular characters of the individuals that ensure the stability of public credit between regimes. It is a virtual system rather than the particular individuals who comprise it, but the system itself is nonetheless starting to develop a character of its own.

While there is an impersonal director, always guiding the machine, Defoe's further work complicates the theological (or indeed, secular or even laissez-faire) component of the argument. Defoe's notion of public credit comes with a caveat: It must be managed in the same way, with the same techniques, as private credit. This development in his theory is particularly complicated, especially given that private credit was subject to personal trust and reputation, or the belief that someone would repay that had to do with emotional knowledge of other humans. This requires one to examine very closely the way Defoe understands the relationship between reputation – the older "culture of credit" (to use Craig Muldrew's terms)[45] – and this newfangled system whose very existence seems to be precariously tangled up with the new way it is described and discussed in the public sphere.

Defoe argues that public and private credit should be treated in exactly the same way, for "experience tells us the same thing in all Cases, whether private or publick, Personal or National."[46] Reflecting his stance in *Projects*, he says that public credit, like private credit, is a matter of "Management."[47] Credit, generally, "is produc'd, and grows insensibly, from fair and upright Dealing, punctual Compliance, honourable Performance of Contracts and Covenants, in short, 'tis the Off-spring of universal Probity."[48] He repeats this more than once: "Our Credit in this Case is a Public Thing; it is rightly call'd by some of our Writers, NATIONAL CREDIT; the Word denominates its Original; 'tis produc'd by *the Nations* Probity, the Honour and exact performing *National Engagements*."[49] An emphasis on exactness and probity is reiterated throughout the document, terms he will also use to discuss what is required of the tradesman.[50] Exact management of public credit is to "put Life into the Nation" and help "those People that had Money think it *as safe*, as well deposited, and the Principle in as *good Hands* as in their own."[51] Suggesting that a person's money is in "good hands" begins to do the work of rendering that which is abstract concrete through literary vehicles – metonym and simile. But this passage also suggests another aspect in the constitution of public credit: One must transfer his trust to the nation, hence the term *national credit*. Investments are not actually 'in' someone's hands – it is only a figure for the mechanical workings of a system. What, then, happens to the personal culture of credit that Muldrew says persists throughout this period when trust shifts from the personal to the virtual?

The call for exactness and probity in addressing individual contracts will require a theory of accounting, another system that, as Mary Poovey shows, works with honest, plain writing that inspires confidence in other people.[52] Poovey also helps one to make sense of why, in discussing public credit, Defoe cannot take recourse to the ledger alone:

> In theory, the system of double-entry bookkeeping displayed the honesty of individual merchants and of merchants of a group by prominently featuring the easily monitored balances of that signified virtue. In practice, however, not all the double-entry books were public, in the sense of being open to inspection.[53]

Trust in the person holding the ledger mattered. But with public credit, there is no one person to evaluate for his reputation for being able to repay his debts.

An Essay upon Publick Credit demonstrates an interesting tension. On the one hand, particular interests are out of the picture because public credit is a system that is free of particular actors. On the other, Defoe resorts to proto-literary techniques in order to help his readers imagine that their particular interests are being served by a system managed by individuals imbued with the virtue – or the reputation – of someone who operates on the principles stemming from honest trade, including practices of diligent double-entry bookkeeping. This has to do with the delicate balance between interest and disinterest. The end effect of these descriptions is a notion that the public good is being served.

This seems a sleight of hand. No one person is interested, but a system nonetheless serves each individual's interests: It serves the public good, and we know this because it takes on the virtues of the tradesman. We trust the nation imagined as an honest tradesman that keeps his books and honors his contracts. The reputation of the depersonalized, mechanistic system, then, is still required, for, despite the qualities of numbers that seem intrinsically neutral, the ledger has no way of demonstrating that it is tethered to the real (which would seem necessary if one is to completely align accounting with emergent scientific or systematic-empirical practices). As *The Review* will show, without management, credit in general suffers, and therefore Defoe's description of management is also very much a prescription for it.

A call for better management: Lady Credit in *The Review*

Much of *The Review*, especially the parts that follow in the wake of "the loss of the City," reiterates what Defoe discusses in *An Essay upon Publick Credit*. In an issue of *The Review* dated December 26, 1710, Defoe articulates a complicated relationship between public and private credit. While private credit historically pre-exists public credit, Defoe argues that the former is dependent on the latter, for "all Pubiick [*sic*] Credit is deriv'd, tho' at some distance, from private Credit, and yet it reciprocally Contributes to the Support of its said remote Parent."[54] But conversely, public credit requires private credit in order to thrive because the former is dependent on the wealth of the nation's constituents: "If private Credit falls off, the Stock, the Trade, and by Consequence the Wealth of the Nation decays; and if the Trade of the Nation dies, the Fund of Publick Credit fails."[55] Here, individual private credit seems to 'add up' to public credit, but is also derived from it. This formulation seems related to the question of interest that gets worked out in *An Essay upon Publick Credit.*

In Defoe's representation of the system, credit in general is necessary for the whole of the nation, not just for particular interests. After arguing for the reciprocal connection between public and private credit, Defoe also explicitly condemns political factionalism in the same issue of *The Review*, arguing that all individuals are supported by the same system of public credit. To these assertions, Defoe adds a third and significant term. "Power" is also a factor in the interconnected relationship between public and private credit: "Publick Credit Supports Power, Power Supports Commerce, and Commerce Credit; an endless *Circulation* runs through these things, their Affinity, Connection, and Dependance is such, that they ever Influence one another, and rise and fall together."[56] Defoe thus presents a triad of terms: commerce, credit, and power. Here again, the description seems mechanistic. The structure allows for circulation, but this circulation is between abstractions and not interested individuals.

Reading on, one finds that *The Review*'s underlying polemic aims to get all political interests in a general agreement on the necessity of managing public credit. "Credit is the Health of Every party, 'tis a general Good; whatever your private Feuds are, whatever your Party Quarrels are, you should join her. For you are all concern'd in it."[57] Here, Defoe refers explicitly to public credit (although what is implied is that a neglect of public credit entails the loss of private credit). He then addresses the Tories and Whigs:

> Gentlemen, you that are Ruining the Publick Credit, you are at War not with *Tories*, not with *Whigs*, but with Trade; you are *at War* with Industry, *at War* with general Improvement; in short, in some respects, you are *at War* with Mankind.[58]

Without the support of all parties, public credit (and thus private credit, according to Defoe's logic) suffers. The third term, power, can then be read as the political apparatus that thrives when the system of credit and commerce function accordingly. This text echoes *An Essay upon Publick Credit*, this time more explicitly spelling out the case that power is based upon non-factionalized consensus. A political consensus helps to provide public credit with the reputation of stability it requires.

The interrelation between public and private credit (or the analogy between them) is somewhat convoluted in *The Review*, in which Defoe develops his characterization of credit through an elaborately drawn figure of Lady Credit. Lady

Credit's identity lies somewhere between public credit and private credit. People of various ideological persuasions represented credit as an "inconstant, often self-willed but persuadable woman,"[59] and often anti-feminist metaphors were used to produce female "figures of disorder."[60] Sherman notes the way "Lady Credit can be no (consistent) lady because, embodying the whimsicality of the market, her female 'honesty' is a punning, metaphorical register of the mercurial honesty of marketplace representations."[61] Sherman's study entices one to consider an important question: What happened to the exactness and probity that Defoe attaches to the movement of a system in *An Essay upon Publick Credit*? While Sherman emphasizes the way Defoe discursively produces "products appealing to a desire for truth while withholding data to verify indicia of truth," *The Review* can also be characterized as being a bit less postmodern than this.[62] Indeed, Defoe works very hard to render credit as something that can be stabilized by telling stories about Lady Credit, who is constructed like a natural human being – an aristocrat, even, who is an element of the older system of trust and reputation. She works as a character to create a coherent public perception, "supplying the social order with its impersonal mechanisms of coherence and comprehensibility."[63] *The Review* discusses credit as a female character with a singular identity who is easily influenced by her environment. Lady Credit serves as a means for consolidating the character of a system and introducing a need to manage it. Such a reading, however, requires a context for Lady Credit's role in *The Review*.

Before Lady Credit, there had already been a tradition of using female figures as national icons, often originating from instantiations of familiar contemporary figures of patron goddesses, namely that of Lady Britannia. Lady Britannia was a symbol inscribed all over the Bank: on the earliest notes, on the building, and in its ledgers. Other writings were more critical, such as the Tory *Moderator* when it satirizes Defoe's Lady Credit through "the False Fits of Whiggish Credit Discovered; or, an Account of the Turns and Returns, Comings and Goings, Visits and Departings of that Subtle Pharisaical Lady Call'd Whiggish Phanatical Credit."[64] And Joseph Addison would also use a female figure in his own characterization in *The Spectator* (No. 3, March 3, 1711), which I will discuss in the following chapter. The Bank of England itself would, by the end of the century, be called "The Old Lady of Threadneedle Street," a figure that would be important for the Bank's self-image at the turn of the nineteenth century. Importantly, what Defoe accomplishes with Lady Credit renders intelligible the political and economic dimensions of the discourse. In effect, Lady Credit brings the problem of inherent risk home to readers whose interests are not specifically economic or political by finding a common language for talking about credit, using the beliefs and expectations of the landed elites. Michael McKeon calls Lady Credit an example of "narrative concentration," in which credit is "domesticated" and made understandable in familial terms.[65] Lady Credit becomes a single figure – almost but not quite a literary character – who needs management. In order to manage her, one must know her.

To answer the question of why Defoe chooses a female character, it is important to reflect on the patriarchal social relationships that prevailed in this period, traditional ties characterized by trust and reputation, having more of an emotional basis than ones facilitated through an economy. In an issue of *The Review* dated January 10, 1706, Defoe states that, in some countries, Lady Credit is called "honour," to make her comprehensible in terms of aristocratic ideology.[66] Indeed, much of what the Lady undergoes in the various short allegorical narratives Defoe goes on to provide are threats to her honor – her virginity, in other words. This had an economic value for families under the laws of primogeniture. Defoe translates credit to honor, because, as he says, "[h]er Name in our Language is call'd CREDIT, in some Countries Honour, and in others, I know not what."[67] Whatever their background, individuals reading *The Review*, and those predisposed to an aristocratic ideology that was so opposed to public credit, would have understood what it meant for an aristocratic woman to lose her honor. As Defoe says, "to recover Credit to any place, where she has been ill Treated, and persuade her to return, is almost as Difficult as to restore Virginity, or to make a W–re an Honest Woman."[68] From the first mention onwards, therefore, Defoe brings home the notion of credit, domesticating it for those operating under the ideology situated within a framework of aristocratic honor and, more specifically, female virtue.

Like a natural human, Lady Credit eats and sleeps, takes walks, and enters periods of health and periods of sickness. On Thursday, June 16, 1709, Defoe provides one of his many long histories of the "Coy Mistress of Treasure" that must be managed. She has a healthy diet of "Flowing Cash, unquestion'd Funds, punctual Compliances, Faithful, exact Payments, Due Interest, and, which is the Foundation of all, Intrinsick Value."[69] However, she is often ill, such as when she succumbs to the "falling sickness" during the Sacheverell events of 1710, a disease to which her whole "family" (such as Reputation, Virtue, and Prudence) is susceptible.[70]

In his depiction of Lady Credit, Defoe emphasizes the accurate management of contracts. Some enemies of this mistress are, of course, the stock-jobbers, whose propensity to speculate means that the value of these quantitative contracts becomes threatened.[71] As the metaphor of Lady Credit and her extended "family" develops, so too will Defoe's insistence that what nourishes Lady Credit (representing credit in general) is a combination of proper business practice and the maintenance of a trustworthy reputation. What hurts the Lady is a government that will not protect her by ensuring that she stays grounded in a solid reputation, and not on the speculative practices of the stock-jobbers who barter for their own interests. Lady Credit is not inherently fickle, therefore, but can be subjected to outside influences that render her unstable. Again, Defoe uses a traditional framework to convey this: "[I]f you will entertain this Virgin, you must Act upon the ... Principles of Honour, and Justice; you must preserve Sacred all the Foundations, and build regular Structures upon them."[72] Lady Credit is, after all, a Lady with a reputation to maintain.

Tellingly, early passages (January 10, 1706) on Lady Credit feature a history of the Bank, which – the reader is told – was designed to overcome problems of the seventeenth century in which the "lady run away and left us." To

Court her Ladyship's Company, and procure her Return, a Knot of her Friends got together, and invited her to come and live with them, and promised, that for her Security they would establish a General Fund for running Cash, that should at any time furnish what quantity of Money she should have occasion for, and supply either a Government or private Persons upon reasonable Terms; and this they call'd, A BANK.[73]

Friends, a term that meant something more like extended family, is striking even a few years later (August 8, 1710) because the Bank becomes, in effect, Lady Credit's household.

Her walk was daily between the Bank and the Exchequer, and between the Exchange and the Treasury; she always went Unveil'd, dress'd like a Bride; innumerable were her Attendants, and a general Joy shew'd itself upon the Faces of all People, when they saw her; for the whole World was pleas'd with her Company.[74]

In summary, Defoe imagines Lady Credit as presiding over her household in the Bank. Defoe domesticates public credit by bringing it into the realm of the private sphere. In this position, Lady Credit is protected from the stock-jobbers by being managed properly. This has a social dimension, as well, as the various protectors are separate entities that do not necessarily naturally cooperate with one another and must be encouraged to do so.

Lady Credit develops as a response to a crisis in public credit, one that passed in the ensuing years. However, a new crisis would emerge a decade later in the wake of the South Sea Bubble. The anti-public credit sentiment that ensued after the Bubble would require a shift in rhetoric, from imagining credit abstractly to understanding it as a set of virtuous practices that everyone should follow. This Defoe would accomplish by writing a manual on how individuals use credit in trade, which has the effect of elevating the tradesman to the status of a gentleman, and by suggesting that financial literacy is of the highest virtue.

The South Sea Bubble and *The Compleat English Tradesman*

For most commentators, contemporary and modern, the South Sea Bubble was a worrisome time in which one private – but chartered – joint-stock company that dealt in cloth, agricultural goods, and slaves was held responsible for what was perceived as the reckless speculations of investors. In August of 1720, stock values dropped from £1,000 to less than £400 in a matter of weeks.[75] The person often considered to be England's first prime minister, Robert Walpole, who both supported and invested in the South Sea scheme, rose to power after the ensuing investigation and its aftermath. He worked diligently to save investors by bailing out the South Sea Company, convincing the Bank of England to take nearly £4 million of South Sea government debt as well as establishing a sinking fund. These acts of "creative accounting" had the added impact of further empowering the Bank and therefore contributing to the restructuring of the State.[76] What was perceived by some to be a manipulative act led to public outrage, prompting Thomas Gordon and John Trenchard to publish *Cato's Letters* (1720–3), which decried Walpole's practices and called for transparency.

The South Sea Bubble is usually cited as one of the most detrimental market crashes in history in which many lost fortunes, and corrupt individuals were often blamed for what happened. Contemporaries (and historians) often attribute the event to a "gambling mania" and liken the stock market to other moral vices of the time.[77] While, as Helen Julia Paul points out, within today's economic framework, the behavior of the investors may not have been all that irrational, contemporaries were made anxious by the event, especially because of the company's status as one of the primary public creditors.[78] The aftermath was also troubling insofar as many were skeptical of the interests that benefited from the bailout.[79] And of course Defoe weighs in, continuing his defense of public credit by calling for virtuous management. *The Compleat English Tradesman*, published in 1726, takes on the question of accounting in private credit transactions, dealing with ways it can be used manipulatively as well as virtuously. While this text deals mainly with private credit, it reveals a post-Bubble notion that virtuous accounting behooves an individual as much as the State. Indeed, it puts the onus on the individual to be financially literate for the good of the whole, to cultivate a personal reputation by knowing how to handle accounting.

What is at stake in private credit is knowing whether one can trust other people and their accounts of themselves, and this was dependent on a whole array of social and communal factors that conveyed credibility. While the majority of economic analyses of early markets are grounded in rational choice theory (and therefore reflect the modern liberal tradition), Muldrew characterizes a "public means of social communication and circulating judgment" in earlier lending networks facilitated by local markets within small communities, which contrasts to the later impersonal system of finance.[80] Arguing against the functionalist (rather than historicist) method of Niklas Luhmann and others, he maintains that there was no circulating capital in the modern sense of bank money until the founding of the Bank of England, and thus "the market cannot simply be interpreted mathematically as an abstract means of exchanging goods on the basis of individual desire or self-interest."[81] When merchants and tradesmen began to use the new quantitative financial instruments, they still relied on a qualitative means of knowing how and when to trust each other. The trust they had acquired from earlier networks, and the model they used to derive such trust, governed their transactions even though quantitative credit instruments were at their disposal.

What emerges in Muldrew's work on credit is a strong emphasis on reputation. Despite a gradual shift to a quantitative means for trust, qualitative reputation is what governed trade practice. Margot C. Finn, like Muldrew, emphasizes the importance of reputation as a way of understanding early modern credit. Finn argues that people formed qualitative conceptions of what others were like, whether they were creditworthy, and this required an analysis of "character":

Where early modern debt relations had been predicated on conceptions of mutual trust, modern consumer credit was shaped most decisively by notions of personal character.... Perceptions of personal worth, in turn, registered the successful use of goods and services obtained on credit to construct creditworthy characters. Credit thus reflected character, but also constituted it.[82]

Finn, like Muldrew, challenges the thesis that credit, even as a form of money, can be grounded on quantitative abstractions alone. Rather, credit is a product of character and reputation, two qualitative registers, which Defoe also explores.

Sherman writes that *"The Compleat English Tradesman* imports the language, the concepts of public credit into the shop."[83] While *The Compleat English Tradesman* ostensibly covers the topic of private credit, I will be providing a counter-intuitive reading that suggests it is also another text in support of public credit, reflecting a post-South Sea Bubble need for stabilizing credit by insisting that the way public credit is managed has nothing to do with the whims of the stock-jobbers, a way of using the accounting ledger that led to the downfall of the South Sea Company at the expense of the public good. Accounting, while serving as a means for conferring "cultural authority on numbers," was insufficient for grounding a credit economy.[84] Rather, Defoe is concerned with the intertwining of two abstract systems after a crisis – that of the State as the government and that of the economy of private individuals – that he strategically links together in a text that seems to be about the private interests of the English tradesman. *The Compleat English Tradesman* prescribes a way for the individual tradesman to behave while also evoking public credit as a model of virtue for the tradesman to follow, a reversal of what seems to be the case in *Projects*, in which he suggests that the tradesman is the model of virtue (or at least a model of "intelligence").

Stock-jobbing, the enemy of Defoe's tradesman ethos, resurfaces throughout his writings as an antithesis to what I have called his virtuous projecting. What these attacks suggest is that, counter to the many historical accounts of the Enlightenment project growing out of accounting – which hold up when one primarily focuses on political arithmeticians like Petty – in Defoe's case, accounting was seen as a problem more than a ground for a public credit system. Defoe was ambivalent about the authority of double-entry bookkeeping, even while he praises the Bank of England for its impeccable accounting ledgers and highlights its centrality for the tradesman. The *Compleat English Tradesman* suggests that accounting, while central to credit, requires a supplement in order to become trustworthy. Defoe's understanding of accounting, in other words, precludes the possibility of it becoming a self-sufficient and self-regulating system because the value of the ledger cannot be detached from the qualitative reputation of the person holding it.

Defoe's earlier writings provide an example of how credit as an abstraction produced through accounting can be manipulated. *The Villainy of Stock-Jobbers Detected* (1701) condemns the way some brokers used the financial system for their own ends, and it addresses why runs on banks occur. He refers to the Bank of England in describing this problem:

> The Credit of the Bank of England does not immediately consist in the reality of their Foundation: Sir, sure it does originally depend upon the Goodness of their Bottom, but the more immediate Credit of their Proceedings, depends upon the currency of their Bills, and the currency of their Bills depends upon their immediate Pay; *the Bank has no Advantage of the meanest Goldsmith as to their current Bills*, for no longer than their Payments continue punctual and free, no longer will any Man take their Bills, or give them Credit for Money.[85]

After all, there is not enough cash to back the Bank's note issue; the run is an inherent risk in public credit. Through accounting, the Bank ensures circulation in order to produce its credit and not the other way around. But this causes problems when, in a crisis, notes stop circulating and demands for cash are made. This is what happens when people perceive that the public funds are being manipulated for private ends. He calls on the government "*to take Care that their Influence and Power be so restrained by wholesome Laws, as that the whole Command of the Nations Cash and Credit may not be in the Hands of Companies and Stock-Jobbers.*"[86]

In *Hymn to the Pillory* (1703), a satire Defoe wrote in prison the year a glass business for which he did the accounts failed, he worries about the false notion of credit grounded in account books. In this satirical piece, Defoe condemns a reified concept of "intrinsick value" that leads to instability.

> *Jobbers*, and *Brokers* of the City Stocks,
> With forty Thousand Tallies at their backs
> Who make our Banks and Companeys obey,
> Or sink 'em all *the shortest way*.
> T'Intrinsick Value of our Stocks,
> Stated in our Calculating Books;
> Th' Imaginary Prizes rise and fall,
> As they Command who toss the Ball.[87]

This passage opens up questions about how contemporaries saw the authority of account books and asks one to rethink the immediacy of the epistemological impact of double-entry bookkeeping. Here, the "calculating books" are an onerous threat, producing figures that are not tethered to the real. Indeed, rather than being a stable and trustworthy mechanism, they very much seem to be the cause of instability.

But this is not the only problem packed into these two texts. A larger problem seems to be that those who profit from the imaginary values recorded in the ledgers are the jobbers and companies – private interests and not the public good, in other words. From Defoe's perspective, preserving the public good means protecting commerce – and stock-jobbing poses a direct threat to this sector. Defoe reveals his concern about relying on a form of "intrinsick value" that is really an abstraction. His use of this term is facetious: This sort of "value" brings about "imaginary prizes" (ones which are not even necessarily valuable as speculations) for a select few, and, by this, he does not mean prizes for honest merchants or tradesmen. Nor does he mean prizes in tangible goods. Defoe's refusal to use the ledger in a corrupt way suggests that he seeks to protect credit for the future. What is the difference between stock-jobbing (or chartered joint-stock companies like the East India Company and the South Sea Company) and the Bank, according to Defoe? Given what he says in *The Review* and *An Essay upon Publick Credit*, it has to do with the State's management.

Defoe does not change his tune after the South Sea Bubble. In his *A Brief Debate upon the Dissolving of the Late Parliament* (1722), he writes to ensure that parliament, as in prior times, manage credit in a stable way, condemning those who "made use of innumerable Stratagems to deceive the People, deluding and drawing in Innocent People, by Transfering Imaginary Stock by, and a Hundred Imaginary Persons Buying in with the Company's Money, and Selling out their own."[88] Here, the worries of early pamphlets return with a vengeance. Imaginary stocks are again the problem, dependent upon abstract numbers (and "imaginary persons") that are used for private gain and not for the public good. Accounting seems to be a problem for Defoe rather than an authoritative mechanism, but he attempts to resolve this problem through the terms of private credit in *The Compleat English Tradesman*, in which he articulates a difference between good and bad accounting practices.

Despite his anxieties, Defoe also insists on the importance of exact accounting practices. He praises the Bank of England for its perfect ledgers, and he maintains that the proper use of reckoning is central to being an effective merchant or tradesman.[89] But *The Compleat English Tradesman* also spends pages teaching the reader how to behave socially in order to maintain one's reputation, reflecting the older culture of credit in which personal trust determined contractual relations between people. To that end, *The Compleat English Tradesman* even includes pages of fictional scenarios in which reputations are damaged by word of mouth or by the mere suggestion of social impropriety. The text produces an interesting tension: On the one hand, it argues for the necessity of learning arithmetical-algebraic skills to keep one's account books. This is, after all, how all credit instruments work. In this regard, Defoe extols the virtues of numbers and numeracy. On the other hand, the manual provides an analysis of social propriety, teaching readers how and why to trust one another in qualitative terms, training readers to be virtuous financial subjects.

The Compleat English Tradesman is one of many texts published in this period whose purpose was to educate the public on how to keep accounts, among other practices necessary for learning the art of management. While such texts on becoming a merchant or engaging in commerce date back to the Restoration, works in this genre were published in increasing numbers by the late seventeenth and early eighteenth centuries.[90] Indeed, once seen by the aristocratic elite as a profane form of knowledge, these manuals elevated the social role of the trades-man, indicating the new centrality of trade. The proliferation of these texts in this period serves as evidence of the necessity of promoting literacy and numer-acy in using the new instruments of credit, reflecting a feedback loop between the public and the State that serves individuals with interests.[91]

Accounting was understood by many of Defoe's contemporaries as having arisen on the same principles as other emerging sciences. For example, *The Gen-tleman Accomptant* (initially published 1714 but republished repeatedly there-after) was written "by a person of honour" (the traditional word for conveying trustworthiness). It was advertised as a way of teaching the gentry and nobility to manage their accounts and also to understand accounting for the "Publick Affairs of the Nation," and it argued for the importance of "a method so compre-hensive and perfect, as makes it worthy to be put among the Sciences."[92] In this manual, the author argues that it is of the utmost importance to learn how to keep accounts: "To justify this Character of Regular Accompting, I need only say, That Method comprehends all other Methods."[93] The notion that accounting "comprehends all methods" implies that it is a self-sufficient system. This notion of accounting conforms to Poovey's take on history insofar as it is through the way the ledger produces the number – which will, in Poovey's version, serve as a prototype for the modern "fact" – that renders it a systematic method that can be trusted. However, given Defoe's overall anxiety and in light of the way numbers were seen to be manipulated for private interests in the recent South Sea Bubble, one comes to expect something different from Defoe's contribution to yet another genre of didactic reading material. In *The Compleat English Tradesman*, accounting cannot "comprehend all methods," as the author of *The Gentleman Accomptant* argues, because accounting requires a supplementary form of trust in order to be counted as trustworthy. Perhaps this comes as no sur-prise to the reader who has followed Defoe's condemnation of "imaginary" balances in ledgers prior to the Bubble.

What is significant here is the way in which Defoe discusses credit in histor-ical terms. The necessity of keeping exact and regular accounts has only become important in recent times, begins *The Compleat English Tradesman*. While before, a tradesman could remain ignorant of certain business practices, Defoe argues, in modern times it is necessary to learn about the nature of private credit in order to stay in business.[94] An entire section of *The Compleat English Trades-man* is dedicated to the problem of over-trading, or overusing credit. One should not overuse credit, for "credit is stock, and, if well supported, is as good as stock, and will be as durable."[95] Used correctly, credit is like any other form of stock. Defoe is looking towards the future, and accounting is a way of ensuring that one preserves oneself for it.

Using credit correctly implies mastering various systematic practices. In earlier times, Defoe writes, people used to cast accounts once a year. This is no longer the case – the process must now be continual, marking a shift in the tem-poral structure of credit. Defoe warns his readers that a "tradesman without his books, in case of a law-suit for a debt, is like a married woman without her certificate."[96] It is now the tradesman's responsibility to have knowledge at all times of how much he owes and how much is owed to him. The ledger, a sort of mirror for consolidating one's identity, is necessary for understanding where one stands in relation to another tradesman, and this knowledge may need to be summed up at any given time. Because numerous tradesmen fail owing to ignorance of how these credit instruments work, Defoe explains the necessity of learning double-entry bookkeeping.

In Defoe's understanding of accounting, the method fails to "comprehend all methods," but it is nonetheless a necessary system. In his description of why bookkeeping is of the utmost importance, a familiar figure returns: that of the clock. He writes:

> A tradesman's books are his repeating clock, which upon all occasions are to tell him how he goes on, and how things stand with him in the world; there he will know when it is time to go on, or when it is time to give over; and upon his regular keeping, and fully acquainting himself with his books, depends at least the comfort of his trade, if not the very trade itself. If they are not duly posted, and if every thing is not carefully entered in them, the debtor's accounts kept even, the cash constantly balanced, and the credits all stated, the tradesman is like a ship at sea, steered without a helm; he is all in confusion, and knows not what he does, or where he is; he may be a rich man, or a bankrupt – for, in a word, he can give no account of himself to himself, much less to any body else.[97]

Bookkeeping is not only for the practical use of the debtor or the creditor but also for keeping a peace of mind, a clear conscience, by knowing exactly where one stands in a relationship of credit with another merchant or tradesman. It helps to ensure that one remains predictable and stable in the eyes of others. The clock represents a series of slots that have to be filled in a sequence, like Robinson Crusoe's and Clarissa's journals (which I will discuss in what follows). The possibility that one might need to produce the account at any given moment explains why Defoe argues that books should be managed with diligence and regularity.

There is a secularization narrative implicit in this passage. A puritan ideology underlies likening the ledger to a clock and emphasizing that bookkeeping is at the heart of trade. Consciousness of one's own reckoning is analogous to being right with God, evoking a notion of one's fundamental indebtedness to God prevalent in Christian thought. But there is also another puritan element in the *Tradesman*, and that is using the technique of plain style. Clarity, to oneself and to others, is essential to the universal readability of double-entry bookkeeping but also part of what Defoe calls the "trading style" of "easy, plain, and familiar language" because trade needs to be carried out in a "universal language."[98] What is inside the ledger is important, but it is so because it is *legible* to others trading. Bookkeeping is essential to the way Defoe understands credit because all other merchants and tradesmen recognize its regulating capacity.

This does not imply that one turns oneself into a mathematical machine, for there is another layer to the type of legibility Defoe describes. Equally important is the management of one's reputation. Defoe spends pages discussing social interactions, some of which seem at first not to have anything to do with trading practices. One chapter warns about ruining a fellow tradesman's reputation (and thus business) by word of mouth alone. Doing so can harm a tradesman's credit, or "the life of his trade; and he that wounds a tradesman's credit without cause, is as much a murderer in trade, as he that kills a man in the dark is a murderer in matters of blood."[99] Ruining a tradesman's reputation is the same as ruining his credit. One can do this with reason, but one can also maliciously scheme against another, and it is this sort of slander that can be just as damaging:

> A story raised upon a tradesman, however malicious, however false, and however frivolous the occasion, is not easily suppressed, but, if it touches his credit, as a flash of fire it spreads over the whole air like a sheet; there is no stopping it.[100]

Reputation can be made or broken through story-telling, through fictions, and these fictions also have the capacity to transform credit. Fiction and accounting seem to have a similar status here. There is a gap between social appearance (decorum) and substance (virtue) that needs to be managed in order for one's character to be perceived in the right way.

Inserted within *The Compleat English Tradesmen* are fictional examples that demonstrate the way reputation works as a supplement to the ledger. The necessity of maintaining one's reputation is represented through a dialogue about people talking about the trustworthiness or credit of a merchant[101] and a dialogue between a husband and a wife regarding the husband's possible ruin.[102] These passages take the reader from straight exposition to a fictional form in order to help her imagine the rise and fall of credit as an effect of a narrative. This technique operates in a way similar to some of Defoe's novels, such as *Moll Flanders* (1722) and *Roxana* (1724), which feature protagonists whose respective progress depends on the way they are perceived (rather than the money or status they actually possess).

Despite an emphasis on bookkeeping elsewhere, Defoe's discussion of what might now be called gossip shows that interpersonal trust underlies credit. A change in qualitative trust (whether well-founded or not) can lead to a change in quantitative credit. The use of fictions within Defoe's didactic treatise means that he can convey possible non-abstract, qualitative bases for credit. In other words, fictions help to teach his readers the component of credit that is not based on accounting but on the older notion of trust or reputation that still underlies credit transactions. Fiction is, among other things, a tool for social education.

This intimate relationship between reputational trust and accounting gets further elaborated when Defoe discusses what to do when one is on the verge of going bankrupt: "In a word, I speak it to every declining tradesman, if you love yourself, your family, or your reputation, and would ever hope to look the world in the face again, *break* in time."[103] This logic reflects legislation in 1706 that distinguished between honest and dishonest bankruptcies, the latter of which was the road to debtor's prison.[104] Through the logic of accounting alone, if one cannot pay one's debts, one then loses credit with a fellow tradesman. However, according to Defoe, this is not necessarily the case, for

> when a man breaks in time, he may hold up his face to his creditors, and tell them, that he could have gone on a considerable while longer, but that he should have had less left to pay them with, and that he has chosen to stop while he may be able to give them so considerable a sum as may convince them of his integrity.[105]

"Breaking in time" ensures that a tradesman remains honorable in the eyes of his creditors, but, without the legibility of the ledger, there is no means for representing this to said creditor. Defoe lays out what "breaking in time" looks like, an act that requires producing the actual account ledger to the creditor.

> But in a surrender the case is altered in all its parts; the debtor says to his creditors, "Gentlemen, there is a full and faithful account of all I have left; it is your own, and there it is; I am ready to put it into your hands, or into the hands of whomsoever you shall appoint to receive it, and to lie at your mercy." This is all the man is able to do, and therefore is so far honest; whether the methods that reduced him were honest or no, that is a question by itself.[106]

The ledger, showing the quantitative value of what the tradesman still possesses, is proof of what he has to offer his creditor. Whatever the circumstances of his breaking, he "will come off with the reputation of an honest man, and will have the favour of his creditors to begin again, with whatever he may have as to stock."[107] Defoe points to a qualitative, even fictional ground for credit (in the sense that fiction does not have to be an untruth, but a narrative). This act, over and above reckoning within the ledger, suggests that part of preserving private credit is the maintenance of a sound reputation through word of mouth. The fictional ground for credit is the whereabouts of the tradesmen as represented by circulating narratives, but the ledger itself is part of the story, making evident the moral commitment of the beholder.

How do fiction and accounting work in public credit, then, when word of mouth and traditional ways of calibrating reputation no longer apply? Defoe already acknowledges that the Bank is vulnerable because, like stock-jobbing, it requires dealing in imaginary, abstract values. Defoe stabilizes public credit in the very end of *The Compleat English Tradesman* by telling a story, a history. He gives an account of the problem of public credit in the time of Charles II and William III, credit that parliament restored in a way similar to the virtuous tradesman. Parliament recovered credit by "the same method [as] a private person," by doing "justly, and fairly, and honestly, by everybody."[108] Unlike the tumultuous seventeenth century, Defoe argues that the government has recently restored credit in the same way as a private merchant might. The public correlative to reputation in Defoe's interpretation of history is the perception that the government is acting to serve the public good. While describing how to be virtuous at the level of private credit, Defoe argues that the government *is already* virtuous at the level of public credit. Unlike private credit, which requires a feeling of trust in a tangible person, public credit's reputation cannot come from word of mouth alone, but rather through printed discourse. In effect, Defoe provides an early credible commitment thesis.

While Defoe's *Compleat English Tradesman* can be read through the genre of writing about credit like *The Gentleman's Accomptant*, it also breaks from this tradition by theorizing why the ledger is valuable in social terms dependent on fictional narrative. The ledger does not produce credit by referring to values that come from a disinterested mechanism, for this is the very process that gets the nation in trouble when it is used by stock-jobbers. Instead, the ledger is important because it is legible to others. But the holder of the ledger always has to be 'read' in addition. The ledger, in other words, needs a frame because, as a form of expression that bespeaks one's commitment, it must be decoded accordingly. It can be translated into a story that produces someone's reputation or character. Because of this function, it also serves as a self-regulating device.

Credible framing and fiction

Critics have read Defoe's fiction in the context of the Financial Revolution, showing how some of the questions endemic to new forms of credit get explored through various characters. For example, James Thompson shows how "political economy and the novel are not yet separable and distinct discourses" in the time Defoe is writing, and he reads Defoe's fiction accordingly.[109] Sherman writes that Defoe's fictions instantiate "the amoral discourse of the market, where narrative is always potentially fictive hence always evasive."[110] What if one were to use the terminology developed through reading the economic and political concerns of public credit in particular to think about Defoe's other fictional works, ones that critics attribute to the 'rise of the novel'? In all of these texts, Defoe alludes in some way or another to accounting. His works of fiction might be read as thought experiments in which the characters, like Lady Credit, are ideas about how the future will turn out and how management plays a role.

Without the concrete representations facilitated through literary devices, public credit seems to be relevant for politicians, investors, and tradesmen – those whose investments are directly tied to the State. However, with Lady Credit, readers were offered something more: a familiar figure who is mobilized to reach readers not directly connected. This is part of what is at stake when McKeon says that Lady Credit is an example of "narrative concentration": Credit is domesticated, or rendered quotidian and manageable in a way that makes it possible for any reader to understand and even take interest.[111] Defoe mobilizes Lady Credit as a means for understanding a new component of the public through what any individual would have already known from his or her private life. Defoe makes economic principles manageable to readers in other works of fiction as well, using a similar technique of credible framing.

Like *The Compleat English Tradesman*, Defoe's fictions explore the relationship between financial credit and traditional reputation. But, while financial credit becomes increasingly important, it is also supplemented with, and even constituted by, fiction. This is why Moll Flanders and Roxana can pass themselves off as being wealthy even when they are not. Roxana "makes her own identity through her powers of acquisition," which is a direct result of her engagement in trade.[112] Both characters frame their own stories in a way that seems credible to other characters, which takes precedence over the fact that, at some point in each narrative, they have neither money nor honor to their names. In this sense, Defoe's novels can be read as thought experiments having to do with what he attempted to nail down by advocating for public credit: namely, that credible framing from a disinterested authority matters.

John F. O'Brien's work on *Roxana*, for example, supports this thesis because he examines what Defoe's fictions claim to do in their prefaces in contrast to what they actually do in the main narratives. *Roxana* begins with a preface that states "that the foundation of this is laid in Truth of Fact; *and so the Work is not a Story, but a History*."[113] The sense of historicity that Defoe develops in *The Compleat English Tradesman* is here evoked explicitly. This time, however, it is not a national history, but a private one. Here, Defoe attempts to distinguish historical narrative – history which signals commitment – from the earlier romance by suggesting it is grounded in empirical reality. But because the history is supposedly written in first person from the perspective of the woman whose credibility is at stake throughout the novel, the preface must go on to claim that the writer is acquainted with the lady, and that this might "*be a Pledge for the Credit of the rest*."[114] Defoe borrows a convention from contemporary 'true histories' insofar as he claims historicity, defending the account of the central character. The preface requires that someone outside of Roxana's perspective, someone already established as having a trustworthy reputation, frame her story in order to give it this status.[115]

In *A Journal of the Plague Year* (1722), Defoe uses a first-person narrator to discuss the drastic impact of the plague on the city as well as tell his particular story of what he finds. In order to establish that the narrator is authoritative, the title page includes information about the account, which is "Written by a Citizen who continued all the while in London." Readers are meant to trust the narrator through a combination of the fact that he is both a citizen and an eye-witness. Further, the account is "never made public before" – the text offers to bring to light an account of what happened before newspapers and is signed by "H.F.," producing a fiction that it is authored by someone who lived through the actual plague. This time, it is not so important that an honorable person be the author, but rather that the author was present to witness the events. Here, reputation comes more directly from a rhetoric of empiricism. In both of these cases, what is required is an empirical witness to garner readerly trust through a meta-fictional frame. But, in the *Journal* and also in *Robinson Crusoe* (1719), Defoe introduces another way of credible framing a story, one that mimics what he so carefully lays out in his economic writings: accounting.

What makes the *Journal* different from *Roxana* is the way it uses numbers, even presenting them as pseudo-statistical accounts that are embedded within the narrative's text. In contrast to the narrator's description, the *Journal* describes superstitious citizens, people who attempt to encourage the anxiety of others, hearsay about people infecting others with the plague, and other forms of chaos brought about by public panic.[116] Over and against this mass panic produced by the fear of others, the narrator cites pseudo-statistical information on the number of dead.[117] This information, the reader gleans, comes from credible sources outside the narrator's eyewitness perspective. The narrator himself does not see or count the dead but instead uses statistics to ground his version of the way the plague has transformed London. The numbers, which Defoe is thought to have borrowed from actual records from the event, have the effect of substantiating the narrator's account, making it seem trustworthy – a 'true history' rather than a 'romance.' H.F. is a reliable recorder of information in general, and therefore we trust his numbers. Readerly trust, therefore, is not garnered solely from the Baconian epistemology that critics have tended to attribute to Defoe's writings.

In the preface to *Robinson Crusoe*, which is also similar to *Roxana* in terms of its credible framing, Defoe writes that the "editor believes the thing to be a just History of Fact; neither is their any appearance of Fiction in it."[118] The reader is meant to believe that the account is historically believable, or that Robinson Crusoe is a real person who actually lived, but this notion later gets complicated by the way the narrative unfolds. This has to do with the formal way the narrative is presented: Once again, an external narrative frames another narrative within. In addition to the retrospective narrative that we are told is a "true history of fact," Crusoe keeps a journal whose purpose is to help him keep track of, to account for, proceedings on the island, which also supposedly serves as documentary evidence, a material witness, to the experience. But this journal also has the potential to produce a paradoxical effect of rendering the main narrative less trustworthy.

Robinson Crusoe attempts to show that its protagonist is trustworthy through the type of credit Defoe advocates when he discusses "probity" and "exactness" in *The Review*. When Crusoe is stranded on the island, he keeps track of his time in a strict and systematic manner. The desire to keep accounts is present from the beginning, just after the shipwreck. Before Crusoe finds pen and ink in the ship, he finds a way of "reckoning" by other means:

> After I had been there about Ten or Twelve Days, it came into my Thoughts, that I should lose my Reckoning of Time for want of Books and Pen and Ink, and should even forget the Sabbath Days from the working Days; but to prevent this I cut it with my Knife upon a large Post, in Capital Letters.[119]

This resembles the need for accounting in *The Compleat English Tradesman* when Defoe argues that the tradesman's books are like a "repeating clock." In addition, the pagination of Crusoe's spiritual/moral evaluation of his situation is even presented in double-entry form.[120] Crusoe may be utterly alone, but he never knows when he will be asked for an account of himself, much like the tradesman.

After taking an inventory of his goods from the shipwreck, Crusoe uses instruments of reckoning from the ship in order to keep track of his scarce resources: "I found Pen, Ink and Paper, and I husbanded them to the utmost, and I shall shew, that while my Ink lasted, I kept things very exact."[121] After 27 years of being on the island, Crusoe is able to claim that his management had been exact – his "repeating clock" had been effective:

> But as for an exact Reckoning of Days, after I had once lost it, I could never recover it again; nor had I kept even the Number of Years so punctually, as to be sure that I was right, tho' as it prov'd, when I afterwards examin'd my Account, I found I had kept a true Reckoning of Years.[122]

This demonstration has, on the one hand, the capacity to ensure that the reader think the narrative is a credible one. But credible framing is not so simple, and reading on one finds out why: The novel draws attention to its own form through its use of the journal – it is self-reflexive – and in so doing calls on the reader to see if the journal matches the reality whose time it purports to be reckoning with the probity and exactness that Defoe so values.

Ironically, it is the journal's attempt to ground itself systematically (by accounting for time, for example) that renders the text problematic as a true history. McKeon argues that a dilemma of "quantitative completeness" characteristic of contemporary rhetoric of empiricism in the journal undermines the novel's historicity:

> But since at least the first few weeks of the journal must be a retrospective re-creation of events, they have the ambiguous power both to confirm the historicity of those events by referring back to them, and to undermine their factuality by providing an alternative version of "what happened."[123]

Citing moments when there is a discrepancy between the journal and the main narrative, such as in descriptions of the weather on particular days and in the order in which Defoe takes on certain tasks, McKeon argues that the journal violates the narrative's claim to being based in historical reality.[124] Grounding the text in accounting undermines a certain type of credibility, and whether the novel lives up to its status as a true history becomes problematized. The question is not whether one believes the systematic account because it is systematic but rather whether one trusts the character of Robinson Crusoe enough to resist auditing his accounts. The same holds true for the State.

This is where Sherman's discussion about Defoe's concern with the instability of credit becomes most useful, for it is here that the stabilizing component of credit – which I have argued comes from Defoe's need to defend public credit in particular – becomes destabilized. In fact, *Robinson Crusoe* becomes generically unstable as a true history because the credible framing is undermined when the reader decides to reread, to check the 'facts' to see if they match the 'reality.' The books are open, ready for critical inspection by readers of an emergent public sphere. It is in the interest of some to do so, for others not so much. But the regulatory function of accounting means that one is invited to do so either way. Indeed, gesturing to the ledger indicates the presence of a feedback loop insofar as it anticipates the reception and evaluation of others. While Defoe is, by this point, writing fictions for an emergent reading public whose interests are not necessarily political or economic, the logic starts to resemble those of his earlier writings on public credit.

By the 1720s, it seems that the question of public credit was no longer aligned with strict political party divisions but rather with ideologies mapping onto different temporalities, epistemologies, and ideas of progress, ones that McKeon calls "aristocratic," "progressive," and "conservative" in *The Origins of the English Novel* (1987). Defoe's attempt to use credible framing and empirical fact, which can be associated with progressive ideology, is also accompanied by what McKeon calls "naïve empiricism," which would collide with conservative "extreme skepticism" over the next couple of decades. *Robinson Crusoe* anticipates this clash of ideologies by playing with modes of credibility that are on the verge of self-deconstruction.

In the end, however, Defoe is no simple "naïve empiricist." He trains his readers to see and understand the way credit is built, but in this very exposition, he builds credit. He makes problems inherent in credit evident and their problematization possible ultimately for the end of showing how credit can be stabilized through shrewd thinking. What this requires is the internalization of his version of credible framing. One must learn how to represent oneself if one is to have an interest. By suggesting that the narrative account is true because of the systematic and therefore credible way it is framed, Defoe innovates fiction by evoking the question of whether its purpose is really the same as his economic writings: to stabilize fact to garner commitment. Like public credit, fiction develops out of a need to hang onto a tether to the real while training readers to accommodate themselves to disinterested representation. Unlike public credit, however, what is at stake in the transformation of fictional forms is a growing appreciation of the aesthetic.

Notes

1 J.G.A. Pocock, *The Machiavellian Moment*, 425.
2 Ibid., 439.
3 Sandra Sherman, *Finance and Fictionality in the Early Eighteenth Century*, 7–8.
4 John Richetti, *The Life of Daniel Defoe*, 15–16.
5 See Colin Nicholson, *Writing and the Rise of Finance*, 8.
6 James Macdonald, "The Importance of Not Defaulting," 127; Carl Wennerlind, *Casualties of Credit*, 169.
7 In Macdonald's account, the debate over public credit was quickly resolved:

> In 1711, party politics precluded using the 'Whig' Bank of England, and a new Tory-controlled trading company was established for the purpose. The flotation of

the South Sea Company in September converted £9.2 million of the government's floating debt into perpetual annuities, and effectively brought the fiscal situation under control.

(130)

8 See Nicholson, 17.
9 Jonathan Swift, *The Examiner and Other Pieces Written in 1710–1711*, 6.
10 See Helen Julia Paul, *The South Sea Bubble*, 13.
11 See John Brewer, *The Sinews of Power*, 250.
12 Daniel Defoe, *The Review*, 413.
13 Mark Knights, *Representation and Misrepresentation in Later Stuart Britain*, 316.
14 Maximillian E. Novak, *Economics and the Fiction of Daniel Defoe*, 4.
15 See Simon Schaffer, "Defoe's Natural Philosophy and the Worlds of Credit," 13.
16 Richetti, 8.
17 Ibid., 13.
18 Koji Yamamoto, "Reformation and the Distrust of the Projector in the Hartlib Circle," 380.
19 Ibid., 380–1.
20 Ian Watt, *The Rise of the Novel*, 60, 62.
21 Novak, 5.
22 Sherman, 8.
23 Katherine Clark, *Daniel Defoe*, 16.
24 Daniel Defoe, *Essays upon Several Projects*, 1.
25 Ibid., 8.
26 Ibid., 15.
27 Ibid., 29.
28 Ibid., 30.
29 Ibid., 33–4.
30 Ibid., 35.
31 B.W. Hill, "The Change of Government and the 'Loss of the City,' 1710–1711," 395. Hill writes that the outcome of this political crisis of 1710 and 1711 ended well for the City and for public credit:

> A Tory Parliament had been persuaded to undertake maintenance of the national debt, and the Whig City to resume its role as the nation's creditor. Both politically and financially these were important developments for the future; politically because they removed a fear that public credit could crumble as the result of a change of government, financially because the form of organization developed by the "monied interest" since the Revolution was acknowledged and even protected by a ministry which represented the City's greatest critics, the landed gentry. The outcome was a consequence of the ultimate good sense of all parties in recognizing that common interest rose above the rivalry of factional interests.
>
> (Ibid., 411)

32 Geoffrey Holmes, "The Sacheverell Riots," 84.
33 Critics have often attempted to read Defoe's involvement with the Tory government as an attempt to restore trust in the public credit system. Katherine Clark attributes Defoe's concerns with credit to a general worry about the decay of meaning as a fallout from partisan politics:

> Defoe's concern about signs losing their meaning was at its most intense at times of instability in the Stock Exchange, as in 1710 and 1720 when politicians sought to manipulate the national debt for partisan purposes. For Defoe, this had an epistemological significance beyond political tactics.
>
> (97)

Further, she writes:

> In the wake of the Sacheverell trial, the Whigs' failed attempt to use credit as a political weapon, and [Defoe's] own increasingly awkward position as a propagandist for the Tory government, Defoe was also more aware than ever of the distortions that party politics could inflict upon money and meaning.

(112)

34 See Schaffer, 14.
35 Ibid., 30.
36 William Paterson, *A Brief Account of the Intended Bank of England*, 11.
37 James E. Thorold Rogers, *The First Nine Years of the Bank of England*, 11.
38 *A Short View of the apparent dangers and mischiefs from the Bank of England*, 8.
39 Bruce Carruthers, *City of Capital*, 87.
40 Macdonald emphasizes Harley's moderate status: "Harley was a former 'country whig' from a nonconformist background. His objective in 1710 was to establish a government open to all moderates, until the sweeping election result somewhat forced his hand" (143).
41 Daniel Defoe, *An Essay upon Publick Credit*, 15.
42 Ibid., 16.
43 This is not for no reason. *Frame* is a term used by seventeenth-century mechanistic philosophers, as well.
44 Ibid., 22–3.
45 See Craig Muldrew, *The Economy of Obligation*, 3.
46 Defoe, *An Essay upon Publick Credit*, 13.
47 Ibid., 21, 23.
48 Ibid., 9.
49 Ibid., 15.
50 See ibid., 16, 20, 21, 23.
51 Ibid., 18.
52 Mary Poovey, *A History of the Modern Fact*, 167.
53 Ibid., 58.
54 Defoe, *The Review*, 470.
55 Ibid.
56 Ibid., 471.
57 Ibid.
58 Ibid.
59 Nicholson, xi.
60 Catherine Ingrassia, *Authorship, Commerce, and Gender in Early Eighteenth-Century England*, 24.
61 Sherman, 40.
62 Ibid., 73
63 Deirdre Lynch, *The Economy of Character*, 41.
64 *The Moderator* 28, August 25, 1710.
65 McKeon defines *narrative concentration* as "a technique for reducing broadly conceived and widely ramified narratives to stories of simpler scope and more circumscribed dimensions." See Michael McKeon, *The Secret History of Domesticity*, 437, 447.
66 Defoe, *The Review*, 17.
67 Ibid.
68 Ibid., 19.
69 Ibid., 127.
70 Ibid., 59.
71 Ibid., 127.
72 Ibid., 463.

73 Ibid., 18.
74 Ibid., 226.
75 Jacob Soll, *The Reckoning*, 110.
76 Ibid., 108.
77 Paul, 16–17.
78 Ibid., 111.
79 Soll, 115.
80 Muldrew, 3.
81 Ibid., 5. Muldrew examines the instability of the so-called credit system that oper-
    ated before, during, and after the financial revolution, and he analyzes the stunningly
    large number of cases of litigation between creditors and debtors in order to suggest
    that people did not know how to use credit at first, and that the system took decades
    to become stable and trustworthy (see ibid., 199).
82 Margot C. Finn, *The Character of Credit*, 18–19.
83 Sherman, 98.
84 Poovey, 54.
85 Daniel Defoe, *The Villainy of Stock-Jobbers Detected*, 13.
86 Ibid., 17.
87 Daniel Defoe, *Hymn to the Pillory*, 10.
88 Daniel Defoe, *A Brief Debate upon the Dissolving of the Late Parliament*, 10.
89 Daniel Defoe, *A Tour Through England and Wales*, 11; *The Compleat English
    Tradesman*, 15.
90 See Natasha Glaisyer, *The Culture of Commerce in England, 1660–1720*, 5.
91 In addition to these, there were also many financial texts circulating around the
    markets, such as price lists and the course of the exchange, allowing investors to
    bear witness at a distance, creating a feedback loop between the readers of these
    financial press documents and the State and its investors. This printed information
    "defined the boundaries of the market, ordered relevant knowledge and allowed
    the inexperienced and occasional investor to approach the market with a degree of
    confidence" (Anne L. Murphy, *The Origins of the English Financial
    Markets*, 112).
92 *The Gentleman's Accomptant*, 1.
93 Ibid., 3.
94 Defoe, *The Compleat English Tradesman*, 4–5.
95 Ibid., 48.
96 Ibid., 198.
97 Ibid., 15.
98 Ibid., 23, 25.
99 Ibid., 132.
100 Ibid., 142.
101 See ibid., 65–9, 138–41, 144–6.
102 See ibid., 99–104.
103 Ibid., 59.
104 See Julian Hoppit, *Risk and Failure in English Business, 1700–1800*, 20.
105 Defoe, *The Compleat English Tradesman*, 59.
106 Ibid., 130.
107 Ibid., 131.
108 Ibid., 241.
109 James Thompson, *Models of Value*, 90.
110 Sherman, 89.
111 McKeon, *The Secret History of Domesticity*, 447.
112 Laura Brown, *Ends of Empire*, 151.
113 Daniel Defoe, *Roxana, or The Fortunate Mistress*, 1.
114 Ibid.

115 This works in a similar way in *The True Relation of the Apparition of One Mrs. Veal* (1706), in which (what has been attributed to) Defoe attempts to render a ghost story factual through the fact of the reputation of Mrs. Bargrave. However, whether Defoe wrote this text has been called into question. See George A. Starr, "Why Defoe Probably Did Not Write *The Apparition of Mrs. Veal.*"
116 See Daniel Defoe, *A Journal of the Plague Year*, 30.
117 See ibid., 13–14, 55, 104, 119, 123, 158–9, 191–3, 208.
118 Daniel Defoe, *Robinson Crusoe*, 3.
119 Ibid., 55.
120 Ibid., 57.
121 Ibid., 56.
122 Ibid., 209.
123 Michael McKeon, *The Origins of the English Novel*, 316.
124 Ibid.

Works cited

Brewer, John. *The Sinews of Power: War, Money and the English State, 1688–1783*. New York: Alfred A. Knopf, 1989.
Brown, Laura. *Ends of Empire: Women and Ideology in Early Eighteenth-Century English Literature*. Ithaca: Cornell University Press, 1993.
Carruthers, Bruce. *City of Capital: Politics and Markets in the English Financial Revolution*. Princeton: Princeton University Press, 1996.
Clark, Katherine. *Daniel Defoe: The Whole Frame of Nature, Time and Providence*. New York: Palgrave Macmillan, 2007.
Defoe, Daniel. *The Villainy of Stock-Jobbers Detected, and the causes of the late run upon the Bank and bankers discovered and considered*. London: n.p., 1701.
Defoe, Daniel. *Essays upon Several Projects: or, effectual ways for advancing the interest of the nation*. London: n.p., 1702.
Defoe, Daniel. *Hymn to the Pillory*. London: n.p., 1703.
Defoe, Daniel. *An Essay upon Publick Credit*. London: n.p., 1710.
Defoe, Daniel. *A Brief Debate upon the Dissolving of the Late Parliament, and whether we ought not to chuse the same gentleman again*. London: n.p., 1722.
Defoe, Daniel. *A Tour Through England and Wales: Divided into Circuits or Journeys*, vol. 1. London: J.M. Dent and E.P. Dutton, 1928.
Defoe, Daniel. *The Review*. 1704–13. New York: Columbia University Press, 1938.
Defoe, Daniel. *A Journal of the Plague Year*. 1722. London: The Folio Society, 1960.
Defoe, Daniel. *Roxana, or The Fortunate Mistress*. 1724. Oxford: Oxford University Press, 1964.
Defoe, Daniel. *The Compleat English Tradesman*. Gloucester: Alan Sutton Publishing, 1987.
Defoe, Daniel. *Robinson Crusoe*. 1719. Oxford: Oxford University Press, 2007.
Finn, Margot C. *The Character of Credit: Personal Debt in English Culture, 1740–1914*. Cambridge: Cambridge University Press, 2003.
The Gentleman's Accomptant, or an essay to unfold the mystery of accompts, by way of Debtor and Creditor. London: E. Curle, 1721.
Glaisyer, Natasha. *The Culture of Commerce in England, 1660–1720*. Bodmin: The Boydell Press, 2006.
Hill, B.W. "The Change of Government and the 'Loss of the City,' 1710–1711." *The Economic History Review* 24 (1971): 395–413.

Holmes, Geoffrey. "The Sacheverell Riots: The Crowd and the Church in Early Eighteenth-Century London." *Past & Present* 72 (1976): 55–85.

Hoppit, Julian. *Risk and Failure in English Business, 1700–1800*. Cambridge: Cambridge University Press, 1987.

Ingrassia, Catherine. *Authorship, Commerce, and Gender in Early Eighteenth-Century England: A Culture of Paper Credit*. Cambridge: Cambridge University Press, 1998.

Knights, Mark. *Representation and Misrepresentation in Later Stuart Britain: Partisanship and Political Culture*. Oxford: Oxford University Press, 2005.

A Letter to a Friend, concerning the Credit of the Nation: and with relation to the present Bank of England, as now establish'd by Act of Parliament. London: E. Whitlock, 1697.

Lynch, Deirdre. *The Economy of Character: Novels, Market Culture, and the Business of Inner Meaning*. Chicago: University of Chicago Press, 1998.

Macdonald, James. "The Importance of Not Defaulting: The Significance of the Election of 1710," in *Questioning Credible Commitment: Perspectives on the Rise of Financial Capitalism*, edited by D'Maris Coffman, Adrian Leonard, and Larry Neal, 125–46. Cambridge: Cambridge University Press, 2013.

McKeon, Michael. *The Origins of the English Novel, 1600–1740*. Baltimore: Johns Hopkins University Press, 1987.

McKeon, Michael. *The Secret History of Domesticity: Public, Private, and the Division of Knowledge*. Baltimore: Johns Hopkins University Press, 2005.

The Moderator 28, August 21–28 (1710).

Muldrew, Craig. *The Economy of Obligation: The Culture of Credit and Social Relations in Early Modern England*. Houndmills: Palgrave Macmillan, 1998.

Murphy, Anne L. *The Origins of the English Financial Markets*. Cambridge: Cambridge University Press, 2009.

Nicholson, Colin. *Writing and the Rise of Finance*. Cambridge: Cambridge University Press, 1994.

Novak, Maximillian E. *Economics and the Fiction of Daniel Defoe*. New York: Russell & Russell, 1962.

Paterson, William. *A Brief Account of the Intended Bank of England*. London: Randal Tayler, 1694.

Paul, Helen Julia. *The South Sea Bubble: An Economic History of its Origins and Consequences*. Abingdon: Routledge, 2011.

Pocock, J.G.A. *The Machiavellian Moment: Florentine Political Thought and the Atlantic Republican Tradition*. Princeton: Princeton University Press, 1975.

Poovey, Mary. *A History of the Modern Fact: Problems of Knowledge in the Sciences of Wealth and Society*. Chicago: University of Chicago Press, 1998.

Richetti, John. *The Life of Daniel Defoe: A Critical Biography*. Malden: Blackwell, 2005.

Rogers, James E. Thorold. *The First Nine Years of the Bank of England*. Oxford: Clarendon Press, 1887.

Schaffer, Simon. "Defoe's Natural Philosophy and the Worlds of Credit," in *Nature Transfigured: Science and Literature, 1700–1900*, edited by John Christie, 13–44. Manchester: Manchester University Press, 1989.

Sherman, Sandra. *Finance and Fictionality in the Early Eighteenth Century: Accounting for Defoe*. Cambridge: Cambridge University Press, 1996.

A Short View of the apparent dangers and mischiefs from the Bank of England. London: B. Bragg, 1707.

Soll, Jacob. *The Reckoning: Financial Accountability and the Rise and Fall of Nations*. New York: Basic Books, 2014.

Starr, George A. "Why Defoe Probably Did Not Write *The Apparition of Mrs. Veal.*" *Eighteenth-Century Fiction* 15.3–4 (2003): 421–50.

Swift, Jonathan. *The Examiner and Other Pieces Written in 1710–1711*, edited by Herbert John Davis. Oxford: Basil Blackwell, 1957.

Thompson, James. *Models of Value: Eighteenth-Century Political Economy and the Novel*. Durham, NC: Duke University Press, 1996.

Watt, Ian. *The Rise of the Novel: Studies in Defoe, Richardson and Fielding*. London: Hogarth, 1957.

Wennerlind, Carl. *Casualties of Credit: The English Financial Revolution, 1620–1720*. Cambridge, MA: Harvard University Press, 2011.

Yamamoto, Koji. "Reformation and the Distrust of the Projector in the Hartlib Circle." *The Historical Journal* 55.2 (2012): 375–97.

3 The Bank of England, virtue, and the *Pamela* controversy

At the end of his book on political partisanship and representation, which takes on the task of discussing politics, public credit, and the emergent public sphere as interrelated mechanisms that produce "collective fictions," Mark Knights wonders "whether the later Stuart period may have opened significant possibilities for self-fictionalization and fictional biography. There may be an important link," he argues, "between party, a concern with the 'self,' and the emergence of novelistic prose fiction."[1] This chapter takes up Knight's suggestion to research the relationship between the construction of the 'self' and the emergent novel through representational strategies used for discussing public credit.

In advocating for public credit, the tendency was to align *virtue* with *disinterestedness*. What an analysis of Daniel Defoe's oeuvre suggests is that public credit had to be accommodated to contemporaries by being represented as serving the public good rather than particular interests. Disinterested representation overlaps with other discursive transformations in the period, such as the emergence of politeness and the championing of public knowledge in the form of scientific practice.[2] In terms of the way historians have discussed political economy, the emphasis has mainly been on the role accounting played in representing disinterestedness.

Andrea Finkelstein points to William Petty's *Political Arithmetick* (1690) as a major turning point because, in this work, the practice of using numbers came to be regarded as being more important than the authority of particular political interests, an underlying problem for the tumultuous seventeenth century. Petty's political arithmetic

> described the political economies of England and Ireland the way bookkeeping described the political economy of the business or household. In this sense, seventeenth-century economics was political economics because it described the economy of the polis, the commonwealth, the political community.[3]

While the 1690s were an important time for political and economic thought, this chapter will suggest that public credit helped to promote an application of accounting practices for the household, a notion corroborated by the proliferation of accounting manuals in the form of almanac-diaries in the middle of the century, especially between 1753 and 1789.[4] What is at stake in representing the 'self' as a financial subject can be understood through the way the disinterested mode of accounting gets taken up – and also credibly framed – in the domestic novel.

What was significant in the early history of public credit is that, for many contemporaries, it was often viewed as little better than stock-jobbing or project-ing, of using quantitative abstractions in order to promote one's interest. Defoe helps to revise this notion by aligning the practices of public credit with the prac-tices of a virtuous tradesman. His writings make it clear that the values of the tradesman enter public discourse for the service of the State. But it seems to be public credit (in other words, credit discussed at the level of State) that paves the way for the discourse of accounting to enter the private sphere through a gentle-manly ethos observed in Defoe's oeuvre. This happens not only through pam-phlets and conduct manuals, but also through other fictional texts.

Defoe's task was to insist that public credit was a stable and fair mechanism whose purpose was to benefit the public good. To that end, he uses credible framing to represent disinterestedness and trustworthiness. Defoe's representa-tional strategies can be found in both the development of the early novel and in the practices of the Bank of England. This relationship is not causal. Rather, it seems to be part of a larger epistemological shift that, for example, Simon Schaf-fer and Steven Shapin describe when they discuss the separation of the natural sciences and philosophy in *Leviathan and the Air-Pump* (1985). In this book, they state that "[s]olutions to the problem of knowledge are solutions to the problem of social order."[5] This ties in with the emergent novel's concerns of examining questions of truth next to questions of virtue.[6]

Part of what is at stake in the *Pamela* controversy has to do with the instab-ility of economic, political, and social categories which critics have argued are central to the novel's formal development,[7] and these concerns are also what we have seen to be important for the rise of public credit. While Defoe's ventures in pamphleteering gave readers a way of imagining an abstract system, some of the material aspects of public credit that find their way into the public imagination often seem to get lost in this abstraction. That is to say, depersonalizing public credit to ensure that it seems politically neutral (like a clock with no active, interested person at the helm) carries with it a risk that it is too far removed from the empirical world, and an emphasis on materiality (through evoking the trades-man's ledger or Robinson Crusoe's diary) becomes part of the credible framing that one observes in Defoe's fictions. Even in *Robinson Crusoe*, one notes some formal innovations: self-reflexivity through a layering of texts that invites the reader to 'audit' the narrative account and a possibly unreliable narrator who surfaces upon such an 'audit.' The reputation of the person holding the ledger helps to determine whether one takes up the invitation to 'audit.'

Reputation implies that someone has had personal, face-to-face knowledge of another person with whom one enters into a contractual relationship, that one person knows the other's character. There is a difficulty in applying this to public credit, in which a person is replaced by an abstract State. There is, in other words, a price of disinterestedness. Where emergent economic thinking seems to dovetail with emergent scientific thinking is where tangible and material factors play a role in adding up to reputation. In these terms, the descriptive/prescriptive economic pamphlets and other types of fiction perform the work of hearkening to tangible and material anchors that readers can imagine.

But what about the actual institutions that came into being during this time? If, as scholars have pointed out, governmental changes from above were only part of the picture, how did these institutions perform the work of garnering commitment?[8] Is there a relationship between the epistemological questions opened up by the way reputation is conveyed through fiction and the strategies particular institutions used to produce trust? If one conceives of the Bank of England not only as a private company with closer and closer ties to the State but also as an intentional set of decisions for cultivating a *reputation* (both through modes of representation and by internal regulation), the answer to this question is yes. The Bank of England features in many contemporary texts, but it can also be read as a text that simulates the reputation inherent to pre-existing social codes.

Credible commitment requires an epistemological transformation that is staged in the early novel. The relationship between narrative and virtue can be said to emerge historically when the new institutional practices of accounting and older forms of reputation, both necessary for public credit, become a means for producing trust. The Bank of England, the most significant agency that comes to facilitate public credit for a nation that is still unsure of what the former even is, relies on its formal presentation of trustworthy accounting in a way that is similar to that of a key text in eighteenth-century literary history, Samuel Richardson's *Pamela* (1740). What is at stake in this text is what critics, aligning the novel with the rise of a bourgeois or middle-class ethos, have described as the representation of female virtue.[9] What matters is not whether there was an actual Pamela with real virtue but whether the self-representational strategies of a fictional character are convincing enough to simulate virtue.

The Bank of England in texts

Despite Defoe's description of public credit as an impartial system made up of passive individuals, public credit was based in and emanated from an actual place – the City of London – where actual living and breathing individuals worked. Indeed, Defoe reminds his readers of this as he develops Lady Credit and provides her with a setting. In an issue of *The Review* dated August 8, 1710, Defoe writes that Lady Credit's "walk was daily between the Bank and the Exchequer and between the Exchange and the Treasury."[10] Here and elsewhere, Defoe emphasizes the location of the Bank, which, until 1734, was in a rented building in the City, the Grocers' Company on Princes Street. By 1720, the stock market had emerged in the environs of the Royal Exchange on Threadneedle Street, where the government's three major creditors resided: the South Sea

Company, the East India Company, and the Bank of England. The Royal Exchange was described by some, including Petty, as a microcosm of the trading world.[11] These architectural structures had an increasingly symbolic value for people in England, fostering an imagination of existing within a self-contained, prosperous commonwealth that benefitted from international trade. One could, like Lady Credit on her perambulations, visit the same physical location to see for oneself the trading world and all that it entails. Material factors are in this way a significant part of the story of credible commitment.

In 1711, Joseph Addison also described public credit by evoking its physical location, drawing on similar techniques as Defoe's use of Lady Credit in *The Review*. But, unlike Defoe, he begins to describe the interior of the Bank, allowing readers to imagine a physical space housing people who work there. He imagines the

> great Hall where the Bank is kept, and was not a little pleased to see the Directors, Secretaries, and Clerks, with all the other Members of that wealthy Corporation, ranged in their several Stations, according to the Parts they act in that just and regular Oeconomy.[12]

This "just and regular oeconomy," productive cooperation rather than hierarchical subordination, reflects Defoe's description a year before. Addison's account evokes a virtuous female similar to Lady Credit. He dreams that he returns

> to the Great Hall, where I had been the Morning before, but to my Surprize, instead of the Company that I left there, I saw towards the Upper-end of the Hall, a beautiful Virgin, seated on a Throne of Gold. Her Name (as they told me) was *Publick Credit*. The walls ... were hung with many Acts of Parliament.[13]

Addison points to the institutional changes that ensued after the Glorious Revolution. But this is only one detail in what becomes yet another allegory about public credit. By using a reality mode and a dream mode, he shifts between the physical components of the Bank that are organized like a system and the allegorical narrative that Defoe also uses.

Addison's allegory makes a connection between public credit and the emergent public sphere (of which Addison's text is, of course, a part). Like Defoe's allegories, in the moment the dreamer comes across "Publick Credit," she is endangered – she becomes ill because of the "news" she receives in the form of letters.

> I had very soon an Opportunity of observing these quick Turns and Changes in her Constitution. There sat at her Feet a Couple of Secretaries, who received every Hour Letters from all Parts of the World, which the one or the other of them was perpetually reading to her; and, according to the News she heard, to which she was exceedingly attentive, she changed Colour, and discovered many Symptoms of Health or Sickness.[14]

Here, the dream allegory does its work by enticing the reader to imagine the material wealth surrounding public credit as well as the secretaries that work in the Bank. What is more, texts that her secretaries 'read' to her are capable of changing her status.

In a second step, the Virgin that represents public credit is linked to the material supply of money. Addison describes the cash that is stored in the Bank. This precious metal, the dreamer hears, is something that the Virgin is capable of creating – much like in alchemy. Midas is evoked to link public credit to alchemical discourse, which, as Carl Wennerlind points out,[15] surfaces throughout the seventeenth and eighteenth centuries (a topic to which I will return in the following chapter):

> Behind the Throne was a prodigious Heap of Bags of Mony, which were piled upon one another so high that they touched the Ceiling. The Floor, on her right Hand, and on her left, was covered with vast Sums of Gold that rose up in Pyramids on either side of her: But this I did not so much wonder at, when I heard, upon Enquiry, that she had the same Virtue in her Touch, which the Poets tell us a *Lydian King* was formerly posses'd of; and that she could convert whatever she pleased into that precious Metal.[16]

Public credit, Addison says, has "Virtue in her Touch." Usually associated with moral goodness, Addison's use of the term *virtue* suggests something else, which he connects to the creation of gold.

After taking note of the Virgin's remarkable alchemical powers, the dreamer encounters dancing specters. When Tyranny, Anarchy, Bigotry, and Atheism enter the room, the lady faints.

> There was as great a Change in the Hill of Mony Bags, and the Heaps of Mony, the former shrinking, and falling into so many empty Bags, that I now found not above a tenth part of them had been filled with Mony. The rest that took up the same Space, and made the same Figure as the bags that were really filled with Mony, had been blown up with Air, and called into my Memory the Bags full of Wind, which *Homer* tells us his Hero receiv'd as a Present from *AEolus*. The great Heaps of Gold, on either side the Throne, now appeared to be only Heaps of Paper, or little Piles of notched Sticks, bound up together in Bundles, like Bath-Faggots.[17]

However, when a second dance of specters arrives, featuring Liberty, Monarchy, Moderation, Religion, and the Genius of Great Britain, the "Lady reviv'd, the Bags swell'd to their former Bulk, the Piles of Faggots and Heaps of Paper changed into Pyramids of Guineas."[18] This passage is striking because, depending on the health of the Virgin, mere paper becomes money, and money becomes paper. Addison represents this in a way that the reader can imagine – in two sets: pyramids and piles. What is more, the health of the Virgin depends on the "news," which gets represented as dancing figures. Like Lady Credit, the Virgin possesses virtue, but she is also susceptible to what takes place outside of the Bank.

What Addison's version of public credit at the Bank shows is the relationship between the Bank's material components and public discourses outside of the Bank that have the capacity to transform public credit. Addison takes the allegory a step further than Defoe. In this representation, public credit is also not found in the accounting ledgers but in the great hall of the Bank, the area where the public engaged in business. Even more than Defoe, Addison uses tangible features of the Bank to understand credit as being more than a series of devices or a system of State made credible through institutional practices. It is both of these, but it is also dependent on what happens outside of the Bank – the public sphere of coffee houses and print circulation. It is perhaps for this reason that the Bank and its particular stabilizing features are represented in circulating texts, creating a feedback loop between the Bank's virtue and its reputation in the public sphere.

The Bank of England as text

The City – comprised of several buildings in which individuals gathered to barter for their interests (a notion that will resurface in Chapter 5) – had increasing significance for those outside of it. Increasingly, the Bank of England came to have significance as the heart of the City and the hub of public credit. Like pamphleteers supporting the idea of public credit by describing the Bank, the Bank itself did the same by presenting itself as having *virtue*, a term I am using because it emerges in several contemporary social contexts.[19]

Like Defoe's pamphlets that attempted to stabilize public credit, the Bank found ways to present itself as being disinterested and politically neutral. First, its very structure, its architectural form, was designed to separate investors (with their individual interests) from the Bank itself, which needed to appear disinterested in the public imagination. Second, it had to give the impression of keeping good accounts. Third, it had to train and regulate its human employees to obey systematic protocols. Finally, what it issued – bank notes – had to convey integrity; they had to be imbued with Addison's Virgin's virtuous touch.

As stated earlier, the establishment of the Bank of England in 1694 was the first of its kind, having been explicitly designed for the purpose of lending to the Exchequer. In the early eighteenth century, England had three major creditors: the South Sea Company, the East India Company, and the Bank. The South Sea Bubble in 1720 resulted in the strengthening of the Bank as England's major public creditor. The Bank, fortunate enough to resist buying overpriced stock in the South Sea Company just before the Bubble, led in the financial bailout. At this point, Robert Walpole handed over more power to the Bank.[20] By 1734, the Bank moved to Threadneedle Street to be just across from the Royal Exchange. George Sampson, the Bank's architect, designed the first building in world history to be built for the purpose of serving as a bank. As Daniel Abramson's research suggests, the building itself is of great importance in the history of capitalism because of its ability to produce confidence in the public that the Bank was serving the public good. "Sampson's rational and cultivated design claimed for the Bank at least an equality with the government's own institutions in Westminster."[21] This included substituting a solid image of the Lady Britannia, which the Bank had begun to use around the time of its move in 1734 to personify itself through patriotic imagery, for the more fungible image of Lady Credit. Lady Britannia was also used on the first banknotes.[22]

Accounting was important for achieving a reputation that the Bank served the public good. The Bank's General Court records indicate that the issuing of cash, in the form of paper, was intended from its opening. The Bank opened its first accounting ledger in the summer of 1694. On the top of the first page next to the date is inscribed Laus Deo, or "Praise be to God" (see Figure 3.1).

These gigantic royal folio tomes utilized the form of the codex, open pages side by side, to register credits and debts. The left page registered "cash paid to" and the right registered "credits by." The far left side of each page was used to calculate balances of credit or debt respectively, and the far bottom right side kept a running total. Sub-calculations (for example, if multiple payments or credits were received through the same creditor or debtor) were performed in the memo section and then carried over to the ledger space. Keeping a running balance by glancing at the two pages simultaneously, a clerk could get a sense of

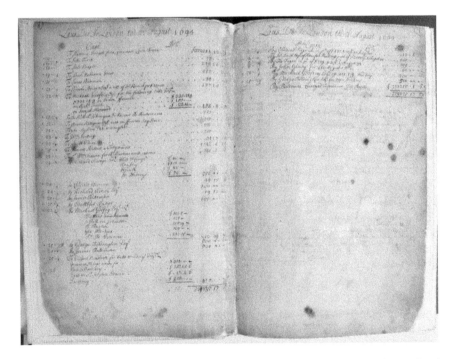

Figure 3.1 1694 Bank of England accounting ledger page (courtesy of The Bank of England Archive (ADM42/1)).

the Bank's available funds almost instantly (or at least with the help of some quick arithmetic).

In double-entry bookkeeping, the function of the zero balance (the part of the account that is formally authoritative) helps to convey a sort of virtue, insofar as this balance is seen as having been arrived at in a disinterested manner. In *A History of the Modern Fact* (1998), Mary Poovey argues that the neutrality of the accounting ledger takes over the authority of classical rhetoric:

> Even though number was not in itself the sign of virtue, *arithmetic*, which followed its own formal rules, constituted a system in relation to which one could judge right from wrong.... The precision of arithmetic replaced the eloquence of speech as the instrument that produced both truth and virtue.[23]

In Poovey's argument, what is significant is not the amount of wealth a ledger indicates, but the form the calculation takes to arrive at that number. Form is what produces virtue, not the number itself. Poovey limits her definition of form to the algebraic system inherent in accounting. According to her argument, because of their seeming neutrality and disinterested basis, facts replaced the traditional use of persuasive rhetoric. Because numbers

> constitute the units of a system of knowledge production that is biased toward deduction – that is, mathematics – numbers inevitably carry within them the traces of a certain kind of systematic knowledge: to assign numbers to observed particulars is to make them amenable to the kind of knowledge system that privileges quantity over quality and equivalence over difference.[24]

What Poovey describes here is the way numbers, placed in a ledger system, come to be trusted to convey the empirical reality they are purported to represent. In theory, each observed particular can be represented by the ledger, and we trust the number not for its own sake, but for its place within the ledger. However, formal decisions outside of the ledger were also important.

The folio-sized tomes, regulated by an increasingly systematized internal procedure, were kept at the teller's counter and in public view, which meant that potential borrowers and lenders could see the tellers registering all credits and debts by glancing at the open book. This massive open tome, visually presenting both sides of the register, was important for a public whose trust was a question for the Bank's success. Just as important as the accuracy of the tellers and accountants was the public perception of this accuracy. The placement of the giant tomes in public view represented a practice of accounting that was done behind the scenes and described in the Bank's internal protocols.[25]

The Bank's layout meant that administrative and market functions were kept separate so that the public would not question whether it had any conflicts of interest. "The spatial clarity of Sampson's plan embodied the Bank of England's desired institutional virtue.... Sampson's building thus functioned as an instrument for producing trust, the Bank of England's most priceless asset."[26] The building served as a marker of individual virtue insofar as it organized the particular people within it and institutional virtue in a climate that questioned the stability of paper money and the financial, political, and social implications of burgeoning public credit. To gain the public's trust, the Bank not only had to balance its books correctly, but it also had to convey its disinterestedness (which Abramson likens to virtue) in spatial terms that regulated people. Members of the public could visit the Bank and be assured that their deposits were safe by seeing firsthand the way the Bank was designed. This architecture can therefore be seen as part of the financial engineering designed to minimize the risk of a run.

The impression of keeping good accounts, partially conveyed through intentional decisions in the formal architecture of the Bank, meant that people might then believe in the integrity of the actual account books. Bookkeeping is an important factor, but the way these books were positioned within the Bank's internal architecture were of the utmost importance.

> The Accountants Office accommodated the Bank of England's book-keeping functions and so symbolized more than any other space in the complex the nation's probity and integrity. Sampson thus helped sustain the Bank's corporate virtue by spatially quarantining stockjobbers and traders away from the rest of the building, its staff and clientele.[27]

As seen from reading Addison in 1711, even the earlier rented building that contained the Bank was notable for its great hall. And what Samson did to the new building heightened the earlier building's impressive qualities by making it seem even more like the mechanistic system Defoe describes.

One of the points that gets lost when one takes accounting as shorthand for virtue is the fact that ledgers are material objects. Within the building, the account books themselves served as representatives of virtue. These books were more important than anything else in the Bank, at least according to its early policies. The Bank required that a porter live on site at all times so that, in case of a fire, he could save the priceless ledger. "Damage to the Bank's books could erase thousands of stockholders' wealth, substantially injure the nation's public credit and financial stability, and likely put an end to the Bank of England itself."[28] Before the Gordon Riots of 1780, the Bank did not arm itself against robbers or intruders. However, extreme care was taken regarding the preservation of the account books, suggesting that the fundamental capital of the Bank lay in its perceived mastery of the algebra of double-entry bookkeeping contained within these material objects.

The ledger itself was not the only apparatus to ensure the Bank remained trustworthy, as the ledger also had to be regulated by very explicit rules. The Bank's accountants were, in other words, accountable to a system of protocols. Correct accounting required a physical process of coordinating multiple human beings and multiple sheets of paper. To manage this feat, the Bank created written house rules for all employees to follow. One internal cash office protocol memo, dated October 19, 1727, specifies the following:

That the Cash Office be enlarged.... That Six persons be imployed at the drawing acctts offices.... That two Check Books be kept, One by Way of Dr and Cr, the other by way of Addition & Subtraction.... That Additions be made in the Book of Dr & Cr at every four Lines.... That the Person who adds shall put the letters of his Name against the Addition.... That a proper time be sett a part, when the Cheque Ledgers are not in use in the Hall, to prick the posting against the Ledger in the accounting office.... That the ledger be locked up every Night.[29]

Pricking, or poking small holes in the parchment, ensured that the ledger lines lined up. Without straight lines, one could not ensure that the correct figure be added or subtracted. Not only was competent arithmetic important, but coordination of all employees in a systematic way was also necessary for calculations to be carried out properly. Such coordination – with a technology used to ensure its systematicity – further reflects Defoe's image of public credit as a clock, an impartial system with passive agents that serve it.

Importantly, and despite Defoe's description of public credit, actual living and breathing people, and not abstract agents, worked inside the Bank. However skilled or precise these accountants were in actuality, they increasingly held a reputation of being unquestionably dependable. Anne Murphy, questioning the credible commitment 'from above' thesis, shows, for example, that it was somewhat difficult for the Bank to find and train tellers who had the impeccable mathematical skills required for the job.[30] By the 1720s, Defoe comes to praise the Bank as a model for all tradesmen to follow. At the Bank,

business is dispatch'd with such exactness, and such expedition and so much of it too, that it is really prodigious; no confusion, nobody is either denied or delayed payment, the merchants who keep their cash there, are sure to have their bills always paid, and even advances made on easy terms, if they have occasion. No accounts in the world are more exactly kept, no place in the world has so much business done, with so much ease.[31]

Whether this passage indicates that the Bank actually possessed these qualities or whether Defoe wanted his readers to imagine that it did is, of course, an open question. But the passage helps one to mark the contemporary terms that get associated with virtue. Defoe's emphasis on "exactness" and "ease" is interesting because in no place does he refer directly to individual workers: He is referring to a system. At the same time, Defoe also seems to imply that it is the virtue of people working inside of the Bank that is important for the flourishing of public credit. This is yet another Defoevean sleight of hand, but it is also one that adds to the overall public perception of the Bank. Whatever the quality of their actual working practices, the accountants had such a solid reputation that the Exchequer Office in Whitehall increasingly handed over portions of publicly subscribed shares.[32] Finally, the Bank issued material objects that circulated outside: paper notes. I will return to banknotes in the next chapter, for these material objects circulated outside of the City, and they also came to symbolize the virtue of the Bank, the City, and the State.

Accounting and ideology in *Pamela*

Critics have pointed out that, in the middle of the century, it is the virtue of the character that drives the ideological and formal development of the domestic novel.[33] In the *Pamela* controversy, what was at stake in the debate was: What constitutes virtue? How can it be signified? These are questions not unrelated to the ones Sampson faced when designing the new building for the Bank or the ones the Bank's board of governors grappled with when they designed various protocols to manage employees. Virtue is at least in part constituted through the form of accounting in the debate that ensues after the publication of *Pamela* in 1740. And by 'form of accounting,' I mean not only double-entry bookkeeping, but also other formal decisions that produce trust. As one gleans from Defoe's *Compleat English Tradesman*, the ledger is a legible means for knowing whether someone can be trusted, and it is also a contract signifying commitment. Representing accounting calls on people to hold the Bank to account – it produces another feedback loop. When a similar logic is applied to *Pamela*, controversy ensues.

At one level, Ian Watt has already addressed the relationship between the rise of the novel and accounting when he argues that

> [b]ook-keeping is but one aspect of a central theme in the modern social order. Our civilization as a whole is based on individual contractual relationships, as opposed to the unwritten, traditional and collective relationships of previous societies; and the idea of contract played an important part in the theoretical development of political individualism.[34]

However, more than Watt, who, through his emphasis on the emergence of a bourgeois middle class,[35] never fully articulates what makes the novel formally different from narrative fictions that come before it, I am following the work of Michael McKeon, who suggests that the novel comes into being because "progressive ideology" meets with resistance from a traditionalist culture, an ideology that evolves from the same social outlook of people who challenged public credit as a threat to landed interests decades earlier. For McKeon, it is this dialectical relationship between conservative and progressive ideologies that are crucial to the formation of the genre.[36]

In *Origins of the English Novel* (1987), McKeon aligns "progressive ideology" with "naïve empiricism."[37] "The instability of social categories registered a cultural crisis in attitudes toward how the external social order is related to the internal, moral state of its members."[38] This means that epistemological questions, which he calls "questions of truth," are inseparable from social and ethical ones, "questions of virtue."[39] Progressive ideology entails a specific, empirically oriented way of understanding moral values because its emphasis on moral agency is fundamentally evidence-based. He asks the question: "What kind of authority or evidence is required of narrative to permit it to signify truth to its readers? What kind of social existence or behavior signifies an individual's virtue to others?"[40] When applied to the *Pamela* controversy, these questions can be related to what is at stake in credible commitment: Authority is constructed through representational strategies that invite people to hold each other to account.

What is important in *Pamela* is that Richardson employs formal strategies to ensure that other characters as well as readers believe Pamela to be virtuous. Truth claims are, in other words, mediators to claims of virtue. This compares to the Bank, in which virtue comes to be defined as the 'truth' of its disinterested management of funds. Respondents to *Pamela* would manipulate the content of the novel in order to suggest that the form of Pamela's letters should not be read as a self-sufficient marker of virtue, even if this is what Richardson intended. Contemporary critics of *Pamela* treat the novel with "extreme skepticism," which correlates to conservative ideology. At a historical moment when national accounting becomes endemic to the functioning of the commonwealth (or at least City interests within it), *Pamela* utilizes similar formal strategies to reflect the progressive ideology that accompanies it.[41]

At the level of content, mid-century domestic novels emphasize the female virtue of household economy. In the eighteenth century, instructional books began to surface whose purpose was to educate women in arithmetic and accounting methods. Such books as *The Accomplish'd Housewife* (1745), Charles Vyse's *The Young Ladies Accountant, and Best Accomplisher* (1771), and the annual editions of *The Ladies Compleat Pocket-Book* and *The Ladies' Own Memorandum Book* were advertised to help women keep track of personal and familial accounts. And, as Nancy Armstrong shows, these texts had a major influence on the domestic novel.[42] Such manuals serve as a combination of diaries, journals, and numerical registers, teaching the management of both fiscal and social debts. Rather than using double-entry columns of "debt"/"credit," ledgers of the domestic memorandum book read "received"/"paid" and were often circulated to friends.[43] Keeping track of one's daily activities in a diary or register conflated social conduct book habits and quantitative practices of accounting used in double-entry bookkeeping.

Richardson's *Pamela* explores a double meaning of the words *accounting* and *tell*, terms that have implied both narration and fiscal counting since the fourteenth century.[44] Rebecca Elisabeth Connor's work explains the relationship between the account as first-person narrative and fiscal reckoning in the household. Discussing the double meaning of the terms *account* and *tell*, Conner writes:

> If to secure one's property is in some sense to stabilize one's history, then the desire to account surely springs from a comparable impulse. And the account – be it spiritual, financial, or narratival – stands as testimony to and template of the individual. All of which would seem to indicate that financial accounting represents a record of experience not dissimilar to the "recording" inherent in narration itself.[45]

Propriety has become a component of one's property, a virtual self that is extended out of one's own body through its carefully framed representation.[46]

Pamela and *Clarissa* (1748) get the reader to believe in the virtue of their respective eponymous protagonists through their recording techniques of writing epistles "to the moment," a practice which seems disinterested in part because the writer has no time to manipulate the truth. In these epistolary novels, the inner selves of the characters are brought out for the scrutiny of other characters in the novel as well as for the reader. The link between deservedness and virtue becomes a central question: Does Pamela possess real virtue whose reward (i.e., upward mobility) is justified? Did Clarissa, despite her false step of absconding with Lovelace, act with propriety? Henry Fielding and Eliza Haywood (key respondents in the *Pamela* controversy) imitate the form of accounting utilized by *Pamela* but then render the content very different from that of Richardson's novel. The result is that characters cannot be seen as virtuous by the same means as Pamela. These parodies provide ironic critiques of Richardson's less-than-ironic project by illuminating the weakness of the form of the ledger by itself as a means for conveying virtue. This extreme skepticism toward the form – this undermining of credible framing techniques – entices readers to reread *Pamela*, and to ultimately question an ideological alignment of the form of accounting with virtue.

The form of Pamela's virtue

What is at stake in *Pamela* is that the reader believes that Pamela refuses her master's sexual advances because she is truly virtuous (and without an 'interested' ulterior motive). It is important that she stays out of obligation to him because by accepting any gifts she might end up owing to him that which he desires: her becoming his mistress. To a certain degree, the novel uses the language of the gift economy reflecting traditional social forms of obligation, but it modifies this form through a logic of accounting. In a sense, Pamela desires to maintain a zero balance with Mr. B. By the end, her supposed virtue is the reason that Mr. B marries her and also why his family comes to accept the marriage. If readers do not really believe Pamela to be virtuous, it would seem that Mr. B was duped into marrying beneath him by a woman only pretending virtue in order to achieve social mobility. Her letters to her parents (and later her personal journal) provide evidence that she is constantly trying to avoid Mr. B's attempts to give her gifts, to seduce her, and to make her his mistress.

In one sense, *Pamela* works very much like Defoe's *Robinson Crusoe* insofar as one text, the inside text of the journal, is meant to corroborate the empirical reality that the outside text describes. Letters that make up the form of *Pamela* are also folded into its content – Pamela's narrative even describes the letters as material objects that she sews to her clothing in order to hide them from Mr. B. Critics have picked up on the material importance of Pamela's written accounts. John B. Pierce's argument that "Pamela's appeal to authority resides in the mediated form of the 'Text'" helps to explain why the materiality of the letters is important in order to produce the reader's trust in what Pamela writes.[47] The text, a material object, is supposed to represent the content of Pamela's subjectivity. The material status of the letters in itself seems to have a rhetorical force, an attempt to credibly frame what they contain.

In Pamela's letters, Richardson goes a step further than Defoe in Crusoe's journal because *Pamela* requires the reader to trust the accounting in the inside text in order to find the conclusion of the outside text socially acceptable. But this time, there is no way to 'audit' the account because the structure of the novel (except for a short third-person introjection in the middle and at the end) is based on Pamela's letters alone. A deeper analysis requires one to examine the way in which Richardson modifies the epistolary form that was employed for fictional texts before *Pamela*. In literary terms, there is no way to determine whether or not Pamela is a reliable narrator. Part of this is owing to the poverty of the epistolary form for stabilizing the character-narrator's self-representation.

Richardson was working out the formal importance of credible letter-writing in his *Familiar Letters on Important Occasions* (1741) prior to the composition of his first major novel, and these formal concerns persist in his fiction. *Pamela* differs radically from epistolary narratives that precede it (such as, for example, Aphra Behn's *Love-Letters Between a Nobleman and His Sister* [1684–5]) because the reader (and Mr. B) must believe that Pamela is virtuous through her letters so that she deserves the reward of marrying up socially. But this requires Richardson to do something to ensure his readers trust Pamela's letters: No third-person narrator is used to ensure that the reader gets a complete picture (as in the case of Behn's *Love-Letters* in certain places). Instead, the fact of staying out of obligation to Mr. B (maintaining a sort of zero balance of social obligation) is reflected in the representational strategies through which Pamela conveys to the reader her actions. The formal quality of "writing to the moment" implies that Pamela cannot be duplicitous. She merely reports the facts of her subjectivity as they occur. Her narration is almost continuous, and it eventually turns into a journal much like Robinson Crusoe's.

Critics have pointed to the way fiscal indebtedness underlies Pamela's behavior and predicament. Catherine Ingrassia writes how readers "see numerous examples of her accounting abilities, her shrewd financial assessment of other (typically male) characters, and her recognition that most aspects of the sociocultural world are determined by the absence or presence of money."[48] Pamela is attuned to indebtedness throughout the novel. Her parents are in debt, after all, and this is why she refuses to take on new debts and keeps her accounts in order.[49] In fact, Pamela's skills as a household manager and accountant are introduced on the first page of the novel. In the very first letter to her parents, Pamela writes of how her mistress had taught her how to cast accounts:

> As my Lady's Goodness has put me to write and cast Accompts, and made me a little expert at my Needle, and other Qualifications above my Degree, it would have been no easy Matter to find a Place that your poor *Pamela* was fit for.[50]

This skill has social implications: It sets her apart from and above other servants. She has the new, much-valued skill of the gentlewoman. But it also has implications for the way the novel is to be read: These skills in accounting encourage us to trust her version of the story – indeed, it is the only story to which we have access. Further, while accounting may be above her station in one sense, what she accounts for shows that she is acting within her station with the propriety proper to her.

Accounting is used explicitly in *Pamela*. Richardson uses the word *account* 83 times throughout the course of the novel. Further, Richardson draws the reader's attention to accounting in the end of the novel, after Pamela has married Mr. B. Here, she discusses the form of the account explicitly once she is in charge of the money of the household:

> I am resolv'd to keep Account of all these Matters, and Mr. *Longman* has already furnish'd me with a Vellum-book of all white Paper; some sides of which I hope soon to fill, with the Names of Proper Objects: And tho' my dear Master has given me all this without Account, yet shall he see, (but nobody else) how I lay it out, from Quarter to Quarter, and I will, if any be left, carry it on, like an Accomptant, to the next Quarter, and strike a Ballance four times a Year, and a general Ballance at every Year's End.[51]

In the final pages of *Pamela*, passages narrated by a third-person 'editor' rather than through the letters themselves, one learns not only of the whereabouts of each character, but one is also provided with a series of morals: "And they charm'd every one within the Circle of their Acquaintance, by the Sweetness of their Manners, [and] the regular Order and Oeconomy of their Household."[52] One of these morals extols the virtues of the household economist and advocates emulating Pamela's accounting skills:

> From the *Oeconomy* [Pamela] purposes to observe in her Elevation, let even *Ladies of Condition* learn, that there are Family Employments in which they may, and ought to, make themselves useful, and give good Examples to their Inferiors, as well as Equals.[53]

Richardson's sequel, *Pamela in Her Exalted Condition* (1742), further explores Pamela's virtues in the household, perhaps attesting to the reason he removed this editorial ending in subsequent editions.

If what is at stake in doubting Pamela's virtue is the possibility that she might be attempting to extract property from Mr. B (a position taken by the pre-reformed Mr. B and anti-Pamelists alike), what matters is that Pamela accounts for her own property well. In fact, she does just this – she produces a zero balance very early in the novel. Here, she separates her true property from the property that does not match her station when Mr. B begins to make sexual advances and she prepares to return home. To show that she owes him nothing, she separates her own clothing from that which does not belong to her. She tells Mrs. Jervis:

> I had no Cloaths suitable to my Condition when I return'd to my Father's; and so it was better to begin here, as I was soon to go away, that all my Fellow-servants might see, I knew how to suit myself to the State I was returning to.[54]

This is less a matter of monetary ownership than one of appropriation to social degree or evidence of her social propriety. She effectively finds a convincing way to signal her propriety.

The way Pamela writes, which to some degree resembles puritan plain style (which is also important for scientific and mercantile rhetoric), is a formal correlative to the way she registers her social propriety through dividing her clothes.[55] The prefatory material, composed by a fictitious editor who compiles Pamela's letters and authoritative readers who reflect upon them, emphasizes the "beautiful Simplicity of the Style, and a happy Propriety and Clearness of Expression (the Letters being written under the immediate Impression of every Circumstance which occasioned them...)."[56] In the second prefatory letter, the author contrasts Pamela's writing to eloquent writing that might "disguise the Facts, marr the Reflections, and unnaturalize the Incidents."[57] By contrast, the novel is persuasive (at least according to its own paratext) because it represents "*Pamela* as *Pamela* wrote it; in her own Words, without Amputation, or Addition."[58] Plain style, pioneered by the seventeenth-century merchant Thomas Mun, was grounded in experiential knowledge and avoided eloquence and rhetoric and is often associated with good business practice and tidy accounting. The novel's paratext also makes the parallel to clothing: "Such a Dress will best edify and entertain. The flowing Robes of Oratory may indeed amuse and amaze, but will never strike the Mind with solid Attention."[59] Like Pamela's narrative, one that is not overdressed, Pamela ensures that her body is not inappropriately dressed with clothing that is not rightfully hers. Pamela, owning herself properly, acts with propriety. Her sense of social propriety is backed up with an awareness of the most proper way of representing herself. She prepares Mrs. Jervis and Mr. B for her assumed departure through physically registering her lack of indebtedness, her zero balance, to them.

But, like at the Bank of England, accounting by itself is not enough to convey virtue. Accounting must be represented to, produced for, others. To ensure that Mrs. Jervis and Mr. B notice her propriety, Pamela makes a formal choice in representing her act. She separates the clothing into three distinct piles. She writes:

> I took all my Cloaths, and all my Linen, and I divided them into three Parcels;... I beg you will look over my poor Matters, and let every one have what belongs to them; for, said I, you know, I am resolv'd to take with me only what I can properly call my own.[60]

She places things her mistress gave to her in the first pile. In the second, she sets aside gifts from Mr. B. She places items she brought with her, and thus rightfully owns, in the third pile:

> But, said I, come to my Arms, my dear third Parcel, the Companion of my Poverty, and the Witness of my honesty; and may I never deserve the least Rag that is contained in thee, when I forfeit a Title to that Innocence that I hope will ever be the Pride of my Life.[61]

The explicit enumeration of these piles stresses the truly formal way she achieves a zero balance. There is nothing left over, and the reader has nothing with which to impute her impropriety. By separating her clothes into what does and does not belong to her, she creates a sartorial register for Mr. B; he and the reader are welcome to hold her to account, but if they were to do so, they would find that she owes him nothing.

The form of the zero balance is not merely folded into the content of the novel, but it also structures the form of an important discursive exchange between Pamela and Mr. B. The piles of clothing, visual indicators that Pamela has cleared her debts and is thus free to leave, might be compared to the way she (and even the printed pagination of *Pamela*) structures Mr. B's proposed contract with her later in the novel. Mr. B lays out the terms of his proposal that Pamela become his mistress through a numbered format, offering to settle her with money and property if she accepts his offer.[62] See Figure 3.2 for the first two pages of the contract and its refusal.

What is striking is the way each proposal is paginated alongside a response from Pamela, who declines each proposal with an explicit reason. At the surface, the passage seems like a contract. But the form of this passage also resembles a ledger because each proposal attempts to put Pamela in Mr. B's debt, and each response clearly negates the debt. By scanning the contract, the reader quickly finds that Pamela has maintained her propriety. As in an accounting ledger, Pamela persuades through producing a zero balance.

Despite the way *Pamela* mobilizes the form of the zero balance and plain style, Pamela's letters are nonetheless moving, and it is because they are moving that Mr. B sympathizes and is converted to believing her. Her accounts seem to bear witness to her honesty, and many details convey a sense of spiritual torture and despair. Pamela's account of her near-suicide by the pond, for example, has affected Mr. B to the degree that he no longer believes she is manipulating him. Lady Davers, at first skeptical of Pamela's intentions, is likewise moved by her narrative account.[63] Pamela's accounts have proven her virtue and thus her deservedness, and have also caused Lady Davers to accept her. Thus, it seems to be a combination of the factual and the moving that allows for the plot of *Pamela* to work: The story of her heart is counted as fact, reflecting Richardson's blending of newfangled accounting with older amatory fiction.

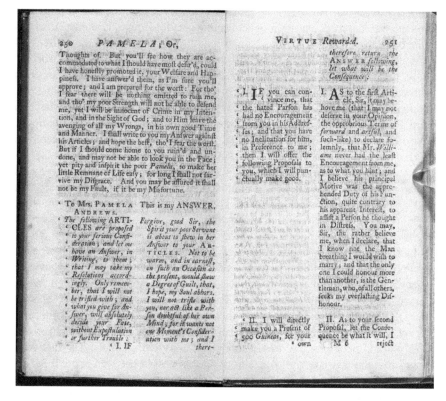

Figure 3.2 Mr. B's proposals and Pamela's refusals (© The British Library Board (Cup. 403.y.8)).

Representing the counter-fact in the *Pamela* controversy

One reason that the novel was subjected to immediate critique is that Pamela's accounts are presented as factual and yet are so utterly moving. William Warner argues that the publication of *Pamela* resulted in a "media event" whereby the public could not help but respond to *Pamela*.[64] Titillating, entertaining details are co-opted into similarly didactic projects, making readers reflect on whether they had been duped into sympathetic identification for and/or critical judgment of the protagonist.[65] The anonymous *Pamela Censured* (1741), for example, accuses the novel of being pornographic, exposing the "Most Artful and Alluring Amorous Ideas." Much of the *Pamela* controversy hinged on whether the truth of her letters (and thus her virtue) was in fact to be believed. Thomas Keymer and Peter Sabor write: "Pamelists and Antipamelists concerned themselves with the obvious areas of dispute opened up by the ambiguities of Richardson's presentation: Pamela's motivation, her veracity, her piety…. *Pamela* was not only a novel but also a site of ideological contestation."[66] This ideological contestation is tied to a debate about naïve trust in the form through which the story presented. The story of Pamela's heart that is counted as fact, garnered through its formal construction (and the way the particular form of accounting gets folded into its content), creates a famous debate about literary technique. And this debate might also be discussed by understanding the way the form of accounting is utilized in subsequent works.

To undermine *Pamela*'s factual pretenses, parodists wrote counter-narratives with counter-facts. *Pamela*, dated in 1741, was published anonymously in 1740. By January of 1741, a second edition was already announced, and by March, a third. Each subsequent edition contained an editorial apparatus praising the novel. Five fictional responses were published immediately after Pamela appeared in 1741: Henry Fielding's *Shamela*, Eliza Haywood's *Anti-Pamela*, James Parry's *The True Anti-Pamela*, Charles Povey's *The Virgin in Eden*, and the anonymous *Memoirs of the Life of Lady H.*[67] Versifications, plays, prose responses, sequels, and graphic representations followed in ensuing years. Of these original five, Fielding's and Haywood's counter-narratives emulate the epistolary form of *Pamela* and can be considered as parodic imitations of the form of accounting.

Fielding's *Shamela*, which Jacob Soll reads as a critique of Robert Walpole's manipulations in accounting after the South Sea Bubble, not only emulates the epistolary structure of *Pamela* but the promotional apparatus as well, using Parson Tickletext (a telling name) and Parson Oliver as correspondents debating the value of the work.[68] The letters themselves replicate the form of those in *Pamela*, only to suggest that the letters included in the original narrative had been partial, incomplete, and even fabricated narrative accounts. The title page claims that the text is a "full Account of all that passed between her and Parson *Arthur Williams*," containing "exact Copies of authentick Papers." The letter as a documentary object is once again preserved as the material witness to the truth. The epistolary form is mobilized to make readers skeptical of Pamela's virtue when given a new set of contexts.

At the level of content, the reader learns that particular details had been wrong in the original *Pamela*. Pamela's name is actually Shamela. Her mother is actually a whore rather than a pious Christian. And Pamela has been pursuing an illicit sexual relationship with Parson Williams the entire time, performing – misrepresenting herself – in order to get Mr. Booby to invest in her through marriage. By contrast to Pamela, who presents herself as being disinterested, Shamela is utterly interested. And we learn that the difference between these two terms is merely a matter of what is presented to the reader.

Significantly, in contrast to Pamela, Shamela is a poor accountant. After her marriage, Shamela says:

> I believe I shall buy everything I see. What signifies having money if one doth not spend it.... It would be hard indeed, that a woman who marries a man only for his money, should be debarred from spending it.[69]

This differs drastically from Pamela's comments on household management throughout the novel, especially at the end when she discusses meticulously accounting for all of her purchases.[70] Even though the novel borrows formally from *Pamela*, *Shamela* explicitly refutes the necessity of maintaining a zero balance. Shamela, unlike Pamela, only thinks on one side of the ledger – Mr. Booby plays no role for our understanding of the protagonist as Mr. B does.

In Haywood's *Anti-Pamela*, Syrena Tricksey writes to her mother asking for advice on how to extract money from various men. Syrena's mother coaches her not to follow her passion but instead her economic interest: "No Woman ever made her Fortune by the Man she had a sincere Value for."[71] Syrena's mother, by contrast to Pamela's parents, who warn about losing her virtue, warns her not to lose her value. Once again, the language of accounting returns. This time, however, it is used for explicitly financial ends. Syrena is 'interested,' and she manages her accounts only in order to marry a rich man:

> The Motives of her behaving in this Fashion were two; the first was to get as much as she could of him, before she granted him any material Favour, having an After-game in her Head to play upon him; and the other was, that she had another Lover whom she found her Account in managing.[72]

Here, managing accounts has become a mere trope, subverting the alignment of accounting and virtue and thereby collapsing the model of virtue in Richardson's novel. The skepticism inherent in *Anti-Pamela* hearkens to the cultural critic of public credit insofar as it presents individual interest as the reason why trust cannot be guaranteed.

Other works of fiction not usually associated with the *Pamela* controversy also follow this logic. By using accounting as a trope to stand in for virtue, John Cleland's *Fanny Hill or Memoirs of a Woman of Pleasure* (1748–89) serves as a serious, non-ironic imitation of *Pamela* when a prostitute is rewarded, like Pamela, for something like virtue. Pursuing the point of *Pamela Censured*, in which the anonymous author illustrates the sexually alluring (and thus corrupting) undertones to *Pamela*, *Fanny Hill* is utterly and explicitly titillating. *Fanny Hill* describes in graphic detail what might now be classified as homosexual sex, heterosexual sex, premature ejaculation, masturbation, fellatio, voyeurism, S&M, rape, revenge sex, spooning, group sex, deflowering, fake deflowering, and sex with the cognitively disabled.

These very different novels seem to have one thing in common: the way virtue can be signified through accounting in the household. While the first volume describes Fanny's learning how to be a prostitute, the second volume of *Fanny Hill* foregrounds household economy, a topic that the last quarter of *Pamela* and the entirety of Richardson's 1742 sequel pursue. Fanny Hill's experience in the house of Mrs. Cole serves as a training ground for the ideal domestic female. Becoming domesticated in the household contributes to the possibility of marriage (and thus the exaltation of virtue even despite her sexual immorality) at the end of the novel. Through the way in which she learns to manage her body *and* her pocketbook, Fanny enacts a Pamela-like practice of legitimating her upward mobility by insisting on her own virtue.

Mrs. Cole's household is what enables Fanny eventually to marry the man who initially deflowered her – Charles – despite their gap in social status. Managing a small household of her own, however, is only the first step toward her eventual success in marriage. The second factor that renders Fanny marriageable is her coming into financial affluence. Fanny's final client, a wealthy man who remains nameless, bequeaths her money because he respects her for her artless, disinterested companionship. This final non-marital sexual relationship makes explicit the domestic virtues Fanny learns at Mrs. Cole's. The fact that the gentleman has left Fanny his possessions results from the training she had received from her mentor: "I owed his opinion of my management of the vast possessions he left me to what he had observed of the prudential economy I had learned under Mrs Cole."[73] Significantly, Fanny ends up with the man who took her virginity – Charles has hit financial hard times, and she redeems him from financial loss at the same time as he redeems her from whoredom. Charles, according to Fanny, is "broken down to his naked personal merit" while she has improved her social status by coming into financial affluence.[74] The social playing field is leveled in the last few pages of *Fanny Hill*.

By the end of the narrative, not only has Fanny managed to balance her account of virtue and vice, she also learns to balance the pleasures of the mind with those of the body in her achieving social propriety. Indeed, the virtues of propriety seem to 'count' more than the sexual vices that pervade the novel. Fanny's account of coming into a state of self-ownership through Mrs. Cole's influence modifies the sort of virtue that Richardson puts forth in emphasizing the domestic realm of *Pamela*. *Fanny Hill*, unlike more subversive parodies of *Pamela* such as *Shamela*, takes on a narrative view of virtue that allows the reader to 'balance' the explicitly pornographic elements of the text with the knowledge that Fanny has attained a sort of propriety. In other words, the novel, full of erotic sexual acts, nonetheless legitimates itself by teaching the reader to manage herself. But because the novel is full of titillating acts of sexual transgression, its definition of virtue, like Pamela's, must extend beyond that of mere virginity.[75]

Virtue is beginning to take on more of a financial definition, reflecting a public that has begun to internalize a form of accounting and even apply it to extra-economic questions. This also reflects the transformation of a subject who is starting to learn the procedures of a new economy and to incorporate such procedures into daily practice. The form of accounting seems to dominate the various ethical and moral values shown to be in competition with one another in mid-century fiction. But this was precisely what was at stake in the conservative backlash against progressive ideology in Richardson's novels: that social distinctions could be done away with by hearkening to a newer definition of virtue.

As soon as *Pamela* appeared, parodists were co-opting accounting in order to use it for various ends, showing how accounting cannot be aligned strictly with older notions of virtue; indeed, accounting even seems to have the capacity to transform virtue. The literary debate about the way *Pamela* attempts to represent virtue opens up the novel for development in an unprecedented way. We might observe, for example, the way Henry Fielding's *Joseph Andrews* (1742) begins as another *Pamela* parody but then loses interest in critiquing *Pamela* and develops into a narrative of its own, exploring a sort of male virtue in the character of Joseph through a more fully depersonalized, disinterested narrator. And yet, at no point does *Joseph Andrews* pretend seriously that it is grounded in empirical reality. Fielding is content to simulate virtue through fiction: He produces virtue not through insisting on historicity, but by approximating it through fictional narrative strategies. Virtue is virtual, and none of Fielding's characters are paragons of moral perfection, revealing the relationship between the formal development of the novel and the rise of the aesthetic.

The account as contract in *Clarissa*

The feedback loop between the public and the State is analogous to the feedback loop between the producer of aesthetic works in a literary marketplace and the reader. In Richardson's letters to various correspondents, such as Aaron Hill, his longtime literary friend and correspondent between 1736 and 1758, Richardson tests some of his ideas with Hill and his household before publishing. In these letters, Richardson admits to having tested Clarissa's absconding with Lovelace with his female friends:

> They have both confessed, that they think Clarissa had sufficient Provocations to throw herself into Lovelace's Protection (She not knowing him so bad as he was–And at the same time, as I have said, he *meant* her no Evil).... That her Motives for meeting him ... were justifiable and Characteristic.[76]

The opinion of others – and the way authorial propriety is calibrated from the outset by vetting works to readers before publishing – pertains to *Clarissa* and not *Pamela*. Looking out for his reputation on the literary marketplace as a bookseller as well as an author, Richardson registers the interstices between literary value and ideological consistency.

Despite the ways contemporaries utilize accounting to transform the definition of virtue put forth in *Pamela*, Richardson does not abandon the form of accounting in its critical aftermath. On the contrary, he refines it (and despite Cleland's innovation, preserves the alignment of female virtue with sexual propriety). This is demonstrated by the way his contemporaries often mark a formal and ethical difference between *Pamela* and *Clarissa*. For example, an anonymous critic ("a LOVER of VIRTUE") writes:

> I think your writings have corrupted our language and our taste; that the composition of them all, except Clarissa, is bad; and that they all ... have a manifest tendency to corrupt our morals. I have likewise shewn that your principle characters are all, except Clarissa's[,] faulty, ridiculous, or unmeaning.[77]

How might one account for the way this critic affirms that *Clarissa*, unlike all other works in Richardson's oeuvre, is not somehow corrupting?

In refining the way accounting works through bringing in more narrator 'accountants,' *Clarissa* is able to represent Clarissa as being less 'interested' than Pamela. Although Clarissa loses her virginity, she remains virtuous precisely because she can demonstrate that she is guiltless in her struggle with Lovelace through the way she establishes herself as a household and narrative accountant. Unlike *Pamela*, it is not only propriety that the form of the accounting produces. *Clarissa* utilizes a very strong zero balance to demonstrate that she is not indebted to Lovelace and is thus not guilty for having lost her sexual virtue through the rape. The form of accounting more literally balances credits and debts, albeit in social (qualitative) rather than economic (quantitative) terms.

The most obvious formal difference between *Pamela* and *Clarissa* is the proliferation of points of view, and letter-writers, in the latter. We read an exchange of correspondence not only between Clarissa and Anna, but also between Lovelace and Belford. Minor characters often write letters to these primary recipients, as well. The proliferation of perspective is a focal point for critics who debate whether or not Richardson comes to acknowledge the arbitrariness of interpretation. Terry Castle, for example, writes:

> Confronting the dissolution of *claritas*, the replacement of a so-called objective narrator by a multiplicity of *interpretative* events, we are made conscious in turn of our own subjectivity, the arbitrariness of the ways we try to make sense of contradictory accounts.[78]

On the one hand, therefore, it looks as if the novel experiments with subjectivity.

An emphasis on subjectivity seemed to be a critical consensus until the work of Sandra Macpherson. By contrast to criticism that emphasized interiority or subjectivity, Macpherson argues that intention is precisely what is under attack in the novel, as "Richardson comes to understand that interpretation is crucially at issue precisely when social relations and obligations are configured as contractual."[79] Macpherson reads *Clarissa* as an example of strict liability law, arguing that "[t]he language of constructive intent is everywhere in *Clarissa*."[80] Constructive intent, which means that the agent has to have demonstrated intent before being accused of a crime (regardless of internal state), is modeled on the logic of accounting I have been describing. This has implications for how we come to understand the liberal social contract insofar as what is at stake is that the individual (as the emergent financial subject) must take it upon herself to represent virtuous intention from the outset, regardless of her internal, subjective state.

In *Clarissa*, Richardson shifts from the production of truth telling by way of accounting to the production of different systems of mutual obligation. But, as in the case of *Pamela*, *Clarissa* begins by linking accounting practices to virtue. The novel is organized so that Clarissa is incapable of accounting for that which would make her morally culpable: being raped by Lovelace. This formal blind spot gets registered through her ultimate forgiveness of Lovelace for the act (rather than acquiescing to marriage, which he desires). This works very much like the forgiveness of a debt. And this narrative strategy has its basis in the logic of accounting. Indeed, even more so than *Pamela*, *Clarissa* almost didactically internalizes a social-spiritual practice of accounting.

Evidence for this comes not only from within the text itself. Reading *Clarissa* inspired contemporaries in the practice of keeping accounts. In a letter to Richardson, Lady Bradshaigh writes:

> You made her early hours appear so charming, that I determined to become in that her imitator, and find numberless conveniencies in it, unknown to me before.... She has also taught me to keep an account of my time; but that, compared with her's, only serves to put me out of conceit with myself.[81]

Similarly, in the 1750s, the shopkeeper Thomas Turner wrote in his journal that his wife read *Clarissa* to him aloud while he kept his books.[82]

In understanding Lady Bradshaigh's or Thomas Turner's enthusiastic responses to accounting in *Clarissa*, one might point to Anna's eulogical statements contained in letter 529, which bring to light Clarissa's particular daily practices of time-management, and which, as in *Pamela*, utilize accounting to signify Clarissa's virtue. Anna begins her lengthy description of Clarissa's daily tasks by quoting Clarissa thus: "No one could spend their time properly, who did not live by some rule: who did not appropriate the hours, as near as might be, to particular purposes and employments."[83] Attention to particular duties regulated within a 24-hour cycle demonstrates the novel's diurnal nature, a term Stuart Sherman uses to discuss the production of temporality in the eighteenth-century novel.[84] Keeping track of time shares with financial accounting the capacity to translate moral obligations into an economic language. Like the double-entry ledger that calculates quantities of fiscal indebtedness, keeping track of one's time is used as a marker to show that one has maintained one's social obligations. Whereas most of the novels Sherman discusses mark time through a single narrator, I want to emphasize the way Clarissa's letters use accounting for time as a way of signifying her innocence – not in a subjective way, but in a way that allows her to produce a contractual grid of intention that neither Lovelace nor the reader can call into question.

Clarissa's diurnal duties range from private time in her closet to the material management of household property. Being a woman who has the potential to inherit, Clarissa's relationship to property is crucial to the plot. Whereas Pamela has much to gain, Clarissa has much to lose. The businesslike and profane nature of the Solmes marriage plot establishes an obsession on Clarissa's part to not become dependent upon him. As Christopher Hill's work has pointed out, the issue of property, inheritance, and marriage for money is essential to reading *Clarissa*.[85] Perhaps this is why Clarissa's refusal to marry Solmes for the purpose of her family's aggrandizement presents a preliminary conflict between her values and those of the Harlowes. What Hill reads as Richardson's critique of the corrupting forces of material wealth occurs as a reaction on Clarissa's part: She keeps tight accounts to stay out of obligation in a system of value she despises, and, more importantly, she defines her own value system explicitly through her letters in order to be held accountable to it alone. Clarissa wants to be audited, and the representation of this desire is – like the Bank of England's – why we trust her.

Clarissa's virtuous intentions, like those of Pamela, become believable because of the credibility of her narrative account, which one sees through her correspondence with Anna. Accounting for time shares with credit the quality of being quantifiable. Anna's representation of Clarissa's account contains subtitles to help the reader visualize the break-down of each part of Clarissa's day. Anna's description shows how Clarissa spent time in study, devotions, domestic management, crafts, meals, conversation, and (as in the case of *Pamela*) charity to the poor. What is significant about Anna's description is the way Clarissa's accounting for time includes a concept of both debt and credit. Four hours of the day serve as potential credits based on whether Clarissa has satisfied her debts. She calls these variable hours her "fund," "upon which she used to draw to satisfy other debits."[86] Further, Clarissa carries over her balance of hours to the end of each week and notes whether she is in credit or debt. Anna writes:

> Once a week she used to reckon with herself; when, if within the 144 hours contained in the six days she had made her account even, she noted it accordingly: if otherwise, she carried the debit to the next week's account; as thus: *Debtor to the article of benevolent visits* so many hours. And so of the rest.[87]

Anna's example gives the reader a sense of what Clarissa might have written in her actual account book. Just as she allocates her hours, Clarissa imbues her narrative accounts with a similar function: to demonstrate and regulate her virtue by ensuring she stays out of problematic obligation to others.

Like the accounting ledger, writing takes on a regulatory function in *Clarissa*. Words as signifiers of intention even come to guide Clarissa's conduct. Clarissa's description of her own writing practice to Anna in letter 135 places writing in the service of a structure of both intention and conduct:

> You have often heard me own the advantages I have found from writing down everything of moment that befalls me; and of all I *think* and all I *do* that may be of future use to me…. But when I set down what I *will* do, or what I *have* done on this or that occasion; the resolution or action is before me, either to be adhered to, withdrawn or amended; and I have entered into a *compact* with myself, as I may say; having given it under my own hand, to *improve* rather than go *backward*, as I live longer.[88]

This differs from *Pamela* insofar as Pamela writes about an *underlying truth* of her heart. By contrast, Clarissa writes explicitly in order to *produce the truth* of her heart. Her writing is a contract to herself, serving a regulatory function. The act of writing is an act of self-improvement through self-objectification, a splitting of self. She enters a compact with someone else she reproduces within herself. In so doing, she produces in the reader a way of measuring whether she lives up to her own intentions. Clarissa's holding herself accountable to her own narrative has a parallel function to the merchant or the banker with a ledger, the contract in its more overtly financialized form. To use Defoe's terminology, accounting serves as Clarissa's "repeating clock," giving her a means of knowing at any time how she stands in relation to others.[89] She suggests it is for herself – just like Defoe's advice to the tradesman – but it is her self-representation that matters the most here. In this sense, Clarissa's own account is a means of arriving at a zero balance with her readers, one that suggests she holds herself accountable to the particular truth she tells. This is how the ledger works as a contract.

When Lovelace rapes Clarissa, there is little account from Clarissa's perspective. Clarissa's description of the act is fuzzy at best. She cannot account exactly for what happens to her, and this contrasts very starkly to the detailed analyses of her intentions and actions that normally characterize her letters. Frances Ferguson's analysis of the relationship between rape law and this lack of account explains why Clarissa categorically cannot be read as culpable for the rape, and why she therefore can be read as virtuous even despite this sexual act. Ferguson writes:

> The very fact that the rape counts as rape necessarily depends not on Clarissa's mental state but on a formal account of that state. It therefore looks as if *Clarissa*, like rape law and unlike the "psychological novel" that it is supposed to represent, argues for the primacy of the form by framing the rape so that it cannot depend on the victim's mental state.[90]

But here we need to take Macpherson's critique of intentionality seriously: In her reading, Clarissa accounts for herself in such a way that she anticipates from the outset that she will be 'audited.' Macpherson's term for this is *emplotment*:

> a formalist account of action indifferent to questions of motive and practices of interiority ... emerges not as a challenge to the possibly of responsibility, as it is, for example, in the deconstructive account of *Clarissa*, nor as a challenge to the possibility of personhood, as it is for Ferguson. Emplotment is the form responsibility and personhood take.[91]

The rape is framed so that legal culpability cannot be measured because its very definition depends on the account, which is not represented. Thus, because Clarissa is in state of unawareness (or pseudo-awareness), her (non-)account of the rape means that we can trust her. She is virtuous even though she has absconded with Lovelace in the first place, is raped by him, and has refused to marry him afterwards. She is virtuous because, in all other cases, she meticulously accounts for her time, which asks the reader to try to 'audit' her account of the rape. The reader finds nothing, and it is therefore assumed that it was impossible for her to have consented.

The account in *Clarissa* anticipates its own critique by self-consciously registering differing definitions of social obligation in order to ensure that *Clarissa* ends with Lovelace on the debt side of a ledger. But the account is much more than this: It is also a contract. Through the manipulation of the account, Richardson renders Clarissa more virtuous after the critique opened up by anti-Pamelists. The form of novel ensures that the reader:

1   knows that Clarissa holds herself to her own account;
2   sees other letter-writers corroborating the strictness by which Clarissa maintains accounts of her time; and
3   sees that Clarissa, despite keeping a strict account of all her time spent in the hands of Lovelace, cannot account for the sexual act perpetrated against her.

It is for this reason that *Clarissa* partly overcomes the "naïve empiricism" associated with *Pamela* (a belief that Pamela is a paragon of virtue because of her self-representation within her accounts, which leaves the novel open to critique by skeptical satirists). Clarissa demonstrates her sincerity by showing that she cannot display all of the information. Her devotion to the factual perspective of the account is so strict that she does not even try to explain herself outside of the framework she has created.

This, of course, has important implications for the questions the novel asks about the various social modes mapping onto the respective characters. Lovelace serves as a representative of an outmoded aristocratic ideology whose values are made to seem more like corruption than virtue, a reversal of the original debate on public credit a few decades before. This even has implications for the form of the novel. John Richetti calls *Clarissa* a "massive rejection of romance."[92] Like McKeon, Richetti's analysis of form is deeply wedded to what is at stake in the social work the novel performs.[93] Clarissa is the representative of a modern, impersonal order, whereas Lovelace

> is both an embodiment of [a traditional] hegemony and a shameless exploiter of the extra-legal privileges that it confers upon him. In the moral and social economy projected by *Clarissa* in which an individual earns his or her status by original moral action in the face of a surrounding fatality, Lovelace is an archaic and dangerously nostalgic figure who must be repudiated and turned from an aristocratic exemplar into a psychological subject.[94]

The effect of Clarissa's letters reveals Lovelace to others in this light. Lovelace's behavior, represented as a product of broader social tendencies, conveys to the semi-public within the novel a dark side of the old order now pushed out by the new, contractually ethical financial subject. The older order has become, by stark contrast, entirely unethical.

The work of the novel in particular, therefore, is an ethical reversal of the virtue/corruption dichotomy, one that serves as a unifying force for garnering commitment to public credit insofar as each individual becomes a representative of it through a new financial ethic. What matters here is the way the reader comes to trust the experience of the protagonist through the way her story is framed by narrators that can corroborate her account. Because Clarissa is in the habit of accounting just like the tradesman, what is glaringly missing – an absence serving as a sign – is her consent. In both of these examples, one gets a sense that the logic of accounting important for public credit mechanisms such as the Bank has begun to be internalized within domestic frameworks. In each case, what is at stake is not reputation alone, nor is it accounting by itself. Rather, it is the way such reputation is a product of representational strategies that anticipate critique and therefore offer themselves up for inspection. This is the ethics of the new financial subject.

From virtue to the virtual

Clarissa explicitly contrasts traditional patriarchal structures to a newer ethos, that which emphasizes rationality and predictability by holding oneself to account. When one examines the conservative responses to *Pamela*, one observes a resemblance to the debate between landed interests and proponents of public credit. But, in the case of Cleland's *Fanny Hill* and *Clarissa*, one sees at the same time an accommodation of the traditional framework (with traditional definitions of virtue) to the newer economic model. It seems that an underlying logic prevails: How can we trust a self-presentation when we suspect it of being interested? It must be *re-presented* to anticipate the critique from the outset.

Representation, which is especially of interest for political historians, seems to have a strong tie to public credit and also to credible commitment.[95] If what is at stake in credible commitment is a process whereby each individual comes to hold the State to account, it would seem that the novel's domestication of accounting does more than just reflect what is going on: It also helps to disseminate an economic model. These novels demonstrate that holding oneself to account is the new predominant virtue. Perhaps, then, when one considers the way financial thinking enters the private sphere, one should add a certain logic of self-accounting that seems to structure the novel, domestic or otherwise. The novel's roots, therefore, seem much more complex than what can be gleaned through the rise of individualism alone. Indeed, the transition to financial capitalism seems to entail almost a spiritual change, one that carries and is carried by other epistemological and spiritual authorities, such as protestant Christianity.[96]

In the way they each configure gendered virtue by using a formal means, *Pamela* and *Clarissa* also teach readers something about the logic of accounting insofar as it relates to public credit in particular and to credible commitment in general. *Pamela* opens itself up for critique because it relies so heavily on Pamela's self-presentation of her virtue, a presentation that, in translated terms, resembles the zero balance of a ledger. *Clarissa* attempts to remedy this problem by proliferating subjects keeping accounts so that, ultimately, readers trust Clarissa's version even if, 'objectively,' they might find her blameworthy. Through accounting, *virtue*, a term used to convey an interior quality of persons or things, quickly transforms into the *virtual*, a related concept that implies that the interior quality is an effect and not necessarily grounded in actuality.[97]

Double-entry bookkeeping is a translation of complex relationships into an abstract form, and this abstraction has a price. Accounting served as a partial basis for a public credit system because of a growing public perception of its disinterested fairness. But accounting by itself, the algebra of double-entry bookkeeping, did not suffice in order to convey this virtue. The Bank made decisions to emphasize its keeping of trustworthy accounts through its architecture and through its assurance that its tellers were doing their jobs perfectly. It explicitly – and visibly – held itself to account because it anticipated that the public would hold it to account. Public credit is another instance of the movement from virtue to the virtual, for it is only when the public believes that national accounting is trustworthy that it becomes virtuous. That is to say, public credit is virtual because it is an effect before it is a ground.

The *Pamela* controversy, a significant moment in the history of the English novel, is governed by an attention to the formal production of virtue in a way similar to the Bank of England. Just as the reader of the novel must imagine Pamela and Clarissa to be virtuous for the novels to serve their ideological praxis, so must the constituents of the commonwealth believe that the Bank of England is sound for public credit to persevere. But this virtue, the virtue of public credit and the virtue of the novel, is virtual – it is the effect of representation and not an interior quality captured by empirical method, the material document, or the true history.

Clarissa seems to offer an example of what happens to the individual when the logic of public credit becomes domesticated: Indeed, perhaps it even requires us to revise our notion of what it means for culture to shift from "status to contract."[98] The modern contract, as Roy Kreitner suggests, is about producing individuals capable of calculating:

> The borders of contract refer to the active role of the framework of discourse in creating individuals: individuality, in the sense of the calculating subject, is created through enframing, the positing of borders – the roping off, defining, delimiting – that generates *individuation*. Calculation is based on singularity, on eliminating competing impulses and undefined responsibilities to others.[99]

Part of what is at stake in the transition from the true history to the novel is the way readers came to value that which is not necessarily empirically or historically true, but that which conveys a virtual truth through a feedback loop in which the representer anticipates from the outset that her account will be audited.

In this version of the story, the rise of the novel is indebted to the financial structures that came into being just before it, and the question of the novel's origins deserves even further critical attention as a product of the epistemologies required for public credit in particular in addition to the social categories and their inherent ideologies, which have already been thoroughly covered by critics. The novel serves as a machine for simulating virtue by using various markers, and the character of the novel is the subject who calculates – who ropes off, defines, and delimits possibility – in anticipation of future responsibilities and obligations.

Notes

1 Mark Knights, *Representation and Misrepresentation in Later Stuart Britain*, 5, 328.
2 On politeness, see Anna Bryson, *From Courtesy to Civility*, 50; and Lawrence E. Klein, "Politeness and the Interpretation of the British Eighteenth Century," 869. On public knowledge and scientific practice, see Robert Markley, *Fallen Languages*, 22; and Larry Stewart, *The Rise of Public Science*, 108.
3 Andrea Finkelstein, *Harmony and the Balance*, 252.
4 See Rebecca Elisabeth Connor, *Women, Accounting, and Narrative*, 19.
5 Simon Schaffer and Steven Shapin, *Leviathan and the Air-Pump*, 332.
6 See Michael McKeon, *The Origins of the English Novel*, 20.
7 See ibid., 410.
8 Anne L. Murphy, "Demanding 'Credible Commitment,' " 180.
9 See Ian Watt, *The Rise of the Novel*, 60.
10 Daniel Defoe, *The Review*, 226.
11 See Natasha Glaisyer, *The Culture of Commerce in England*, 50.
12 Joseph Addison, *The Spectator*, 14.
13 Ibid., 14–15.
14 Ibid., 16.
15 See Carl Wennerlind, *Casualties of Credit*, 44.
16 Addison, 16.
17 Ibid., 17.
18 Ibid.
19 Indeed, this is the term J.G.A. Pocock uses for a similar reason. In his reading, civic virtue is the antithesis to corruption often framed in terms of commerce. See *The Machiavellian Moment*, ix.
20 Daniel M. Abramson, *Building the Bank of England*, 24.
21 Ibid., 53.
22 Ibid., 53–4.
23 Mary Poovey, *A History of the Modern Fact*, 55.
24 Ibid., 4.
25 Abramson, 53.
26 Ibid.
27 Ibid., 52.
28 Ibid., 14.
29 Bank of England Archive Minutes Committee of the Bank of England, 6A30/1, October 19, 1727.
30 Anne L. Murphy, "Learning the Business of Banking," 157.
31 Daniel Defoe, *A Tour Through England and Wales*, 11.
32 Murphy, "Learning the Business of Banking," 157.
33 See Nancy Armstrong, *Desire and Domestic Fiction*, 87.

34 Watt, 63–4.
35 See ibid., 300.
36 McKeon, 212.
37 Ibid., 171.
38 Ibid., 20.
39 Ibid.
40 Ibid.
41 Like Defoe, Richardson (who worked as a printer) wrote handbooks before novels. In 1733, he published *The Apprentice's Vade Mecum*, which taught rules and behaviors for the apprentice, including a strict condemnation of theaters, taverns, and gambling.
42 See Armstrong, 87.
43 See Connor, 54.
44 *Oxford English Dictionary Online*, s.v. "Account" and "Tell."
45 Connor, 45.
46 Pocock shows how this happens in legal terms a century earlier:

> "[P]ropriety" defines the individual in terms of what is "his own" and at the same time in terms of all the legal, social and moral relations in which he is properly involved and to which he may properly lay claim in law and justice. This is the bridge over which we pass in journeying from "property" in the economic sense to "propriety" in the ethical and moral; and the social reality expressed in the language in that of common-law England, in which a law which was essentially a law of tenures had become the main regulating, identifying and describing device whereby both the propertied individual and the kingdom knew themselves to exist.
>
> ("Propriety, Liberty and Valour," 242–3)

47 John B. Pierce, "Pamela's Textual Authority," 10.
48 Catherine Ingrassia, " 'I am Become a Mere Usurer,' " 303.
49 Ingrassia sees Richardson's attitude toward credit as being very different from earlier writers: "Richardson's texts ... illustrate how, by the 1740s, the notions of speculative investment, fictional duplicity, and paper credit so troubling twenty years earlier, are increasingly normalized" (*Authorship, Commerce, and Gender in Early Eighteenth-Century England*, 14). Ingrassia thinks of Pamela as a domestic stock-jobber because of her attention to her future worth, like a speculative investment. She gets Mr. B to invest in her through the "paper credit" of her journal (ibid., 304). By contrast, I would be inclined to see Pamela functioning more like public credit, which is not exactly the same thing.
50 Samuel Richardson, *Pamela: Or, Virtue Rewarded*, 11.
51 Ibid., 471–2.
52 Ibid., 499.
53 Ibid., 502.
54 Ibid., 55.
55 Plain style and accounting can both be linked to the emergence of the empirical sciences. Thomas Sprat calls for a one-to-one relation between words and things in his *The History of the Royal-Society of London, for the improving of natural knowledge*. One should "reject all the amplifications, digressions and swellings of style: to return back to the primitive purity, and shortness, which men delivered so many things, almost in an equal number of words" (113).
56 Richardson, *Pamela*, 5.
57 Ibid., 9.
58 Ibid.
59 Ibid.
60 Ibid., 77.
61 Ibid., 79.

62 See ibid., 188–92.
63 Ibid., 455.
64 William B. Warner, *Licensing Entertainment*, 178.
65 Ibid., 22.
66 Thomas Keymer and Peter Sabor, "General Introduction," xiii.
67 Thomas Keymer and Peter Sabor, *Pamela in the Marketplace*, 83.
68 Jacob Soll, *The Reckoning*, 115.
69 Henry Fielding, *Joseph Andrews and Shamela*, 331–2.
70 See Richardson, *Pamela*, 471–2.
71 Eliza Haywood, *Anti-Pamela*, 19.
72 Ibid., 113.
73 John Cleland, *Fanny Hill or Memoirs of a Woman of Pleasure*, 212.
74 Ibid., 217.
75 Whereas Richardson takes the form seriously, Cleland may have merely wanted to cynically capitalize on it. After all, Cleland, a medical science researcher and linguist, wrote *Fanny Hill* while he was in debtors' prison.
76 Samuel Richardson, *Letters written to and for particular friends*, 247.
77 *Critical Remarks on Sir Charles Grandison, Clarissa and Pamela*, 57–8.
78 Terry Castle, *Clarissa's Ciphers*, 28.
79 Sandra Macpherson, "Lovelace, Ltd.," 100.
80 Sandra Macpherson, *Harm's Way*, 77.
81 Samuel Richardson, *The Correspondence of Samuel Richardson*, 264.
82 Margot C. Finn, *The Character of Credit*, 64.
83 Samuel Richardson, *Clarissa*, 1470.
84 Stuart Sherman, *Telling Time*, 224.
85 Christopher Hill, "Clarissa Harlowe and Her Times," 39.
86 Richardson, *Clarissa*, 1471.
87 Ibid.
88 Ibid., 483.
89 Daniel Defoe, *The Compleat English Tradesman*, 15.
90 Frances Ferguson, "Rape and the Rise of the Novel," 100.
91 Macpherson, *Harm's Way*, 66.
92 John Richetti, *The English Novel in History, 1700–1780*, 99.
93 Richetti writes:

> Richardson articulates a network of connections encompassing the Harlowes and Lovelace clan, a tangled web of alliances, inheritances, obligations, courtships, rivalries – all of these actions and accidents remembered, analyzed, and almost endlessly rehearsed…. This complex past that suffuses *Clarissa* from its opening pages renders the present as it emerges paralyzingly contingent and provisional, subject always to the heroine's obsessive contemplation of her narrowing options to revisions and adjustments mandated by her developing grasp of the history of her family and those connected to it.
>
> (Ibid., 100)

94 Ibid., 117.
95 See Knights, 37–41.
96 See R.H. Tawney, *Religion and the Rise of Capitalism*; and Max Weber, *The Protestant Ethic and the Spirit of Capitalism*.
97 *Oxford English Dictionary Online*, s.v. "Virtual."
98 Macpherson, *Harm's Way*, 4.
99 Roy Kreitner, *Calculating Promises*, 12.

Works cited

Abramson, Daniel M. *Building the Bank of England: Money, Architecture, Society, 1694–1942*. New Haven: Yale University Press, 2005.

Addison, Joseph. *The Spectator*, vol. 1, edited by Donald F. Bond. Oxford: Oxford at the Clarendon Press, 1965.

Armstrong, Nancy. *Desire and Domestic Fiction: A Political History of the Novel*. New York: Oxford University Press, 1987.

Bank of England Archive. Minutes Committee of the Bank of England. 6A30/1. October 19, 1727.

Bryson, Anna. *From Courtesy to Civility: Changing Codes of Conduct in Early Modern England*. Oxford: Oxford University Press, 1998.

Castle, Terry. *Clarissa's Ciphers: Meaning and Disruption in Richardson's Clarissa*. Ithaca: Cornell University Press, 1989.

Cleland, John. *Fanny Hill or Memoirs of a Woman of Pleasure*. 1748. Harmondsworth: Penguin, 1985.

Connor, Rebecca Elisabeth. *Women, Accounting, and Narrative: Keeping Books in Eighteenth-Century England*. London: Routledge, 2004.

Critical Remarks on Sir Charles Grandison, Clarissa and Pamela. London: J. Dowse, 1754.

Defoe, Daniel. *A Tour Through England and Wales: Divided into Circuits or Journeys*, vol. 1. London: J.M. Dent and E.P. Dutton, 1928.

Defoe, Daniel. *The Review*. 1704–13. New York: Columbia University Press, 1938.

Defoe, Daniel. *The Compleat English Tradesman*. 1726. Gloucester: Alan Sutton Publishing, 1987.

Ferguson, Frances. "Rape and the Rise of the Novel." *Representations* 20 (1987): 88–112.

Fielding, Henry. *Joseph Andrews and Shamela*. 1742, 1741. Boston: Houghton Mifflin, 1961.

Finkelstein, Andrea. *Harmony and the Balance: An Intellectual History of Seventeenth-Century English Economic Thought*. Ann Arbor: University of Michigan Press, 2000.

Finn, Margot C. *The Character of Credit: Personal Debt in English Culture, 1740–1914*. Cambridge: Cambridge University Press, 2003.

Glaisyer, Natasha. *The Culture of Commerce in England, 1660–1720*. Bodmin: The Boydell Press, 2006.

Haywood, Eliza. *Anti-Pamela*. London: n.p., 1741.

Hill, Christopher. "Clarissa Harlowe and Her Times," in *Essays on the Eighteenth-Century Novel*, edited by Robert Donald Spector, 32–63. Bloomington: Indiana University Press, 1965.

Ingrassia, Catherine. *Authorship, Commerce, and Gender in Early Eighteenth-Century England: A Culture of Paper Credit*. Cambridge: Cambridge University Press, 1998.

Ingrassia, Catherine. "'I am Become a Mere Usurer': Pamela and Domestic Stock-Jobbing." *Studies in the Novel* 30.3 (1998): 303–23.

Keymer, Thomas and Peter Sabor. "General Introduction," in *The Pamela Controversy: Criticisms and Adaptations of Samuel Richardson's Pamela, 1740–1750*, vol. 1, edited by Thomas Keymer and Peter Sabor, xiii–xxix. London: Pickering & Chatto, 2001.

Keymer, Thomas and Peter Sabor. *Pamela in the Marketplace: Literary Controversy and Print Culture in Eighteenth-Century Britain and Ireland*. Cambridge: Cambridge University Press, 2005.

Klein, Lawrence E. "Politeness and the Interpretation of the British Eighteenth Century." *The Historical Journal* 45.4 (2002): 869–98.

Knights, Mark. *Representation and Misrepresentation in Later Stuart Britain: Partisanship and Political Culture*. Oxford: Oxford University Press, 2005.

Kreitner, Roy. *Calculating Promises: The Emergence of Modern American Contract Doctrine*. Stanford: Stanford University Press, 2006.

McKeon, Michael. *The Origins of the English Novel, 1600–1740*. Baltimore: Johns Hopkins University Press, 1987.

Macpherson, Sandra. "Lovelace, Ltd." *ELH* 65.1 (1998): 99–121.

Macpherson, Sandra. *Harm's Way: Tragic Responsibility and the Novel Form*. Baltimore: Johns Hopkins University Press, 2010.

Markley, Robert. *Fallen Languages: Crises of Representation in Newtonian England, 1660–1740*. Ithaca: Cornell University Press, 1993.

Murphy, Anne L. "Learning the Business of Banking: The Management of the Bank of England's First Tellers." *Business History* 52.1 (2010): 150–68.

Murphy, Anne L. "Demanding 'Credible Commitment': Public Reactions to the Failures of the Early Financial Revolution." *The Economic History Review* 66.1 (2013): 178–97.

Oxford English Dictionary Online.

Pierce, John B. "Pamela's Textual Authority," in *Passion and Virtue: Essays on the Novels of Samuel Richardson*, edited by David Blewett, 8–26. Toronto: University of Toronto Press, 2001.

Pocock, J.G.A. *The Machiavellian Moment: Florentine Political Thought and the Atlantic Republican Tradition*. Princeton: Princeton University Press, 1975.

Pocock, J.G.A. "Propriety, Liberty and Valour: Ideology, Rhetoric and Speech in the 1628 Debates in the House of Commons," in *The Political Imagination in History: Essays Concerning J.G.A. Pocock*, edited by D.N. DeLuna, 231–60. Dexter: Owlworks, 2006.

Poovey, Mary. *A History of the Modern Fact: Problems of Knowledge in the Sciences of Wealth and Society*. Chicago: University of Chicago Press, 1998.

Richardson, Samuel. *Letters written to and for particular friends*. London: n.p., 1741.

Richardson, Samuel. *The Correspondence of Samuel Richardson*, vol. 4. New York: AMS, 1966.

Richardson, Samuel. *Clarissa*. 1748. London: Penguin, 1985.

Richardson, Samuel. *Pamela: Or, Virtue Rewarded*. 1740. Oxford: Oxford University Press, 2001.

Richetti, John. *The English Novel in History, 1700–1780*. London: Routledge, 1999.

Schaffer, Simon and Steven Shapin. *Leviathan and the Air-Pump: Hobbes, Boyle, and the Experimental Life*. Princeton: Princeton University Press, 1985.

Sherman, Stuart. *Telling Time: Clocks, Diaries, and English Diurnal Form, 1660–1785*. Chicago: University of Chicago Press, 1996.

Soll, Jacob. *The Reckoning: Financial Accountability and the Rise and Fall of Nations*. New York: Basic Books, 2014.

Sprat, Thomas. *The History of the Royal-Society of London, for the improving of natural knowledge*. London: n.p., 1702.

Stewart, Larry. *The Rise of Public Science: Rhetoric, Technology and Natural Philosophy in Newtonian Britain, 1660–1750*. Cambridge: Cambridge University Press, 1992.

Tawney, R.H. *Religion and the Rise of Capitalism*. New York: Harcourt Brace Jovanovich, 1954.

Warner, William B. *Licensing Entertainment: The Elevation of Novel Reading in Britain, 1684–1750.* Berkeley: University of California Press, 1998.

Watt, Ian. *The Rise of the Novel: Studies in Defoe, Richardson and Fielding.* London: Hogarth, 1957.

Weber, Max. *The Protestant Ethic and the Spirit of Capitalism,* translated by Talcott Parsons. London: Routledge, 1930.

Wennerlind, Carl. *Casualties of Credit: The English Financial Revolution, 1620–1720.* Cambridge, MA: Harvard University Press, 2011.

Part II

Framing fiction through credible commitment

4 Paper contracts, public fictions, and the money it-narrative

Part II of this book examines various types of fiction that take on some of the cultural conflicts owing to the rise of public credit. I examine various narrative strategies to get a sense of how the novel differentiates itself from other forms of fiction in the later eighteenth century, arguing that the virtualization of trust, new to contemporaries, puts additional pressure on the novel's generic concerns which can be seen as an extension of the representational questions discussed in Part I. The remainder of *Representing Public Credit*, therefore, takes a certain liberty: the extension of the credible commitment thesis into discursive territories it has not yet ventured – deeper into the part of public credit that is dependent on public opinion. A reason for this is that in the early eighteenth century, the public itself, as Mark Knights points out, can be seen as a collective fiction with new importance because "for the first time a National Debt was funded by the public and based on public credit."[1] What follows is an attempt to continue reading through eighteenth-century texts by looking for evidence that credible commitment might have still been a problem, still an ongoing process of negotiation between creditors and the State.

If the credible commitment thesis is, as Anne Murphy says, also about getting public creditors to demand commitment 'from below,' has the task been completed by the middle of the century?[2] By the end of the century? Since public credit – and attitudes about the National Debt – depends on public opinion, one place to begin is to continue examining texts that discuss public credit, the burgeoning National Debt, and the proliferation of paper credit instruments. For this, I read contemporary political economic writings next to two it-narratives featuring circulating monetary objects that serve as characters. These narratives serve as a way of registering the status of money and credit later in the eighteenth century in order to consider the relationship between the emergent financial subject and a newer form of money whose value – produced virtually – comes from public credit in particular. More so than in political economy, the type of cultural work performed in fiction serves as a means for training individual readers to participate in the public of public credit. This framework will thereby provide new readings for more texts that have already been covered by critics.

While the State and the Bank of England were separate entities in 1694, later developments meant that they became increasingly interdependent. To contemporaries, it seemed that the State's repayment of the loan from the Bank was no longer possible after the middle of the century.[3] By 1750, the Bank had been granted a quasi-monopoly over short-term lending to the government, and it had by then become the primary public creditor.[4] This meant that the government gave sanctions to the Bank of England that it did not provide for other private banks. The Bank of England was no longer merely a mechanism for financing war because it became increasingly implicated in transactions between private investors and thus served a larger function than merely being the government's creditor. And it actively intervened to ensure its continued existence, as well. By 1764, the Bank made a direct non-refundable payment of £100,000 in return for an extension of its charter.[5] This was also the year that the Bank handled about 70 percent of the total National Debt and managed lotteries and annuities.[6] The Bank had to get its charter renewed until 1844, when it became legally permanent.[7] By the end of the eighteenth century, public reliance on the Bank had increased so much so that when its charter was renewed in 1781 it was described by Lord North as "the public exchequer."[8] What began the century as a temporary solution to the problem of government finance therefore ended the century as a revolution in credit – and money.

While commitment for public credit took time to develop, its uniqueness has to do with the fact that the Bank, from the outset, created what Christine Desan calls a "fiat loop." Because of the way the currency was attached to the public debt, "the government began to accept in payment what it spent in payment."[9] This mean that

> [p]ublic officials could take the essential step with popular support because while private contracts separated parties into debtors and creditors, all individuals were debtors where public payments were concerned. Taxpayers had little reason to object to a practice that accorded value to the notes they held to pay off an obligation to a common creditor – the government.[10]

While there was always an inherent risk of a run, the "image offered of gold or silver in the vault gave those holding paper the sense that an anchor existed – even if the anchor was actually elsewhere, in the sound functioning of the fiscal system."[11] Despite the tightening of the relationship between the Bank and the State into a "fiscal system," it is important to note that most people had no direct connection to the Bank of England, as banknotes in general were still mostly used by investors and tradesmen. Indeed, the Bank of England was not yet even a national bank or a central bank in the modern sense. By the end of the century, however, this would start to change when the Bank issued notes in smaller denominations that more types of people were likely to use.

In terms of influential events, the strengthening of public credit had much to do with the Seven Years War with France and the resulting necessity of increasing government borrowing between 1756 and 1763. While at the beginning of the war, the National Debt stood at £72,289,000, by the end of the war it had nearly doubled, rising to £139,516,800.[12] It is in this period that the Bank of England became a pre-eminent institution with the right to discount treasury bonds, and, from this point on, it monopolized the servicing of the National Debt.[13] Peter de Bolla argues that it is during the Seven Years War that "the Bank became inexorably linked to, if not the sign of, the bank of the nation."[14] Alongside this was more of a consensus that debt could be infinite, as long as it is regulated and managed.[15] This is a very different attitude, then, from the example found in the early seventeenth century in *The Debt Book* (1625), which reflects a moral economy that condemned financial indebtedness. The rise of the financial subject seems very much tied up with public credit insofar as being in debt now signifies that a subject-citizen is in support of – committing himself to – a State project.

De Bolla, borrowing from J.G.A. Pocock, writes:

> Public credit is both the individual's expression of confidence in the constitution and the index to the individual's public standing. These two facets of public credit are brought together through the agency of the individual's mortgage of his own standing to the state, for just as each person who "promises to pay" another must be in good standing with his creditor – his public credit must be good – so the public debt represents the individual's faith in the government.[16]

If one accepts the interpretation that private individual investors began to internalize a logic of public credit even in private transactions, what is implied is a transformation to what historians have called the emergence of a "citizen creditor," which is signaled by a willingness to buy treasury bonds and circulate banknotes – to participate in an economy – as an index of commitment to the State that serves the individual's interests. The proliferation of banknotes in this period, which were not only issued by the Bank of England but also by smaller banks, offers another way of re-examining credible commitment as an ongoing process. Further, pamphleteers in this period begin to distinguish between public credit (meaning confidence and economic participation in the nation) and the National Debt (the money required by the government to pursue war).[17]

The historical process by which Charles Taylor's "economic model" comes into being is one of getting individuals to see themselves in a society of mutual benefit in which each person possesses an economic interest. If this is indeed what is further cultivated during the Seven Years War, it seems that commitment flows in the opposite direction here, or at least it reveals another feedback loop. This time, commitment would imply that individuals see themselves as representatives of the 'public' of public credit, or as part of the State. The way the Bank (having become the primary public creditor) helped to achieve this was through the dissemination of its loan to the State to more and more investors. As one notes from ongoing mid-century debates on the viability of public credit, credible commitment has not yet fully completed the second aim that Douglass C. North and Barry R. Weingast describe, that of allowing private rights and markets to prevail in large segments of the economy.[18] In this reading of credible commitment, the next step would be to bring in more investors with accompanying economic interests into the network of trust that became institutionalized around the time of the Glorious Revolution. Banknotes and other credit instruments would be seen as the key to the process, but this would require that these credit instruments be used correctly by more sectors of the emergent economy. Following de Bolla's logic, each person holding a note would signal a belief in the future of the State, which now seems even more intimately connected to the holder's own future. The issue is no longer one of representing public credit as a virtuous system, but rather each person becoming a representative of public credit.

Paper credit or paper money?

One might say that anything that functions as money can be called money – money is what money does.[19] However, the project of this book has been to discuss public credit by using the concepts of the time. For the sake of consistency, therefore, it would be necessary to try to distinguish between credit and money, even if the two begin to blur together at some point in the eighteenth century when the shortage of coin and the growth of market for financial paper grows exorbitantly. It is important to remember that, from the seventeenth century onwards, it was increasingly difficult to use specie to facilitate trade. Furthermore, specie had begun to be hoarded by banks in exchange for the issuing of credit instruments, which were becoming preferred as a means for exchange. Merchants and tradesmen preferred private credit instruments to handling cash. However, banks were still "the institutional tip of a larger private structure of credit."[20]

Social scientists have often discussed circulating money, with a quantitative basis for its value, as a means for explaining or understanding modern social organization. Some traditions in sociology, for example, have supported the notion that modern social systems are based on money. Writing in the latter half of the twentieth century, Niklas Luhmann argues that money indicates that interpersonal trust is no longer relevant.[21] Money is central to Luhmann's concept of the modern social system because it makes it possible to have a shared faith in the future, reducing what he calls "social complexity," which is the function of any social system. Even Georg Simmel's more eccentric *The Philosophy of Money* (1900), which ultimately argues that money brings people together in closer proximity through a negotiation of desire like a language, assumes a reduction of the complexity of the interpersonal.[22] He argues that money "objectifies the external activities of the subject which are represented in general by monetary transactions, and money has therefore developed as its content the most objective practices, the most logical, purely mathematical norms, the absolute freedom from everything personal."[23] Traditions of thought that view money as a negotiation between the objective and the subjective assume that money's objectifying capability arises from its quantitative form. (Simmel has a separate section on credit, supposing that money and credit are categorically different.)

It is in the eighteenth century that money takes on a coherent quantitative form that allows for the "freedom from everything personal," and it gets this form because it is a particular type of credit. It is important to note here that both money and credit both still required a process of interpersonal social negotiation rather than existing as self-sufficient entities of the economy.[24] Therefore, a twentieth-century definition of money as that which reduces social complexity begs the question of when money in general – and banknotes in particular – can claim this status. Modern accounts of money are helpful when viewed in light of the rise of public credit, in which what is at stake is investment in the State which had to ensure that it represented itself as a depersonalized and disinterested entity that used a private (but depersonalized and disinterested) institution to consolidate credit from private, interested individuals.

Because of the increasing stability of paper credit, it was eventually able to function as money, a process that Matthew Rowlinson argues is part of "the abstraction and rationalization of British currency on a national basis."[25] The transition from paper credit to paper money, according to Rowlinson, is the early history of the monetization of English currency dependent upon techniques of double-entry bookkeeping. Circulation was reshaped in such a way that it not only extended to more people, but it also transformed goods into commodities with quantitative value. Bank of England notes circulated in London, but other regional banks produced their own paper currencies that circulated in their respective areas.

> A bank can sustain a local paper circulation only on the condition that it is always ready to exchange its own notes for money that can be used elsewhere. The heterogeneous British paper currencies therefore articulated not only their differences from one another, but also their identity as *different instances of a single abstraction*. Even when these currencies, as they passed from hand to hand, supported regionally specific forms of class identity, they also remained oriented toward another circulation external to their own, with respect to which they functioned as a sort of place-holder.[26]

The fact that a pound sterling could be rendered abstractly and quantitatively, for example, meant that it could assume multiple forms.[27] While the Bank was not yet a central bank in the modern sense, it came to serve this function once the notes were seen as the unit of account.

Paper credit is by no means the first instance of abstraction through quantification. A numerical abstraction is already implicit in specie, which is perhaps one reason why Karl Marx bases his analysis of money on an examination of gold – it already has a universal value owing to its measurability by weight.[28] Marx argues that one reason for specie holding universal value is because these precious metals have standard weights and thus have a recourse to universally agreed-upon measurement.[29] And yet, custom is insufficient by itself to maintain this universal value:

> Historical processes have made the separation of the money-name from the weight name into a fixed popular custom. Since the standard of money is on

the one hand purely conventional, while on the other hand it must possess universal validity, it is in the end regulated by law.[30]

In this sense, the process of abstraction happens even earlier than the paper money Rowlinson describes, and even in this process a governing authority is implied (which one observes even in the Locke–Lowndes debate at the end of the seventeenth century). How, then, is paper different from metals that exist in an abstract and quantified form? Whereas gold has already achieved its status as a store of value, paper credit is meant for circulation alone. And what is implied in a paper credit instrument is that someone is earning interest on it.

This difference might be formulated along the lines Marx provides when he differentiates between money, which is used to buy (and value) commodities (M-C-M), and capital, which is used to buy commodities for the purpose of attaining more capital (M-C-M').[31] The value of capital, he says, is "value in process."[32] Bank-issued paper, because it is intrinsically valueless, only has value when it circulates. But what allows it to circulate is more than quantification – or accounting – alone: Its standard comes from the logic of public credit discussed in the previous chapters, which is partly grounded in the 'public faith' or 'public opinion.' This implies that people believe bank-issued paper can be redeemed for gold, but they also believe this to the extent that they would not demand it. They believe it enough, in other words, not to 'audit' the accounts of the issuing bank. This is why paper money needs to be read in light of the rise of public credit – and the inherent risks entailed by it – even though quantification and accounting are the core mechanisms that allows it to proliferate, circulate, and multiply itself. Abstraction through quantification and accounting is only part of the story, for it is by orienting public credit through the standard established by the Bank of England, which has a history of having to represent itself as serving the public good rather than private individuals or interests, that makes the difference.

In defining money, whereas Luhmann emphasizes trust in institutions, Simmel suggests that it is the mathematical norm that matters most. This replicates an earlier question this study posed: namely, whether proto-scientific accounting practices were self-sufficient in producing trust or whether it was institutions and their practices that formed the basis for trust. The Bank of England as an institutional 'text' that serves as the government's creditor for financing war also becomes the producer of trustworthy printed texts – paper notes that serve as transferable credit but also come to be seen as the most trustworthy of all paper instruments – that implicate more citizens in the State's functioning. Between 1640 and 1770, "early modern people regarded the money they encountered as laden with qualities that indicated its character and connections within broad social networks of meaning."[33] This changes as the virtue of the beholder is translated into, is displaced onto, the virtue of the State. The network becomes, like other forms of representation examined here, virtual. In this sense, answering the question of whether paper credit can be equated with paper money is very much tied to credible commitment.

The scholarly discussion of credible commitment has so far not extensively considered the relationship between paper money and public credit, but two questions that seem tied to the discussion are: Who owes the debt held in the form of a banknote? Who supports its value, thus maintaining its currency? Who is going to translate it back into cash? It is very easy to assume that a credit economy entails the automatic depersonalization of individuals, but, as Craig Muldrew points out: private credit by itself was personal and reputation-based, which is why there was so much litigation over the course of the eighteenth century. How do these credit instruments become like cash, 'ready money'? How does the personalized 'debt owed to me by King William' turn into the depersonalized form of money that Luhmann and Simmel describe two centuries later?

The contractual banknote

Public credit cannot be equated with money – for stocks and other financial instruments also play a role – but paper money is perhaps the most effective heuristic for making sense of the virtual public it binds together. While private credit instruments pre-date the founding of the Bank of England, and while it may be the case that banks were only the tip of the iceberg for credit transactions, such credit instruments became increasingly dependent on the Bank of England, the Bank of Scotland (founded in 1695), and the City interests that relied on these banks. People in the eighteenth century also relied on regional banks outside of the City, which issued their own paper credit as a result of the high demand for it.[34] The effect of public credit in general was that paper credit proliferated, by the end of the century taking on diverse forms such as Bank of England sealed bills and running cash notes, lottery tickets, and exchequer bills.[35] Bank of England notes, however, began to climb the hierarchy of credit instruments, eventually coming to be seen as the most trustworthy.

Significantly, the State also began to take on a role of policing the use of Bank of England credit instruments. In 1729, parliament passed a law that meant that people who forged Bank of England notes faced the death penalty rather than punishment by other means.[36] With the advent of capital punishment as a response to forgery, Bank of England notes begin to look more like State-authorized contracts rather than ones exchanged merely between private creditors. There is a similarity between the way John Locke writes about money (not as a bullionist, as some argue, but as one who theorizes a contract with civil government) and the transition from paper credit to paper money. In Locke's theory (discussed in Chapter 1), the public stamp is only a guard and voucher of the quality of the coin. Any manipulation of the form of coin is an act of treason. Over the course of time, banknotes would develop with a similar logic. While at first, the security of credit instruments was in the private hands of the Bank of England, the State would later take on a policing role in order to secure the quality of the notes, just as they did with the coins.

Notes do not contain bullion; they represent it, a representation that has to be stabilized and managed, even despite the factual quantitative figures that can be placed in the ledger. In theory, all one had to do was to take the note to the Bank, and the teller, referring to his accounting ledger, would exchange the note for the equivalent in cash. In the eighteenth century, this required one to physically go to the Bank (as there were no branches of the Bank of England until later in the nineteenth century), and one could have his contract fulfilled. The Bank served as the third party that authorized a contract between the private creditor and the State.

Running cash notes, which were available at the Bank's inception, read like contracts between two private creditors. Stamped with an image of Lady Britannia, they bear the following language: "I [and occasionally 'we'] promise to pay the Bearer of this Intended Note the summe of ... pounds on demand."[37] But, unlike most contracts, the bearer of the paper could be anyone, not only the person to whom the note was issued – they were, from the outset, intended to function *in lieu of* money, addressing the ongoing coin shortage. From the very beginning, these paper documents were transferrable contracts – whoever was in possession could demand payment in cash. This created a problem, insofar as transferrable notes could be forged. At first, the Bank produced a stamp with an elaborate framework of coins surrounding Lady Britannia, but they soon discontinued this practice because there was not yet capital punishment for forgery and this was too easy to imitate. The Bank then used handwritten notes, but soon after developed a watermark scroll in order to make them difficult to forge.[38] Forgery, however, was an ongoing problem, which is why the Bank from very early on needed the State to intervene on its behalf.

Its note-issuing policies, backed by State authority, proved very effective, and over the course of the century there was an increased demand for notes. The Bank's early policy was not to issue notes lower than £20, and typical denominations were £20, £30, £40, £50, and £100.[39] By 1745, there were 14 more denominations, up to £1,000.[40] During the Seven Years War, the Bank added £10 and £15 notes.[41] By 1793, during the outbreak of war with France, the £5 note was issued. During the Restriction Period, in which the Bank temporarily suspended its controvertibility, £1 and £2 notes were issued to meet increasing demand for currency.[42] Over time, demand for Bank of England and other notes increased, which led to smaller and small denominations to facilitate more and more types of transactions. By 1844, the Bank Charter Act gave the Bank of England exclusive note-issuing rights.

The proliferation of banknotes over the course of the century, with bursts during wartime, can be read as evidence of a gradual transition to a credit economy, in which individual contracts between private investors – already in place well before the Bank – become a contract between individuals and the State, mediated by the Bank (which is, in effect, a pool of individual private investors). This form of credit is endlessly transferable, which people accept because of trust in the contract that (even to this day) is explicitly guaranteed upon each note. Tested in 1793 during the Restriction Period in which the Bank stopped redeeming notes for cash, by 1812, private Bank of England notes officially become public legal tender. However, there is much evidence that people became increasingly comfortable using these pieces of paper well before the legal definition was established.

The process of converting private credit instruments to public legal tender is a historical one, which Mary Poovey describes in terms of "naturalization," in which people gradually forget the distinction between an object's material form and the ground of the value it represents. Poovey attributes this to "a *campaign* on the part of the Bank to naturalize its notes – to make them so familiar and so reliable that users would simply take it for granted that they were worth the sums on their faces."[43] But, as is the case with public credit in general, the process of commitment was not merely institutional. Indeed, the Bank of England's protecting of its notes (and its management of its image in general) was certainly part of the equation. The other part came 'from below' – a process of more individuals coming to participate and more individuals holding the State to account.

In distinguishing between credit and money, the State's role now seems key. Geoffrey Ingham writes that

> [m]oney is *assignable* trust. In the face of real-world radical uncertainty, self-fulfilling long-term trust is rooted in a social and political legitimacy whereby potentially personally untrustworthy strangers are able to participate in complex multilateral relationships. Historically, this has been the work of states.[44]

If one accepts Ingham's assertion about money, in which the State is the facilitator of trust between potentially untrustworthy strangers, this sort of money can and should be read in the context of credible commitment, for what is implied in the work of States is historical development and precedent rather than the amassing of authority by means of rationalization through quantification and accounting alone.

This historical process, however, was not intended at the outset, nor was it complete by the middle of the century. Further, there is no implied conspiracy theory here implicating the Bank of England as a calculating engine of capitalist exploitation. Indeed, Ingham emphasizes the unintendedness of the long-term consequence of the Bank's early decisions when he spells out what renders the Bank of England unique:

> From a monetary perspective, the most important, but *unintended*, long-term consequence of the establishment of the Bank was its monopoly to deal in bills of exchange. This arrangement practically fused the private money and public currency. The purchase of domestic bills of exchange at a discount before maturity was a source of monopoly profits for the Bank. But it also proved to be the means by which the banking system as a whole became integrated, and the supply of credit-money (bills and notes) was influenced by the Bank's discount rate. The two main sources of capitalist credit-money that had originated in Italian banking – that is, *public debt* in the form of state bonds and *private debt* in the form of bills of exchange – were

now combined for the first time in the operation of a single institution. But, most importantly, these forms of money were introduced into an *existing sovereign monetary space* defined by an integrated money of account and means of payment based on the metallic standard. The Bank's notes were at the top of the hierarchy of moneys, and were introduced widely into the economy when they were exchanged for the discounted private bills and notes.[45]

What Ingham's work on money demonstrates is that the type of credit money that the Bank issued unified the public debt and private debts through the operation of a single institution. The Bank of England is special because it allowed for its issue to climb the hierarchy of monetary forms through its interwovenness with public credit, gradually becoming the unit of account that formed the standard of value for measuring other credit instruments by using metallic standards already in place. This happened when these most sought after 'promise to pay' contracts became accepted as a means of paying state taxes and final settlements.[46] At this point, whatever monetary theory one subscribes to, one can probably accept that paper credit has become paper money, as it is the unit of account and store of value as soon as it reaches the top of the hierarchy.

The banknote is a depersonalized contract that represents the quantification of a metal that one does not actually see. There is no need to examine the object for evidence of clipping or to examine the beholder of the object in order to evaluate his or her reputation. The social life of money that Deborah refers to has come to an end, and modern money – *à la* Simmel and Luhmann – has come into being, the effect of which being that the individual transfer his trust of the other individual to trust in institutions such as the Bank and the State. 'We are all representatives of public credit now,' and this is what is at stake in the virtualization of trust. But this outlook took discursive work in addition to social and ideological change. Mid-century political economy simultaneously reflects this transformation and produces it.

Public credit and paper money in political economy

For the reason that it took time and discursive momentum for paper credit to become naturalized (to use Poovey's term) or to reach the top of the hierarchy (to use Ingham's), it is not entirely accurate to conflate public credit with paper money, but contemporaries did so as do some modern historians. In the middle of the eighteenth century, one observes a proliferation of pamphlets advocating for public credit – this time through writing even more explicitly about the National Debt. In *An Essay upon Public Credit in a letter to a friend occasioned by the Fall of Stocks* (1748), the anonymous author argues that "the *Debts* of the *Public* are a Part of the *Constitution*, interwoven with all kinds of *Property*, and … they cannot be separated, without *subverting the constitution*."[47] One already registers a difference in rhetoric from Daniel Defoe's pamphlets, for example. Rather than forcefully arguing that one should support public credit, public credit seems so deeply tied to property that its perseverance seems no longer in question. However, there were still many detractors, David Hume being one of them.

The relationship between various forms of property and the National Debt is most famously articulated in Hume's famous critique of public credit. Hume's "Of Public Credit" (1752) was highly influential, arguing that public credit would eventually ruin the nation despite the fact that it faciltates consumption.

> In short, our national debts furnish merchants with a species of money, that is continually multiplying in their hands, and produces sure gain, besides the profits of their commerce. This must enable them to trade upon less profit. The small profit of the merchant renders the commodity cheaper, causes a greater consumption, quickens the labour of the common people, and helps to spread arts and industry throughout the whole society.[48]

However, Hume worries about the spread of an unstable form of money, which is accompanied by the accumulation of precious metals by the banks:

> Public stocks, being a kind of paper-credit, have all the disadvantages attending that species of money. They banish gold and silver from the most considerable commerce of the state, reduce them to common circulation, and by that means render all provisions and labour dearer than otherwise they would be.[49]

Hume, concerned about the effects of the National Debt on trade (with a precarious form of money) and war, famously concludes that "either the nation must destroy public credit, or public credit will destroy the nation. It is impossible that they can both subsist, after the manner they have been hitherto managed."[50] Hume's suspicion comes from a notion that the military ventures attached to public credit would undermine the basis for commercial prosperity, and therefore institutions that promote war should be eliminated.[51] His language reveals distrust in institutions, a question of whether certain institutional practices will lead to prosperity or disaster. If public credit and paper money are, as Hume suggests, interwoven, credible commitment seems still very much an ongoing process of negotiation in the middle of the century.

R. Wallace, attributed author of a pamphlet entitled *Characteristics of the Present Political State of Great Britain* (1758), would write a response to Hume's critique of public credit, arguing that there are "*natural* checks and limits, beyond which credit will not be extended."[52] With this premise, Wallace links confidence in public credit to having confidence in the nation at large, or at least in an aggregate of prudent investors:

> A private man may be obliged to borrow, and may borrow with great advantage to his private affairs. The same thing holds in the case of a nation.... If the people have confidence in the Government, the securities

given by the Public, bearing a certain interest, may not only become a fund of paper-money, which may be easily transferred from hand to hand, but become so convenient for merchants or others, that they may very reasonably rise above par. Thus there may be a solid foundation for stocks and public funds.[53]

Wallace makes an explicit connection between the stability of public credit and the success of paper money, suggesting that the latter is a guarantee for the former. This is further justified by the political stability of the nation, owing to another feedback loop between politics (where credible commitment is key) and a credit economy. In a later section, Wallace uses historical examples to suggest that the government *has already* achieved the confidence of its people:

When a free government is able to contract great debts by borrowing from its own subjects, this is a certain sign, that it has gained *the confidence* of the people.... 'Tis by this firm credit, among other things, that the Government ever since the Revolution has been remarkably distinguished from the Government during the four preceding reigns.... Before the Revolution the nation could place no confidence in the administration; for they were continually giving them ground of jealousy, and were secretly undermining, or openly invading, their constitution.[54]

The prescription of the earlier passage here morphs into a description of why public credit is already stable and hence why individual confidence is justified – going beyond the necessary presumption of individual prudence to that of the dependability of the whole system. Like Defoe, in justifying public credit, Wallace evokes an early version of the credible commitment thesis. The thesis – a history of virtuous institutions – has become internalized as part of the persuasive, but descriptive, rhetoric of political economy. Wallace not only conflates private and public credit, he also links paper credit explicitly to the National Debt.

The conflation of public credit and paper money is a premise in the even more systematic writings of political economy. Sir James Steuart published *An Inquiry into the Principles of Political Economy: Being an Essay on the Science of Domestic Policy in Free Nations* in 1767, a work which many consider to be the first properly systematic treatment of modern economic principles, featuring a detailed analysis of the operations of public credit. In this work, public credit is understood as a functional, operative system functioning around credit and debt. Steuart's approach to political economy acknowledges a need for imagining public credit through the same principles as private credit, which is

established upon the confidence reposed in a state, or body politic, who borrow money upon condition that the capital shall not be demandable; but that a certain proportional part of the sum shall be annually paid, either in lieu of interest, or in extinction of part of the capital; for the security of which, a permanent annual fund is appropriated, with a liberty, however, to the state to free itself at pleasure, upon repaying the whole; when nothing to the contrary is stipulated.[55]

While private credit is "inseparable, in some degree, from human society," public credit is "but a late invention."[56] He writes:

> The ruling principle in private credit, and the basis on which it rests, is the facility of converting, into money, the effects of the debtor; because the capital and interest are constantly supposed to be demandable. The proper way, therefore, to support this sort of credit to the utmost, is to contrive a ready method of appretiating every subject affectable by debts; and secondly, of melting it down into symbolical or paper money.[57]

Here, Steuart uses the logic of private credit to explain the workings of credit in general. Tellingly, "melting it down," used repeatedly to talk about the way coin turns into paper in order to circulate, does not refer to metal (as a literal interpretation of the language would suggest). The passage serves as a metaphor for how paper money abstracts particular relationships between people into a virtual system. The private credit described in the passage seems already part of public credit, a system of placing subjects in virtual relationships with one another. And the best way to facilitate this is to dissolve older forms of social obligation, such as entails upon lands.[58]

In his description of how credit and money work, the Bank of England plays a key role: "The bank of England is to the exchequer, what a private person's banker is to him. It receives cash of the exchequer, and answers its demands."[59] Further, he argues that each individual benefits from this arrangement, as the use of paper implies a trickle-down effect from the rich to those in trade:

> All the landed men who reside in London, and many other wealthy people not concerned in trade, constantly keep their money either in the bank or in some banker's hand without interest: this enables bankers in general to discount foreign bills at 4 per cent. as has been said, even when the rate of interest is rather above this standard. This is, as it were, a contribution from the rich or idle, in favour of the trade of the nation.[60]

Banks are starting to become more than private businesses: They seem to be enablers of the economy. Furthermore, Steuart repeatedly provides a moral prescription to use banks:

> But I say it becomes a national concern to assist the bank; because the loss incurred by the bank in procuring coin, falls ultimately on every individual, by raising exchange; by raising prices; by raising the interest of money to be borrowed; and, last of all, by constituting a perpetual interest to be paid to foreigners, out of the revenue of the solid property of the country. Upon

such occasions, a good citizen ought to blush at pulling out a purse, when his own interest, and that of his country, should make him satisfied with a pocket book.[61]

This passage reveals the eventually important role played by central banking. It is no longer feasible to do without such an entity, one that exists somewhere between the political and the economic realms.

By the time he published *An Inquiry into the Nature and Causes of the Wealth of the Nations* in 1776, the way had been paved for Smith to claim as though self-evident the existence of a "system of natural liberty."[62] His treatise is a prescription for how to dismantle mercantilism by embracing a commercial type of political economy. And yet, despite the polemical project of advocating for free trade without government restriction, *The Wealth of Nations* describes a political apparatus that allows paper money to be recognized as a form of generally accepted credit. In *The Wealth of Nations*, Smith argues that the abstractions inherent in paper credit can substitute for the traditional trade relationships mediated by specie: "The substitution of paper in the room of gold and silver money, replaces a very expensive instrument of commerce with one much less costly, and sometimes equally convenient."[63] Paper and specie can be called equivalents through a banking system just as subjects who are unrelated to each other can be said to be connected through a system that mediates debts.

> The judicious operations of banking, by substituting paper in the room of a great part of this gold and silver, enables the country to convert a great part of this dead stock into active and productive stock; into stock which produces something to the country. The gold and silver money which circulates in any country may very properly be compared to a highway, which, while it circulates and carries to market all the grass and corn of the country, produces itself not a single pile of either. The judicious operations of banking, by providing, if I may be allowed so violent a metaphor, a sort of waggonway through the air; enable the country to convert, as it were, a great part of its highways into good pastures and corn fields, and thereby to increase very considerably the annual produce of its land and labour.[64]

This metaphor, the distinction between the "normal highway" and "the waggonway through the air," is telling, for it suggests that paper, and not bullion, serves as the capital form. It is not merely a means for facilitating trade. It is also productive stock with the capacity to create prosperity. But the equivalence between specie and paper comes from its circulation, one that renders all subjects part of a shared network: a public. One notes a tendency of movement from the actual to the virtual in these descriptions. First, traditional trust between tangible people gets replaced by trust in the theoretical dependability of a Bank with its mechanisms of "appreciating subjects affectable by debts." Second, actual metals (with supposed intrinsic value) become represented by paper money, but they circulate just as well and are justified on the ground that they have productive powers with trickle-down effects.

Smith's polemic develops the link between the banking system and the commonwealth's role in ensuring stability of credit. While he is adamant in his attack on monopolies that undermine a "natural" price for goods,[65] he nonetheless insists that the "stability of the bank of England is equal to that of the British government."[66] For the Bank, Smith makes an exception to his attack on monopolies. In this case, the centralized bank (that had not hitherto been a part of the State) is necessary; if paper money is abused, it can be a detriment to the commonwealth. One notes ambivalence in the following passage:

> The commerce and industry of the country ... cannot be altogether so secure when they are ... as it were, suspended upon the Daedalian wings of paper money as when they travel about on the solid ground of gold and silver.[67]

Implicit in Smith's writings is a 'natural' economy that proceeds from a division of labor ending in prosperity and growth, which many modern commentators take as an important foundation for laissez-faire theory. However, Smith also admits the need for an overseeing authority – a State – that regulates paper money, which he identifies as the key to national prosperity.

The upside of paper money is that it is productive because it is, in the end, credit with interest. The downside is that it is not stable because it is tied to public credit, which is, as we have seen, intimately interwoven with public opinion. When public confidence is high, paper money is equal to coin or bullion:

> A paper money consisting in bank notes, issued by people of undoubted credit, payable upon demand without any condition, and in fact always readily paid as soon as presented, is, in every respect, equal in value to gold and silver money; since gold and silver money can at any time be had for it.[68]

Here, Smith does not delve into what happens when public opinion wanes, even though strong public confidence seems a necessary condition for equating the 'effect of coin' with coin itself. Rather, Smith advocates the need for strong ties between the Bank and the State, a relationship that manages the public perception that the effect of coin really is equal in value to gold and silver.

Credit, consumption, and the it-narrative

Concurrently with the rise of public credit (and its tie to the imperial project with its capacity to bring in material goods from afar) came an increase in consumption. With the expansion of credit also came the increased demand for consumable goods, goods which were not necessarily produced in the region (or nation) in which one lived. Valenze suggests that the consumer revolution is directly related to the advent of public credit, for credit through banking meant that "[n]ew forms of promissory notes ... signaled the ability of parties to carry out exchanges at greater geographical distances and transfer debt to unknown third parties. This set the stage for greater liquidity of all forms of debtor/creditor relationships."[69] Because credit money circulated outside of its normal boundaries, people could purchase consumable products with greater ease. And some of these products were other paper commodities.

The turn toward consumption is also reflected in political economic writings. Contemporary writers suggest that public credit is a necessary supplement to trade, a necessary currency that brings people what they need and desire. In *A Proposal for the Restoration of Public Wealth and Credit* (1760), for example, argues in support of public credit based on the way it raises one's buying capacity.

> As a Medium, *Money*, or that *Material to which Public Credit is annexed*, answers the Purpose of Air in conveying any desirable Object to our Eye, or of a Conduit that contains and carries Water from the Fountain to the Cistern. Or, rather, as the Liquid or Serum in the Veins of a human Body, that bears along the nutrimental Particles to the Glands, where they are secreted and assimilated to their relative Members and Offices, and, thereby, preserve, nourish, and actuate the whole System. For, though the *Material of Credit* is no Part of the *Wealth*, for which it is exchangeable; yet, in containing the political Value which Public-Consent hath annexed thereto; It is therein supposed to contain and circulate whatever it can purchace.[70]

Like earlier writers on the topic of public credit, this author distinguishes between public credit and wealth. But, unlike earlier writers, he emphasizes the way public credit's medium, money, serves as the means for purchasing "every desirable object to our Eye." Public credit facilitates consumption.

In the latter half of the eighteenth century, objects were often personified as characters in novel-like texts, what scholars have called "it-narratives." These stories, very popular within the burgeoning reading public, featured purchasable items that ranged from animals to clothes to children's toys. Since these objects (and sometimes animals) usually had something to do with new products that could be bought and sold in the marketplace, it is probably not surprising that, from the 1750s onwards, it-narratives about different types of financial instruments were also quite common.[71] What one observes when one compares two very popular examples – Charles Johnstone's *Adventures of a Guinea* (1760–5) and Thomas Bridges' *Adventures of a Bank-Note* (1770–1) – is two distinct but nonetheless related notions of money, which means that these texts also implicitly (and sometimes explicitly) participate in the question of the nature of money one observes in works of eighteenth-century political economy.

Different attitudes toward commitment provide for a new way of reading eighteenth-century it-narratives, which critics have more recently begun to explore. Scholars working on it-narratives have emphasized the way they offer "a bitingly satirical account of a society characterized by greed, ignorance, and self-interest."[72] Christopher Flint defines the object of these narratives "as a product of manufacture rather than a part of nature, and [its] satiric vision of the world arises from its particular experience of human commerce."[73] Liz Bellamy defines two key characteristics of these texts: the item must be a manufactured object lacking independent agency, but it also must be able to transgress social barriers.[74] The object of the it-narrative must, in other words, be moved around through the whims of various humans who have different needs for and interests in trading with one another. Money fits these criteria very well.[75]

What it-narratives have in common is that the objects have the capacity to illuminate or evaluate the social milieu in which they circulate. It-narratives are particularly striking in the way they present the monetary object as being self-assured of its own value – indeed, the value of money is taken for granted because it is able to connect together members of society through circulation, and this is central to narrative development.[76] From a literary standpoint, therefore, a key element that each of these texts share is that the circulation of the central object (which is also the point of narrative focalization) is what drives the plot. A gold guinea and a banknote are both objects of "manufacture" that circulate widely, and this wide circulation endemic to the it-narrative is also a prerequisite for the monetary object in the real world. While it is tempting to suppose that these fictions merely *reflect* contemporary notions of credit and money, I will suggest that by simulating a financially interested public through fictional narrative strategies, these two narratives help to *produce* commitment by exposing more types of people to forms of money that they would not have necessarily been familiar with. These it-narratives helped to construct the "imagined community" that Benedict Anderson has identified insofar as they unfold in space that begins to map out what nations look like as coherent sites of economic transaction.[77]

In distinguishing between credit and money, one notes a conflicting logic that has to do with different types of temporal thinking. Money allows for people to disregard the origins of its value, but credit also implies a shared social construction about the future.[78] Credit is not real insofar as it has a correlative in the form of a precious metal, but "rather it was a print phenomenon that could be known primarily through print sources" which "existed discursively, to be accessed on the page and recreated imaginatively in the mind of the investor."[79] Using credit as money requires a shared imagination of the future. It-narratives conflate credit and money on purpose, expressing a difficulty in distinguishing between them. These texts self-reflexively examine the conditions under which money circulates, while at the same time the character-objects also serving as the narrators circulate without difficulty within the imagined communities they represent.

Chrysal: naturalizing alchemy

Chrysal: or, The Adventures of a Guinea, Wherein are exhibited views of several striking scenes, with curious and interesting anecdotes of the most noted persons

... whose hands it passed through, in America, England, Holland, Germany, and Portugal was published initially between 1760 and 1765, and is signed "written by an adept." According to the *Oxford Dictionary of National Biography*, Johnstone's hugely popular novel went through 20 editions by 1800 and was also translated into French. While written on a trip to Devon, *Chrysal* was first published in Dublin (where Johnstone had been educated), and later editions issued from various publishing houses in London. Billed as the "Best Scandalous Chronicle of the Day," it details the corruption of known public figures and satirizes the famous Hell-Fire Club, referring to actual public figures that contemporary readers would have recognized. The narrative fulfills Bellamy's two criteria for the it-narrative insofar as the character-narrator circulates due to human agency external to it and it also transgresses social barriers, ending up in the hands of various people from various walks of life.

The way the text is said to have been discovered draws attention to its status as a material printed object. The text that makes up the narrative is a found and fragmentary one. Taking shelter in Whitechapel during a storm, the frame (first) narrator breakfasts with a family who use sheets of paper as plates.[80] This peculiarity piques his curiosity and he immediately seeks the origins of the manuscript, which he eventually traces to a chandler's shop nearby. There, he finds that the female shopkeeper has been using the paper to wrap her wares, and, being interested in what is written in the manuscript rather than the paper's use value, he buys the remaining paper from the shopkeeper. The shopkeeper tells him that the author of the manuscript had been a lodger who taught her to read, and he had also "been a schemer, who had wasted his whole fortune, in the search, after the philosopher's stone."[81] The frame narrative reminds the reader that the story is a product of an author's labor, a paper manuscript that failed to be printed, but one with the potential to contain worthwhile secret knowledge. The man, we learn, became possessed by the spirit of Chrysal, which is where he has attained the secret knowledge the work will reveal.

The reader is then promised pseudo-scientific knowledge on the secret of the creation of gold, and the first pages of the central narrative refer to alchemy. The reader is promised the "grand secret" that underlies the power of gold.[82] The adept, a person who has access to hidden or restricted knowledge, is also the second narrator who learns secret knowledge from possessing (and being possessed by) Chrysal. So far, the layers of narration are very complex: These layers become even more convoluted in what follows. After the author is possessed, we move further into the layers of narration to the third narrator, Chrysal, who is also the spirit of gold. Chrysal introduces himself as if he were a religious official, his power originating from the occult:

> [W]e of superior orders, who animate this universal monarch Gold, have also a power of entering into the hearts of the immediate possessors of our bodies, and there reading all the secrets of their lives. And this will explain to you the cause of that love of gold, which is so remarkable in all who possess any quantity of that metal.... When the mighty spirit of a large mass

of gold takes possession of the human heart, it influences all its actions, and overpowers, or banishes, the weaker impulse of those immaterial, unessential notions called *virtues*.[83]

In this passage, Chrysal tells us that each individual is overpowered by his spirit, which is why the narrator gains insights into each person he possesses. Rather than being about alchemy as the frame narrative suggests, the story will emphasize the power money exerts over human beings. But this power has little to do with the material out of which the currency is coined. Indeed, I am suggesting that gold is a ruse – a fictitious imaginary space through which value can be stabilized, a gold standard in a period in which there was no gold standard.

At first glance, it may seem as if *Chrysal* has nothing to do with public credit and is merely a personification of a trustworthy form of commodity money, the "universal monarch" of gold. However, in light of Carl Wennerlind's research on the relationship between the establishment of public credit and the discourse of alchemy a century earlier, this introductory passage is telling. Wennerlind shows how the new credit system led to the "rapid falloff in patronage of alchemists, and credit-money was elevated to the position of the best available system of money creation."[84] Wennerlind also explores the philosophy of the Hartlib Circle in the 1640s, a group that used alchemical principles in order to attempt to expand the money supply by discovering ways to convert base metals into gold. He shows how

metallic transmutation and credit money shared the same underlying idea of using an expansion in the money stock to launch a process of continuous economic change, improvement, and growth. As such, for the Hartlib Circle, the idea of making money through metallic transmutation or credit were both rooted in the same alchemical and Baconian worldview and were part of the same universal reform project.[85]

These 'projectors' believed that finding the philosopher's stone enabled one to manipulate change and growth ad infinitum, a philosophy which differed greatly from the neo-Aristotelian political economies (for example, balance of trade theory that posited a finite supply of money) that preceded them. While alchemists never achieved the production of gold through transforming base metals, this philosophy persisted in the discussions on how to increase the money supply through the establishment of credit money.[86] It is perhaps little wonder then that *Chrysal* promises the reader secret knowledge of alchemy since the idea of accessing ways to produce more money was part of contemporary debates. Despite being about commodity money or specie, therefore, *Chrysal* reflects newer thinking about credit money insofar as alchemy shaped the early philosophy of money. Alchemy is a symbol for a transition whereby riches come to be seen as infinite.

Despite this narrative's being about gold – which is eventually minted into the commodity money form of the guinea – it turns to an analysis of human behavior, partly through traditional allegory, partly through the political exposé for which it was famous. Chrysal says: "It is contrary to the rules of our order, ever to give up an heart of which we once get possession."[87] The narrator explains to the reader his own value from his secret knowledge, as he is a moti- vator for human action and also an observer. In a bizarrely experimental move, the beginning scenes combine the roles of the main character and narrative focal- izer: Chrysal *becomes* the person he first possesses, Traffick. By merging the (third) narrator with the first possessed character, Traffick, Chrysal's secret knowledge of gold demonstrates absolute power over the bearer.[88] Early sections of the internal plot of the novel begin allegorically – Traffick is the first person to become possessed – but then Chrysal ends up in the hands of a priest, a captain, a gentleman at the gaming tables, an author whom the gentleman pays off in a coffee house, and many others. This seems familiar. The tradesman, Defoe's model gentleman, is the first individual implicated, but circulation extends outwards, encompassing (or 'encircling,' a term I will refer to in the next chapter) more types of people as the narrative progresses.

Throughout the narrative, the tone is quite somber. What the reader learns from the secret knowledge of the adept is that gold is ultimately detrimental to the nation. Traffick's father warns him to trade carefully, so as not to endanger the nation. He "*should never let private interest tempt him to engage in any trade or scheme that can interfere with the publick interest, or is forbidden by the laws of his country.*"[89] Traffick (here, the fourth narrator who has merged with Chrysal) does the very opposite of what his father advises: "I therefore threw off all restraint, and entered into measures the most injurious to my country, which was then engaged in a just and expensive war."[90] The allegorical lesson here is that money – in this case, gold – damages the nation by corrupting the individual bearer in his dealings with others. This text is beginning to look like a criticism of public credit – one very similar to Hume's.

Chrysal is full of stories of people becoming possessed with the 'spirit' and sacrificing the interests of the whole (the state, the public, etc.) for that of private gain. Indeed, gold even has the power to corrupt monarchs. At one point, a duchess comes to possess (and be possessed by) Chrysal:

> I was now at the summit of human grandeur, the favourite of the favourite, of a mighty monarch. For curiosity tempting me to take a view of my new mistress's heart, as she sat at her toilet; I found myself established there without a rival, in the most absolute authority, every passion being sub- servient to my rule; even the love of power, which had, in every other instance disputed the empire with me, being *here* my most abject slave, and encouraged for no other reason than solely to promote my interest; the mighty spirit of the immense mass of gold, which my mistress had accumu- lated, having taken possession of her soul.[91]

Here, the narrative seems to condemn (or satirize) the corruption of the monarch by money. Just as gold ruins Traffick's capacity to engage in fair trade, it also governs the whims and the interests of the monarch who has power over the constituents of a State. The moralizing tone provides the reader with the secret knowledge that money is a corrupter of virtue and a destroyer of commonwealth.

While *Chrysal* reveals a moral anxiety about the power of money, it also reflects a certain type of knowledge about how it works. *Chrysal* shows readers that the power of money must change forms to circulate in various realms, especially when traveling internationally:

> I here came into the possession of a new master, and immediately after changed my *Spanish* appearance for the fashion of the country, and in the shape of *a guinea*, encountered into the most extensive state of sublunary influence, becoming the price of every name, that is respected under heaven.[92]

This passage reflects a form of money that is universally valuable – it has the capacity to name the price for anything, everywhere – but it must change its form to do so. Despite its moralizing tone, therefore, the narrative has a secondary function, that of educating the reader, and this also includes an explanation of the Bank's (or a bank's) role. While circulating within England, Chrysal takes the form of a guinea. Immediately after being minted, he ends up in a place of central financial authority, the Bank (or a bank):

> From the *Mint*, where I put on the shape of a guinea, I was sent to the *Bank*, where the pleasure I had felt at the beauty and convenience of my new figure was considerably cooled, at my being thrown into so large an heap, as took away all my particular consequence, and seemed to threaten a long state of inactivity, before it might come to my turn to be brought into action. But I soon found myself agreeably mistaken, and that the *circulation* there was too quick to admit of such delay: for I was that very day paid out to a noble lord, in his pension for the ministry.[93]

The narrator here expresses panic at the thought of not continuing to circulate, his "particular consequence," but circulate he does.

Chrysal goes from bearer to bearer, exposing the flaws of each (those exacerbated by becoming possessed by Chrysal). The story ends when Chrysal returns from his time abroad and ends up in London (which is significant since London was and is a hub of finance). There, he ends up back in the hands of the adept. After telling the adept (conveyed through the frame narrator to the reader) a great secret, which is blocked out in the printed text with asterisks, Chrysal disappears. The adept faints, and this is where the shopkeeper in the preface finds him. In the end, *Chrysal* provides a moral conclusion, presumably what the adept has learned from his time with Chrysal. Whether one is a tailor, a cobbler, a senator, or a poet, the narrator says, one must bear the following in mind:

> Seize the present moment, nor depend upon the future; let reason curb expectation: reduce imagination to common sense; and bring your wishes

within the bounds of your real wants: so shall industry banish necessity from your habitation; and content turn all your possessions into gold.[94]

The moral of the story is to stop pursuing the philosopher's stone, to reject the alchemical project of creating something out of nothing. If we follow Wennerlind's account of the Hartlib Circle and its influence on the development of public credit, one might say that *Chrysal*'s somber tone about the power of a gold coin is ultimately a warning about the social effects of a newer form of credit money as well. This reading is corroborated by what the adept says about how one should imagine the future.

The reading I have presented so far is partially complicated by the way later versions of the text emphasize the value of paper. Drawing on the comic moments from the first edition, in which the first narrator discovers that a manuscript is being used for practical purposes, the 1762 edition plays with the fact that the value of the paper has now risen since the initial publication of *Chrysal*. This edition contains many emendations, which the editor says result from more paper manuscripts used for practical purposes being sought out.

> Such an attempt was necessarily tedious, troublesome, and expensive in going to all the customers of the chandler's shop, where it was first met with, prevailing upon them to search cup-boards, holes and corners, wherever they might possibly have laid up anything that was wrapped in it, and purchasing the scraps which could be found; for such an enquiry made them naturally imagine, that the papers were of some considerable value, and of course demand an extravagant price for them.[95]

This comical explanation for the new text sheds light on the narrative's new value. Those using the paper for its use value come to revalue the paper based on what they surmise the editor sees in the discourses it contains and its consequent capacity to circulate through its exchange value.

This later version reflects the logic of credit money, and not gold. Gold was merely the way for the narrative to ask the question: what is money? The narrative returns to the fetish that contemporaries had to believe in to circulate money that has taken the form of public credit. Money is what money does, and, at least by the second edition, it is paper and not metal that serves as the locus of value and key to the philosopher's stone. This version, given its own moralizing condemnation of future speculations, seems ideologically conflicted and also deeply tied to a mid-century transition in thinking about the nature of money, public credit, and the subject who is implicated in either.

As with many texts from the early modern period that deal with money, *Chrysal* is anti-Semitic. This narrative is one of many that reflects nostalgic attitudes about nationhood that spring from financial innovation, representations which function by scapegoating Jewish people – also seen in William Shakespeare's *The Merchant of Venice* (1605) as well as in reactions to the South Sea Bubble. Ann Louise Kibbie discusses the anti-Semitic subtext in *Chrysal*, as it participates in "the backlash against the Jewish Naturalization Act" and "intensifies that genre's intrinsic interest in anxieties surrounding national identity and citizenship."[96] In this case, gold represents the stereotype about the Jewish money-lender in the years following the Jewish Naturalization Act of 1753, a piece of legislation that granted Jewish people the right to citizenship in the country where they had lived for centuries. Johnstone's themes of national identity, currency debasement, and blood libel are irreducibly connected.[97] Given that anti-Semitic themes feature in many fictional texts that discuss money and credit in the period, a separate study on the rise of public credit and anti-Semitism is perhaps also in order.

Adventures of a Bank-Note: the virtual publics of public credit

While Johnstone's *Chrysal* is somber and satirical in tone, Bridges' *The Adventures of a Bank-Note* is playful and lighthearted. While gold would have been seen by a general readership as having almost self-evident value as commodity money, paper money (as fiat money) required an outside authority, one based in and around the City of London, to give it value. This produces a different effect, one that, as Bellamy points out, means that the banknote comically draws attention to the issue of his own creditworthiness even while he is circulated without question.[98]

Before Bridges published *Adventures*, he had worked as a partner in a banking company in Hull (Sell, Bridges, and Blunt) that failed in 1759, and therefore he would have had a certain type of knowledge – he would have been another type of "adept" – on financial instruments that were not accessible to much of the public in this period. Earlier, he had also delved into writing with the publication of two burlesque parodies, *A Travestie of Homer* in 1762 and *The Battle of the Genii* in 1764, two works he published under the pseudonym "Caustic Barebones," and therefore he was also familiar with the ins and outs of publishing and circulating literary works in the literary marketplace.[99] Two overlapping publics, one which circulates the banknote and one which comes together through literacy nurtured and sustained in a growing print market, are illuminated in *Adventures*. Bridges' initially unsigned work features a banknote as a main character, one who is 'born' of a poet who exchanges £20 he received for his poetry at the Bank.[100]

In the first chapter, a classical muse instructs the poet, "Timothy Taggrhime," to go to the Bank for the following reason:

> Go ... to the Bank; give them twenty pounds for a bank-note, payable to Timothy Taggrhime, Esq. After the Bank has dubb'd you an esquire, no man will dare to say a word against it; you may then boldly add the title esquire to your name the very next work you publish. Your title will then be as indisputably a title, as your own title to your title page. How many fellows are there that never saw a bank-note of their own in their lives, yet have the assurance to tagg the word esquire to their names.... Now you,

when you are a Bank-dubb'd esquire, may look on all these self-dubbed esquires with as much contempt as my lord's pimp, when he first gets into his coach, doth on the honest stable-keeper that help'd him to his place.[101]

This somewhat cheeky explanation for the birth of the banknote with a particularly trustworthy reputation reflects a Bank very different from what one observes in the first decades of the eighteenth century, for it is one that has managed to gain the public trust. The pun of the word "title," which refers to the bearer of the banknote and the author's name on the title page, suggests both the virtue of the Bank's practices to ensure the trustworthiness of its notes and also the importance of reputation for an author selling his works in a growing literary marketplace. The banknote has received a title through honorable work, even though he was not born with it.

Despite its playfulness regarding the origins of the banknote's value, *Adventures* reflects a form of credit that has already become money capable of easy circulation. Deirdre Lynch has argued that the "bank-note's travels can make the circulation seem more tidily circular" and that the type of narrator used can "assuage fears that the social is of unlimited and hence inapprehensible extension.... His social work demonstrates how people are connected."[102] As one might expect, the banknote does not remain with the poet nor does it end up in the Bank's coffers – it circulates throughout London society, illuminating the various members of the public that come in contact with it.

Chrysal's frontispiece promotes the work as follows: "Hold the Mirror up to Nature,/To shew Vice its own Image, Virtue his own Likeness,/And the very Age and Body of the Times/His Form and Pressure." This Shakespearean quote reflects what the adept discovers through his encounter with Chrysal. *Adventures* satirizes this in its own frontispiece. "When I've held up a proper number/Of fools and knaves, and such-like lumber,/To public view, and public scorn, Contented I'll to dust return." The banknote, 'born' with the credibility produced through the authority of the Bank, evaluates the constituents of the public with whom he makes contact. The note ends up in the hands of a doctor, a man called Crispin whose sexual encounters the banknote accounts for in great detail, a stock-broker's wife, a diamond merchant, a bill-man, a milliner, and many others of various ages, social statuses, and predicaments. Like Chrysal, the banknote witnesses secrets and scandals to which only private persons are privy, and these passages often are told in a satirical or bawdy tone, in the same vein as Bridges' other works.[103] These caricatures are not negative but humorous. In other words, it is not the banknote's fault that people behave the way they do, but the banknote is able to get a glimpse of these private misdeeds owing to his status as circulating money. And the vices are beside the point: "private vices, public virtues." Given the banknote's special status, we might ask whether the public that circulates the banknote within this work of fiction is really the same public as that of public credit. What does this do for our understanding of how newly-minted financial subjects imagined themselves as having shared interests? The narrative presents an opposition between the public authority of public credit, which establishes the value and credibility of the "title" of the banknote, and the private subjects that should perpetuate this authority through their participation in a common project.

The potentially volatile value of paper money and the value of literary works on what scholars call the "literary marketplace"[104] are intertwined, *Adventures* shows us, and the narrative's unifying principle is the stabilization of values. Poovey notes how the first two volumes of *Adventures* provide vast amounts of information about how banknotes work, while the second two volumes subordinate the "informational agenda" to the workings of imaginative fiction. In 1770, she writes,

> the vast majority of Britons would not have known how to evaluate the quality of various notes, might never have seen a Bank of England note, and would not have known how to realize the value of notes that passed through their hands.[105]

Paper money was still known only to specialists in 1770, and the first installments of the novel also have the function of making the banknote familiar to readers who had never seen one.[106] Poovey's emphasis on the division of knowledge that occurs in this period, one that separates out facts from scientific discourses and emergent literary fiction, might also be understood as having a shared basis in the circulation of printed texts and the gradual establishment of symbolic value on a literary marketplace as distinct from economic value.[107]

As one notes from explicit discussions on public credit earlier in the century, the imagination of a public as such is one important ground for public credit. The public of *Adventures*, even more so than that of *Chrysal*, is unified based on its shared reception and consequent discussion of print media beginning to separate out what is 'literary' from what is not. This is why *Adventures* not only becomes less informative, as Poovey suggests, but also why it becomes more like a literary text in its final chapters – it assumes that all readers have been steeped in contemporary works bought, sold, and circulated in the literary marketplace. The production of a unified public with a shared future is not merely oriented around financial interest, in other words, but around shared qualitative values, common notions of distinction that come into being through literary debate.

The narrator breaks from his adventures (writ: circulation) in order to comment on literary aesthetics and to fold fictional forms and characters from other contemporary literary works into the content. He starts by saying he will "give a full and true account of my birth, parentage, life, and education,"[108] but then reflects that he "may attempt to account for what is really unaccountable."[109] The novel's break with the expectation that what one reads is true about the way banknotes come into being gets supplanted by an authorial erudition that leads the reader to assume that the author (whoever he may be) has read other literary texts. (This resembles the promises *Chrysal* makes about discovering the philosopher's stone by reading the text.) It comes, then, as little surprise to the reader when "Tristram Shandy" is later referenced as a character in the fourth volume of *Adventures*.[110] The intrusion of this fictional character functions because the reading public presumably has a shared imagination of Laurence Sterne's *The Life and Opinions of Tristram Shandy, Gentleman*, published a few years before, between 1759 and 1767.

Adventures does more than refer to other fictional characters from other printed works: It also emulates the style of the other novels it refers to, including addressing the reader in the manner of Sterne by imagining that the reader has objected to particular literary techniques that it uses. The narrator of *Tristram Shandy*, justifying his style to the reader, proclaims: "Digressions, incontestably, are the sunshine; – they are the life, the soul of reading; – take them out of this book for instance, – you might as well take the book along with them."[111] *Adventures* implicitly mocks Sterne's use of digression when the narrator likens digression to throwing up. In the narrator's guts, he says, anecdotes have been "rumbling," and "every ten days at least, by the grumbling of my bowels, I expect they are coming forth, yet the duce a single hit has stirred: I must be forced to physic 'em out at last." His interlocutor responds: "You had better, my dear Sir ... let them stay where they are, than produce them to the public, after such a kind of digression."[112] And yet, like his fictional counterpart, the narrator cannot help but digress in his own story-telling, for this is precisely what allows him to show off his erudition in contemporary printed texts. He consolidates his own value by citing other valued texts.

Similar to the digressions and interludes which are part and parcel of *Tristram Shandy*, *Adventures* has its own discussions of literary value that take place in between the banknote's being transferred from bearer to bearer. Bridges refers to Defoe's *Robinson Crusoe* early in the fourth volume, for example. He says elsewhere that he has the same right to speak as Samuel Johnson.[113] In one passage, the text features a dialogue between two characters who discuss the aesthetics of Alexander Pope's translation of Homer.[114] In another, the narrator refers to Samuel Richardson's *Clarissa*, suggesting that that novel's enormous length (unlike the present text) is justified by its plot:

> Had the author the spirit of Rabelais, or the fire of a Tristram, he might go through four and forty volumes, without a grain of connection, and people would follow him; but, with such a head as his, it won't do, unless he will let us have a good long story well worked up, of some pretty innocent virgin, that, at last, in spite of all her prayers, tears, and intreaties, gets fairly ravished.[115]

In the end, *Adventures* lacks in terms of internal cohesion and narrative development. There is no moral ending like the reader finds in *Chrysal*. But it offers something to contemporary readers through its engagement with other texts: It celebrates the shared knowledge of other printed works as well as a calibration of their value, and this celebration is paired with the public who circulates the banknote. The shared "grain of connection," missing from the digressions and continually used as a means for making jokes, is made through a shared knowledge of – and a capacity to value – the other circulating works. While political economy discusses paper money by linking it explicitly to public credit (which is somewhat precariously based on pubic opinion), *Adventures* begins to formulate criteria for an emergent literary canon that ties together shared public values.

Adventures is written with an intertextuality that not only allows readers to imagine other people as potential partners of transaction in the English public credit system but also potential fellow readers in a virtual public sphere with a developing notion of what a work of literary fiction should be. To publish is to invest in the public sphere of readers, to commit oneself to writing for a readership with a shared project of defining what is and what is not worthy of being printed.

Just after the Seven Years War, it seems complicated to say what money is and how it mediates relationships between people. Reading these two it-narratives together suggests that the period of the 1760s and 1770s was a time of great ideological change. On the one hand, there was still a great concern that new ways of conceiving of money would lead to the corruption of the country's constituents. On the other, however, there was already belief – if not trust – that the system in place was serving an important function. Public opinion, mediated through print and required for the stability of the State, may have been a shaky political ground for maintaining a public credit system, but one way of ensuring that there was a public of shared interests was to write for a public with shared interests. And these interests, it seems, did not originate solely in the realm of finance, but also in a shared discussion of – indeed, a shared production of – literary value.

Notes

1 Mark Knights, *Representation and Misrepresentation in Later Stuart Britain*, 29.
2 Anne L. Murphy, "Demanding 'Credible Commitment,'" 180.
3 H.V. Bowen, "The Bank of England During the Long Eighteenth Century, 1694–1820," 9.
4 P.G.M. Dickson, *The Financial Revolution in England*, 360.
5 Bowen, 6.
6 See J.H. Clapham, *The Bank of England*, 103; Bowen, 10; and R.D. Richards, *The Early History of Banking in England*, 60–3.
7 The Bank was not nationalized (that is, owned by the government by explicit legal decree) until the twentieth century.
8 Quoted in Clapham, 174.
9 Christine Desan, *Making Money*, 312.
10 Ibid., 313.
11 Ibid., 319.
12 Peter de Bolla, *The Discourse of the Sublime*, 108.
13 Ibid., 109.
14 Ibid. Linda Colley has also emphasized the role secure credit plays (along with English Protestantism by contrast to French Catholicism) in shaping the British national identity. However, she provides no account of public credit's role in this process. See Linda Colley, *Britons*, 67.

15 De Bolla, 111.
16 Ibid., 115.
17 Ibid., 127.
18 Douglass C. North and Barry R. Weingast, "Constitutions and Commitment," 808.
19 See B.L. Anderson, "Money and the Structure of Credit in the Eighteenth Century," 86.
20 Ibid., 100.
21 Niklas Luhmann, *Trust and Power*, 51.
22 Georg Simmel, *The Philosophy of Money*, 470.
23 Ibid., 128.
24 See Deborah Valenze, *The Social Life of Money in the English Past*, 2; see also Craig Muldrew, *The Economy of Obligation*, 17.
25 Matthew Rowlinson, *Real Money and Romanticism*, 43.
26 Ibid., 50.
27 Ibid., 54.
28 Karl Marx, *Capital*, 188.
29 Ibid., 191.
30 Ibid., 194.
31 Ibid., 257.
32 Ibid., 256.
33 Valenze, 2.
34 Rowlinson, 46.
35 Natasha Glaisyer, *The Culture of Commerce in England, 1660–1720*, 6.
36 See Randall McGowan, "From Pillory to Gallows," 110; and see Carl Wennerlind, "The Death Penalty as Monetary Policy," 131.
37 Derrick Byatt, *Promises to Pay*, 13.
38 Ibid., 14.
39 Ibid., 21.
40 Ibid., 29.
41 Ibid.
42 Ibid., 35.
43 Mary Poovey, *Genres of the Credit Economy*, 49.
44 Geoffrey Ingham, *The Nature of Money*, 74.
45 Ibid., 129.
46 Ibid., 135.
47 *An Essay upon Public Credit in a letter a friend occasioned by the Fall of Stocks*, 10.
48 David Hume, "Of Public Credit," 353.
49 Ibid., 355. Hume goes on to argue that public credit's transformation of taxation heightens the price of labor, payments are conferred only in London, foreigners possess too great a share of national funds, and that most of the actual stock ends up in the hands of a few idle people (ibid., 354–5).
50 Ibid., 360–1.
51 See Carl Wennerlind, *Casualties of Credit*, 242.
52 R. Wallace, *Characteristics of the Present Political State of Great Britain*, 34.
53 Ibid., 57–8.
54 Ibid., 64.
55 James Steuart, *An Inquiry into the Principles of Political Oeconomy*, 3:160.
56 Ibid., 3:161.
57 Ibid., 3:163.
58 Ibid., 3:164.
59 Ibid., 3:247.
60 Ibid., 3:246.
61 Ibid., 3:198.

62 Adam Smith, *An Inquiry into the Nature and Causes of the Wealth of Nations*, 2:687.
63 Ibid., 1:292.
64 Ibid., 1:321.
65 Ibid., 1:79.
66 Ibid., 1:320.
67 Ibid., 1:321. Richard Price's *Two Tracts on Civil Liberty*, published two years later in 1778, would theorize paper money in semiotic terms:

> [O]ur wealth, or the quantity of money in the kingdom, is greatly increased. This is paper to a vast amount, issued in almost every corner of the kingdom; and particularly by the BANK OF ENGLAND. While this paper maintains its credit it answers all the purposes of specie, and is in all respects the same as money.... Paper, therefore, represents coin; and coin represents real value. That is, the one is a *sign* of wealth. The other is the *sign* of that *sign*.... Paper, owing its currency to opinion, has only a local and imaginary value. It can stand no shock.
>
> (58)

68 Smith, 1:324.
69 Valenze, 22.
70 *A Proposal for the Restoration of Public Wealth and Credit, in a letter to a truely honorable member of the House of Commons*, 8.
71 An entire volume of Pickering & Chatto's *British It-Narratives, 1750–1830* (2012) is devoted to monetary instruments alone. While the majority of the narratives anthologized in this collection are on coined money, only a few of these feature banknotes, a form of currency somewhat novel to contemporaries not directly involved in trade. See Blackwell, *British It-Narratives, 1750–1830*.
72 Christina Lupton, "The Knowing Book," 403.
73 Christopher Flint, "Speaking Objects," 212.
74 Liz Bellamy, "It-Narrators and Circulation," 121, 122.
75 It-narratives featuring monetary objects were part and parcel of an emergent public sphere from very early on. The 11 November 1710 *Tatler*, probably written by Richard Steele, was the first to feature a monetary object – a shilling – as a subject narrating his adventures, which was a product of Steele's (or an outside narrator's) "delirium" (Angus Ross, *Selections from The Tatler and The Spectator of Steele and Addison*, 186).
76 See Liz Bellamy, "Introduction," 1:xlvii.
77 Benedict Anderson, *Imagined Communities*, 15.
78 Wennerlind, *Casualties of Credit*, 230.
79 Catherine Ingrassia, *Authorship, Commerce, and Gender in Early Eighteenth-Century England*, 7.
80 Charles Johnstone, *Chrysal*, 1:viii
81 Ibid., 1:xii, xxii.
82 Ibid., 1:3.
83 Ibid., 1:6.
84 Carl Wennerlind, "Credit-Money as the Philosopher's Stone," 234.
85 Wennerlind, *Casualties of Credit*, 68.
86 Ibid., 45.
87 Johnstone, *Chrysal*, 1:7.
88 After Traffick's merging with Chrysal, however, Johnstone gives up this bizarre narrative strategy. Chrysal simply becomes an object that comments on the people he possesses.
89 Ibid., 1:17.
90 Ibid., 1:19.
91 Ibid., 2:35.

92 Ibid., 1:77.
93 Ibid., 1:79–80.
94 Ibid., 2:220.
95 Charles Johnstone, *Chrysal: or, The Adventures of a Guinea*, v.
96 Ann Louise Kibbie, "Circulating Anti-Semitism," 243.
97 Ibid.
98 Bellamy, "It-Narratives," 124.
99 *The Monthly Review* of 1771 reviewed both volumes of *Adventures*, saying that "[s]ome parts of this work are very laughable, others are licentious; and the whole ... shews that the Writer has more genius than grace" (152).
100 Again, whether he goes to a bank or the Bank is an open question. I am reading this text through the logic of the latter for the reason that banks in general were beginning to be subordinated to the Bank of England in this period.
101 Thomas Bridges, *Adventures of a Bank-Note*, 1:14–15.
102 Deirdre Lynch, *The Economy of Character*, 98.
103 *The History and Adventures of an Atom* (1769), attributed to Tobias Smollett, shares the structural features of the it-narrative. Its particular qualities allow it to expose what Smollett believed to be corrupt political system during the Seven Years War and attack William Pitt's "Great War for Empire that exacerbated the National Debt" (Smollett, xxxiv). The satire, which works as a 'secret history,' reveals the hidden motivations of all players through an omniscient being – an atom – that is ultimately omnipresent, working very much like *Chrysal*. Narrated by a London haberdasher, it gives an account of a political history of ancient Japan. In its political critique, the minister Yak-strot is unable to undertake political action because of "self-interest," reflecting a traditional morality rather than the new economic model. Yak-strot "summoned council after council to deliberate on conciliatory expedients; but found the motly crew so divided by self-interest, faction, and mutual rancour, that no consistent plan could be formed: all was nonsense, clamour, and contradiction" (ibid., 132). What Smollett, a country gentleman, consistently attacks as being corrupt is a government ruled by the masses, and here self-interest is the culprit. The ideology underlying this work is opposed to public credit. By contrast, Bridges' it-narrative accommodates itself to it.
104 See Dustin Griffin, *Authorship in the Long Eighteenth Century*.
105 Poovey, 148.
106 Ibid., 151.
107 See Pierre Bourdieu, "The Market of Symbolic Goods," 13–44.
108 Bridges, 1:2.
109 Ibid., 1:3.
110 Ibid., 4:194.
111 Laurence Sterne, *The Life and Opinions of Tristram Shandy, Gentleman*, 58.
112 Bridges, 4:202.
113 Ibid., 2:42.
114 Ibid., 4:177–8.
115 Ibid., 4:97.

Works cited

Anderson, Benedict. *Imagined Communities: Reflections on the Origin and Spread of Nationalism*. London: Verso, 1983.
Anderson, B.L. "Money and the Structure of Credit in the Eighteenth Century." *Business History* 12 (1970): 85–101.
Bellamy, Liz. "It-Narrators and Circulation: Defining a Subgenre," in *The Secret Life of Things: Animals, Objects, and It-Narratives in Eighteenth-Century England*, edited by Mark Blackwell, 117–46. Lewisburg: Bucknell University Press, 2007.

Bellamy, Liz. "Introduction," in *British It-Narratives, 1750–1830*, vol. 1, xli–lv. London: Pickering & Chatto, 2012.

Blackwell, Mark, editor. *British It-Narratives, 1750–1830*, 4 vols. London: Pickering & Chatto, 2012.

Bourdieu, Pierre. "The Market of Symbolic Goods." *Poetics* 14 (1985): 13–44.

Bowen, H.V. "The Bank of England During the Long Eighteenth Century, 1694–1820," in *The Bank of England: Money, Power and Influence, 1694–1994*, edited by Richard Roberts and David Kynaston, 1–18. Oxford: Clarendon Press, 1995.

Bridges, Thomas. *Adventures of a Bank-Note*. 4 vols. London: n.p., 1770, 1771.

Byatt, Derrick. *Promises to Pay: The First Three Hundred Years of Bank of England Notes*. London: Spink & Son, 1994.

Clapham, J.H. *The Bank of England: A History*, vol. 1. Cambridge: Cambridge University Press, 1945.

Colley, Linda. *Britons: Forging the Nation, 1707–1837*. New Haven: Yale University Press, 1992.

De Bolla, Peter. *The Discourse of the Sublime: Readings in History, Aesthetics and the Subject*. Oxford: Basil Blackwell, 1989.

Desan, Christine. *Making Money: Coin, Currency, and the Coming of Capitalism*. Oxford: Oxford University Press, 2014.

Dickson, P.G.M. *The Financial Revolution in England: A Study in the Development of Public Credit, 1688–1756*. London: Macmillan, 1967.

An Essay upon Public Credit in a letter a friend occasioned by the Fall of Stocks. London: Carpenter, 1748.

Flint, Christopher. "Speaking Objects: The Circulation of Stories in Eighteenth-Century Prose Fiction." *PMLA* 113.2 (1998): 212–26.

Glaisyer, Natasha. *The Culture of Commerce in England, 1660–1720*. Bodmin: The Boydell Press, 2006.

Griffin, Dustin. *Authorship in the Long Eighteenth Century*. Newark: University of Delaware Press, 2014.

Hume, David. "Of Public Credit," in *Essays Moral, Political, and Literary*, edited by Eugene F. Miller, 349–65. Indianapolis: Liberty Fund, 1985.

Ingham, Geoffrey. *The Nature of Money*. Cambridge: Polity, 2004.

Ingrassia, Catherine. *Authorship, Commerce, and Gender in Early Eighteenth-Century England: A Culture of Paper Credit*. Cambridge: Cambridge University Press, 1998.

Johnstone, Charles. *Chrysal: or, The Adventures of a Guinea, Wherein are exhibited views of several striking scenes, with curious and interesting anecdotes of the most noted persons*, 2 vols. Dublin: n.p., 1760.

Johnstone, Charles. *Chrysal: or, The Adventures of a Guinea*, 3 vols. London: n.p., 1762.

Kibbie, Ann Louise. "Circulating Anti-Semitism: Charles Johnstone's *Chrysal*," in *The Secret Life of Things: Animals, Objects, and It-Narratives in Eighteenth-Century England*, edited by Mark Blackwell, 242–64. Lewisburg: Bucknell University Press, 2007.

Knights, Mark. *Representation and Misrepresentation in Later Stuart Britain: Partisanship and Political Culture*. Oxford: Oxford University Press, 2005.

Luhmann, Niklas. *Trust and Power*, translated by Howard Davis, John Raffan, and Kathryn Rooney. Chichester: John Wiley & Sons, 1979.

Lupton, Christina. "The Knowing Book: Authors, It-Narratives, and Objectification in the Eighteenth Century." *Novel: A Forum on Fiction* 39.3 (2006): 402–20.

Lynch, Deirdre. *The Economy of Character: Novels, Market Culture, and the Business of Inner Meaning*. Chicago: University of Chicago Press, 1998.

McGowan, Randall. "From Pillory to Gallows: The Punishment of Forgery in the Age of the Financial Revolution." *Past and Present* 165 (1999): 107–40.

Marx, Karl. *Capital: A Critique of Political Economy*, 1867, vol. 1, translated by Ben Fowkes. London: Penguin, 1976.

The Monthly Review; or, Literary Journal, vol. XLIII. London: R. Griffiths, 1771.

Muldrew, Craig. *The Economy of Obligation: The Culture of Credit and Social Relations in Early Modern England*. Houndmills: Macmillan, 1998.

Murphy, Anne L. "Demanding 'Credible Commitment': Public Reactions to the Failures of the Early Financial Revolution." *The Economic History Review* 66.1 (2013): 178–97.

North, Douglass C. and Barry R. Weingast. "Constitutions and Commitment: The Evolution of Institutions Governing Public Choice in Seventeenth-Century England." *The Journal of Economic History* 49.4 (1989): 803–32.

Poovey, Mary. *Genres of the Credit Economy: Mediating Value in Eighteenth- and Nineteenth-Century Britain*. Chicago: University of Chicago Press, 2008.

Price, Richard. *Two Tracts on Civil Liberty*. 1778. Cambridge: Cambridge University Press, 1991.

A Proposal for the Restoration of Public Wealth and Credit, in a letter to a truely honorable member of the House of Commons. Dublin: n.p., 1760.

Richards, R.D. *The Early History of Banking in England*. London: Frank Cass and Company, 1958.

Ross, Angus, editor. *Selections from The Tatler and The Spectator of Steele and Addison*. Harmondsworth: Penguin, 1982.

Rowlinson, Matthew. *Real Money and Romanticism*. Cambridge: Cambridge University Press, 2010.

Simmel, Georg. *The Philosophy of Money*, 2nd edn, translated by Tom Bottomore and David Frisby. London: Routledge, 1990.

Smith, Adam. *An Inquiry into the Nature and Causes of the Wealth of Nations*, 1776, 2 vols. London: Oxford University Press, 1976.

Smollett, Tobias. *The History and Adventures of an Atom*. 1769. Athens: University of Georgia Press, 1989.

Sterne, Laurence. *The Life and Opinions of Tristram Shandy, Gentleman*. 1759. Oxford: Oxford University Press, 1983.

Steuart, James. *An Inquiry into the Principles of Political Oeconomy*, 1767, edited by Andrew S. Skinner, Noboru Kobayashi, and Hiroshi Mizuta, 4 vols. London: Pickering & Chatto, 1998.

Valenze, Deborah. *The Social Life of Money in the English Past*. Cambridge: Cambridge University Press, 2006.

Wallace, R. *Characteristics of the Present Political State of Great Britain*. London: A. Millar, 1758.

Wennerlind, Carl. "Credit-Money as the Philosopher's Stone: Alchemy and the Coinage Problem in Seventeenth-Century England." *History of Political Economy Annual Supplement to Volume 35* (2003): 234–61.

Wennerlind, Carl. "The Death Penalty as Monetary Policy: The Practice and Punishment of Monetary Crime, 1690–1830." *History of Political Economy* 36.1 (2004): 131–61.

Wennerlind, Carl. *Casualties of Credit: The English Financial Revolution, 1620–1720*. Cambridge, MA: Harvard University Press, 2011.

5   Abstraction, social mediation, and the novel of sensibility

Over the course of the eighteenth century, a variety of strategies were used for representing public credit, such as virtuous accounting, credible framing, simulating disinterestedness, and describing various members of the public whose interests are tied together. Part of what is at stake in commitment is the general cultivation of trust in a new system that still seems to threaten traditional social values by the end of the century. And this overlaps with what is at stake in the rise of the novel. Novels do much more than represent individuals: They accommodate readers to a set of practices and outlooks that reflect a changing model of society, which this book has read through public credit in particular and the economic model in general. How does the novel, read alongside a more developed public credit system, continue to transform itself in order to adapt to a restructuring of society? This chapter will consider a connection between public credit and the establishment of realism as distinct from romance, and sensibility as distinct from sentimentality, often associated with the rise of the novel.

Tellingly, by the middle of the century, what scholars now consider to be works of fiction only make up about 2 percent of what was published in terms of editions produced. This has caused bibliographers and book historians to question the emphasis on fiction – and especially the novel – in eighteenth-century literary studies.[1] As Christopher Flint argues, "the novel represents a rather modest part of the history of publishing in the long eighteenth century."[2] It "was vying for the attention of consumers among a variety of other equally compelling modes of communication in the print sphere."[3] Therefore, when one looks back on the eighteenth century through the novel, one gets a skewed version of things. There is, however, an important reason for this.

From the point of view of the present, readers have tended to identify with the ethical worlds as well as the modes of representation inherent to the realism of the later eighteenth-century novel, which is part of the reason literary criticism from the twentieth century onwards has valued the genre so highly, which John Richetti calls a "teleological bias."[4] "The history of the novel has thus been handed down to us as the triumph of an enlightened realism over reactionary romance, the development or evolution of a superior literary instrument," he says.[5]

> What is involved is nothing less than a gratuitous imposition of the social
> and philosophical norms (summed up in such terms as bourgeois democracy
> and pragmatism) and the narrative effects (summed up in the term realism)
> we value most upon a body of writing which was at least partly unaware of,
> if not hostile to, them.[6]

Richetti points to the great irony of reading literary history in the eighteenth
century from the point of view of the present: Many contemporaries would not
have viewed novels with the same enthusiasm as today's readers. Indeed, many
thought that works of fiction were corrupting media floating along in a sea of
other corrupting media. And yet, these media proliferated – and evolved – even
despite resistance to them, developing features that we now associate with the
realism inherent to the modern novel. This is why it is problematic to write about
the history of the novel without acknowledging the genre's capacity to provide
the modern world with its ethics and values, values that have meant that literary
critics have possibly overemphasized their importance for eighteenth-century
contemporaries.

To discuss the eighteenth century in terms of its media is also to talk about a
transformation in which direct communication between people became increasingly supplanted (or supplemented) by virtual connectedness through new
systems and technologies that mediated interpersonal interaction. Indeed, these
media allow for the public sphere – made up of private individuals – to come
into being.[7] Clifford Siskin's and William Warner's *This is Enlightenment*
(2010) even goes so far as to call the Enlightenment a media event, one which
united symbolic and technical media. Print was instrumental to this process "not
only because there was more of it, but also because it insinuated itself into other
forms of mediation."[8] Mediation simultaneously enables communication and
requires a network of signification. Public credit is, in effect, a form of mediation that comes into being alongside other forms of mediation. What makes it
so unique – and central to this study – is its capacity to mediate beholden-ness or
social obligation through financial rules or fiscal obligation.

While the former requires the tangible, interpersonal relationship discussed
through Craig Muldrew's and Deborah Valenze's respective concepts of credit
and money, fiscal obligation is a form of mediation whereby trust has already
been transferred to the systematic practices of institutions. Indeed, this is relevant to Siskin and Warner's discussion of how to read the proliferation of texts
on various topics in the latter half of the eighteenth century as an "expanding
array of mediations geared to the goal of 'Universal' encirclement: access to all
knowledge for all people."[9] There was, through the new literacy on finance for
those who did not traditionally need such knowledge, a practical change in the
way people used new forms of media. Public credit has a particular role to play
in the Enlightenment project – that of encouraging participation in a "universal
encirclement" tying financial subjects to a State.

However, by the middle of the eighteenth century, public credit and the
National Debt were still often called into question. As discussed in the previous

chapter, in 1742, David Hume famously worries about the way public credit might harm the nation's constituents. He says:

> It must, indeed, be one of these two events; either the nation must destroy public credit, or public credit will destroy the nation. It is impossible that they can both subsist, after the manner they have been hitherto managed, in this, as well as in some other countries.[10]

Hume's concerns were not merely pragmatic, as public credit also had radical social consequences. He worries in particular about what public credit will do to traditional connections: "Adieu to all ideas of nobility, gentry, and family. The stocks can be transferred in an instant, and being in such a fluctuating state, will seldom be transmitted during three generations to father and son."[11] While Hume is primarily concerned with what a volatile market does to transform inheritance, his words (specifically, the capacity for wealth in the form of stocks to transfer outside of traditional social ties) reveal a conservative outlook on the way public credit restructures society.

Through its capacity to mediate relationships of indebtedness, public credit shifts obligations to the future and transforms social connections by transferring trust to the institutions of the State, which are in turn supported by public opinion circulating in a public sphere. This form of commitment, which takes the shape of a feedback loop, is borne out by the way paper money functions. Money in its modern form is, first and foremost, a medium. It is a medium of exchange, but it is also a way of mediating between individual people. Paper money, whose form is constituted through the systematic operation of public credit, mediates social relationships by decoding traditional, vertical hierarchies and recoding a horizontal network sustained by the virtuous operation of the State.

A fully functional, cooperative society whose power structure is horizontal – Charles Taylor's "economic model" – requires a form of mediation that replaces interpersonal trust. Understanding public credit as the gradual development of a system helps one to historicize modern conceptions of money. Niklas Luhmann, reflecting a twentieth-century perspective, writes:

> Anyone who has money has no need … to trust others. Generalized trust in the institution, then, replaces, through one all-inclusive act, the countless individual, difficult demonstrations of trust which would be necessary to provide a sure foundation for life in a co-operative society.[12]

Money reduces one's need to evaluate another person on a qualitative basis. Georg Simmel, writing earlier, similarly discusses money in terms of the "freedom from everything personal," which comes from a notion that money has the capacity to translate subjective experience, or the purely subjective significance of any object, into objectively understandable terms.[13] In both of these modern theories, money is equated with an abstraction that allows people to interact with one another virtually, which is why Simmel[14] – and others, including Jean-Joseph Goux's much later *Symbolic Economies: After Freud and Marx* (1990) – compare it to a language.[15] Money translates particular social relationships into a universal language by removing personal, qualitative variables.

As discussed in the previous chapter, modern theories about money cannot simply be applied transhistorically, as it was the work of public credit that helped to remove the reputation-based, qualitative components of both coin and credit. James Thompson, examining debates about the value of money, argues that the language of monetary theory gradually became "less subjective, less focused on the trust of the individual subject" and also correspondingly "more objective, imagined more as a system separate and apart from human actors."[16] For Patrick Brantlinger, the fiction of the State as such is dependent on paper money and the way it mediates citizens through circulation.[17] Here, Brantlinger is describing its virtual function, one that requires an abstraction in the first place. Public credit's power to recode social relationships along new lines is *abstract* insofar as it is an idea that has no concrete existence. But it is also *virtual* because it nonetheless functions. If this point seems abstract it might be because what I am describing is a process of *coming to value the abstract*, which contemporary theorists associate with modernity.[18]

This is related to something that historians and literary critics have pointed out: that modern economic values emerge together with other Enlightenment values. As Thompson points out:

> The cultural work of this period revolves around the transition from real to nominal value in semiology and in economics; [Max] Horkheimer and [Theodor] Adorno characterize the Enlightenment as "a nominalist movement." Indeed, economics could be described as the theorization of nominal value – its essential stock in trade. The novel and courtship narratives, on the contrary, assert internal and intrinsic value. The novel, then can be read as an ideological regrounding of intrinsic value.[19]

To read the rise of the novel from the perspective of present through the lens of public credit in particular is a multifaceted act by which one acknowledges that, while things could very well have gone differently, the rules of the game – as transformed by a medium whose capacity to mediate is tied to public credit – are the ones by which we still play. Nostalgia for the concrete or the tangible brings with it an ethical quandary for this reason. The novel of sensibility, more than any other sub-genre, captures the ambivalence of public credit's mediating function by documenting the process of registering new rules of social engagement predicated on abstraction while still seeking to imagine a world in which social mediation – and the virtualization of social relationships – played a much smaller role. This is part of what is at stake in sensibility's emphasis on person-to-person connections, a theme that attempts to counterbalance virtualization.

Sarah Fielding's *David Simple* (1744) and its sequel, *Volume the Last* (1753), both of which have been categorized as novels of sensibility but also share features of the romance, are chock-full of new media. What Fielding herself calls a "moral romance" and its sequel together mark a paradox about social mediation still present today. On the one hand, new media provide new rules and opportunities for engaging with others. The flip side is that when we use media, we do not engage with others directly, and thus mediation inevitably transforms the way we experience other people. And this is part of what is represented in the novel of sensibility, whose didactic function is to train readers to sympathize with the fictional characters it presents, often critiquing a system predicated on new rules and codes while simultaneously being one of these media.

To put it otherwise, I will suggest through my reading of public credit that the emergent novel of sensibility – which borrows features of the romance – tries to get the reader to empathize as if he or she were there as a tangible person even despite the fact that the novel (as a medium) precludes this very possibility. I will use *David Simple* and its sequel as a way of rethinking public credit's role in the development of the novel of sensibility, and will afterwards turn to Frances Burney's *Cecilia* (1782) – a novel that explores financial issues (of credit and debt) explicitly – in order to examine the way the social project of sensibility maps onto the new financial rules that have developed in the wake of public credit. The difference between these novels is one of romance and realism, sentimentality and sensibility. Reading these novels written over a four-decade gap, one filled in by the consequences of the Seven Years War discussed in the previous chapter, helps one to further register the state of commitment as well as the development of the financial subject in the latter half of the eighteenth century.

People of the Royal Exchange: social mediation in *David Simple*

Set in London, *David Simple* begins when David's brother Daniel attempts to cheat him out of an inheritance. He makes a journey from east to west, from Fleet Street in the City by way of the Strand to Westminster, and he meets various people along the way from different stations in life, people who disappoint him when he attempts to befriend them. He finally meets Cynthia, and then later a pair of siblings, Camilla and Valentine, who have also been deceived or forsaken by others, usually for financial reasons. After David hears their respective stories, the four form a family and share a household: David marries Camilla and Cynthia marries Valentine. The novel ends happily with David having found friends and having created a family, at last. But in *Volume the Last*, a reversal of fortune takes place.[20] Members of David's family lose their financial security and thus the capacity to remain together in one household. A relative makes a legal claim on an estate left to David, one which drains him of necessary money. He loses his ability to support his family without outside assistance and becomes financially dependent on creditors. Valentine must get a job in the West Indies, and Cynthia accompanies him. Later, David's house burns down and the family's property is destroyed. All but one of the children die of various illnesses. The sequel ends tragically with David's death.

Many of the mediating devices shown to be disadvantageous for David's community have origins in new virtual forms of property. This is perhaps the reason critics emphasize the way economic factors influence the way characters attempt to cultivate readerly sympathy. In Gillian Skinner's reading, both the novel and its sequel present multiple economic problems whose elusive solutions are true feeling and communal sensibility.[21] Richard Terry argues that the sentimental (or the capacity for characters to sympathize with others) is consistently subverted by commercial interests.[22] Linda Bree's work on Sarah Fielding draws attention to the novel's focus on profit and loss over and above charity and benevolence.[23] This perspective on sensibility (one that positions it in a simple opposition to finance) also requires that one ask the question of which social stakes the novel has in launching such a critique. It is not only finance that is the problem, after all, but abstraction.

By using resistance to public credit as an alternate lens for interpreting the novel and its sequel, one gains a new perspective on the social ramifications of the Financial Revolution as depicted in mid-century fiction. Public credit is not merely about creditors and debtors, for it entails a reorganization of society horizontally through each individual's virtual relationship to the State. This requires that each person become a financial subject who is able to see the world in this way. But public credit is not merely an idea. It is also a medium insofar as the banknote and other forms of authoritative paper come to mediate relationships between strangers. *David Simple* (and its sequel) disaggregate between 'good' media and 'bad' media in an attempt to cultivate an ethic that is not governed by abstraction. Indeed, the novel is preoccupied with social obligation, and it attempts to eschew fiscal indebtedness in the process in describing a clash between the two worlds. What it seems to lament is that there are new rules for a new form of virtual society, rules at odds with the tangible type of friendship David pursues. Moreover, the novel's mode of sensibility also hearkens to quixotism in order to place David's character in a lineage of other figures whose values were out of sync with their time. This turn is also a reaction to part of the "universal encirclement" that Warner and Siskin argue characterizes the Enlightenment project.

It is not a big leap to suggest that the novel does its work systematically, through various iterations of the same problem: the erosion of the tangible by the virtual. Before his family members set up house, David finds people coming together to engage through new systems whose rules mediate interactions but at the same time fail to facilitate the friendship he is looking for. What happens to people in the multiple narratives that make up the first volume seems almost systematically problematic, as if each separate event is predicated on one cause: the pursuit of individual interest. David's brother Daniel wants "in some shape or other to promote his own Interest."[24] Early in the novel, David is in love with Nanny Johnson and she seems to reciprocate his feelings, but she marries the older Mr. Nokes for his money instead.[25] After his heart is broken, David takes lodgings in various places, but "he found all the Women tearing one another to pieces from Envy, and the Men sacrificing each other to every trifling Interest."[26]

Similarly, Valentine's and Camilla's stepmother turns their father against them "because she thought her Interest incompatible" with theirs.[27] Wherever David searches, households seem to be ruined by individual interest, which is over the course of the novel shown to be an abstraction that facilitates the working of virtual, rather than actual, communities. This serves as a stark ideological contrast to the advocates of public credit earlier in the century who argued that public credit must be supported because each individual's interest requires it. Here, interest may be a motivator, but it is also a spoiler. The ascendency of interest is shown to be a problem.

Pursuing the accumulation of money has become the way individuals look out for their interests. When David attempts to relocate Valentine and Camilla to another house, the owners there are distrusting of the group because of what they are wearing until David "pulled out Money enough to convince them he could pay for any thing they had: For nothing but the sight of Money, could have got the better of that *Suspicion* the first sight of them occasioned."[28] The capacity of others to trust David and his new friends is entirely governed by money, insofar as money corrects for the lack of trust that arises when the owners see their humble clothing. Only because of a virtual community mediated by money do the owners decide to help Valentine and Camilla. The way David's tangible community comes together is through a shared experience of the negative effects of individuals pursuing their interests.

Just after his brother attempts to cheat him by forging their father's will, David sets out on a quest for a real friend but soon suffers disappointment in a particularly telling geographical location: Threadneedle Street, home of the Bank of England and the Royal Exchange. At the Royal Exchange, David watches one man luring another man into buying massive quantities of a stock that the former immediately thereafter sells.

> The first place he went into was the *Royal-Exchange....* He could not have gone any where to have seen a more melancholy Prospect, or with the more likelihood of being disappointed of his Design, than where Men of all Ages and all Nations were assembled, with no other View than to barter for Interest. The Countenances of most of the People, showed they were filled with Anxiety: Some indeed appeared pleased; but yet it was with a mixture of Fear.[29]

This passage makes a connection between the pursuit of individual interest through (what we would today call) insider trading and social anxiety, but the setting also helps the reader to imagine a system that makes it possible or even desirable for people to congregate at the Exchange in the first place.

When David goes to the Royal Exchange, the novel seems to be mocking a famous passage from the May 19, 1711 *Spectator* (No. 69), in which Joseph Addison represents the Royal Exchange as a microcosm of the world.

> There is no Place in the Town which I so much love to frequent as the *Royal Exchange*. It gives me a secret Satisfaction, and, in some measure, gratifies

my Vanity, as I am an *Englishman*, to see so rich an Assembly of Country-
men and Foreigners consulting together upon the private Business of
Mankind, and making this Metropolis a kind of *Emporium* for the whole
Earth.... This grand Scene of Business gives me an infinite Variety of solid
and substantial Entertainments. As I am a great Lover of Mankind, my Heart
naturally overflows with Pleasure at the sight of a prosperous and happy
Multitude, insomuch that at many publick Solemnities I cannot forbear
expressing my Joy with Tears that have stoln down my Cheeks. For this
reason I am wonderfully delighted to see such a Body of Men thriving their
own private Fortunes, and at the same time promoting the Publick Stock; or
in other Words, raising Estates for their own Families, by bringing into their
Country whatever is wanting, and carrying out of it whatever is
superfluous.[30]

While it is possible that Addison is being ironic, the Royal Exchange seems to
incite unbridled enthusiasm and emotional outpourings. By contrast, David
leaves the Royal Exchange devastated. *David Simple* offers an alternate universe
to Addison's, dismantling the alignment of "thriving [for one's] private Fortunes, and at the same time promoting the Publick Stock." While Addison's
positive description imagines the elevation of the English individual emanating
from "public stock," Fielding's version reflects the consequences that Hume
points to: the destruction of social ties through the operations of new media.

The novel, and the pleasures of the aesthetic that come with it, allows for a
subversion of the descriptive power of Addison's account. David's experience at
the Royal Exchange turns into an "Emporium for the whole Earth" of its own,
for *David Simple* features various scenarios – iterations – that mimic what
happens at the Royal Exchange in the novel's early pages. One of these iterations takes place in another context in which people come together in order to
'barter for their interest': gambling, which, as Mareike de Goede argues, had no
conceptual difference to finance in early modern Europe.[31] David's experience at
the Royal Exchange might be compared to players of whist he encounters.
Whist, a trick-taking card game invented in the seventeenth century, had become
popular by the middle of the eighteenth century, signified by the publication of
Edmond Hoyle's hugely popular *A Short Treatise on the Game of Whist* in 1743,
a manual which helped the reader learn the basic arithmetical skills to ascertain
probabilities as well as learn the very complicated rules of play. This sort of
entertainment, a reason for bringing people together in a social setting, ultimately has a negative outcome, very much like what takes place at the Royal
Exchange.

Those very People, who, before they sat down to play, conversed with each
other in a strain so polite and well-bred, that an *unexperienced* Man would
have thought the greatest Pleasure they could have had, would have been in
serving each other, were in a moment turned into *Enemies*, and in the
winning of a Guinea, or perhaps five, (according to the Sum played for) was

the only Idea that possessed the Minds of a whole Company of People, none of whom were in any manner of want of it.[32]

This is not a direct moral critique of gambling that de Goede refers to, one that will pick up momentum in the decades to follow. Rather, the emphasis is on what happens to the people at the Royal Exchange. In Fielding's description of gambling, players are overtaken by the game's structure: They are possessed by the rules and ignore each other's company in order to win. Less pecuniary than the stock market, the game nonetheless uses a system of rules proliferated by the medium of print.

This is by no means the only novel that integrates games of chance with new rules into fiction. Jesse Molesworth's research on lotteries, tarot readings, and gambling suggests that novels allowed for older superstitions as well as newer forms of reason. The emphasis on whist is significant because, unlike other games of chance, Hoyle's contribution was to:

> introduce mathematical considerations of the odds to the gambling public, thereby both disseminating the nascent calculus of probability among a wide range of readers and offering an irresistible demonstration of its profits.... Overnight ... Hoyle created probabilists out of people hitherto unable even to compute a simple average of several numbers.[33]

The new rules, therefore, have a direct tie to other forms of mathematical rationality governing other aspects of culture.

In these scenes, an intense focus on individual interest leads people to acts of duplicity, creating the need for distinguishing between 'true' and 'false' friendship alluded to in the subtitle. In the Royal Exchange and the gaming table, people come together through abstract rules whose mediation unites people virtually. This can be read as a metaphor for public credit but also as an extension of its logic into other cultural forms and practices. What is striking about these passages is that Fielding depicts deep ambivalence in the affect of the participants at the stock exchange and at the gaming table. The calculation of individual interest, while seeming to benefit individual people, consistently divides individual advantage from collective pleasure.

Another iteration of what happens at the Royal Exchange takes place by way of legal procedures. What helps people to look out for their pecuniary interests is the legal system, providing another example of a set of rules that prevent David from attaining what he desires. From very early on in *Volume the Last*, we learn that David is involved in a chancery suit over his estate. His opponent's attorney knows all the "Tricks of the Law" leading David to eventually lose.[34] For a "simple" person like David, the system of law is incomprehensible. Law mediates disputes, but because he does not possess knowledge of the rules, it literally breaks up his household. David's community is then forced to take a smaller house. In this period, David's family members (including the children Camilla, Peter, Fanny, Cynthia, Joany, and David), suffer various illnesses, leaving them in dire straits. The family runs out of money, and the household economy, one that had sustained them as an independent unit and community, is insufficient to keep them together. Valentine is offered a job practicing law in Jamaica, and, because of the family's financial pinch, he decides to take it.[35] No longer can Valentine be part of the family – he must take a job as a migrant wage laborer out of necessity, taking on the very profession that broke up his community in the first place. In this iteration of the same problem, the novel takes the reader away from pecuniary matters to reveal how systems of rules (abstractions that allow virtual systems to function) more generally determine the fortune of the protagonist.

This repeated emphasis on systems – tricks or rules – is contrasted to a tangible counterpart that allows for David's family to thrive toward the end of the first volume: the household. One of the values both volumes repeatedly and exuberantly extol is that of household economy, or looking after the property of the household for the sake of meeting the needs of the family. David's family members, even after they lose their home and must live in a smaller one, practice a diligent household economy:

> For every thing in this small Cottage, tho' poor and plain, yet was preserved in so neat a Manner, as visibly proved that the owners of it could not think themselves debarred of every Comfort, whilst they enjoyed each other's Company.[36]

An emphasis on the visual here is a poignant antonym to the invisible and abstract rules governing other projects in the novel. *David Simple* emphasizes taking care of the household for the here-and-now of those occupying it. It is significant, therefore, that David is not able to hold onto the tangible structure that allows him and his family to subsist.

Here, it is important to note that the novel seems not against interest per se because David wants to promote his family's interest (which they achieve through the household). The house is managed so as to ensure each individual's benefit, which keeps them in a state of mutual obligation to one another:

> Therefore in our little Family of Love, each Day was employed in Endeavours to promote its common Welfare. *Camilla* and her eldest Daughter were industrious in their pursuit of Household Business; not groaning or repining under their Labour, but looking cheerfully forward to their principle Aim.[37]

The focus is on what is right in front of them. Speaking in the first-person plural, the narrator entices the reader to imagine the immediate value of a household by contrast to virtual examples of community that I have suggested serve as iterations of the Royal Exchange. Tellingly, the practice of household economy, valued because it ensures subsistence and comfort for the immediate members of the family unit, is not enough to hold the community together when the world outside increasingly privileges interest granted through new rules and new mediating forces. Before David sets up his community, he glances out at men rowing boats and says he

> wish'd all the World would imitate these *Watermen*, and fairly own when they were rowing against each other's Interest, and not treacherously pretend to have an equal Desire of promoting others [*sic*] Good with their own, while they are under-hand acting to destroy it.[38]

In the example of the watermen, the interest of the individual is at one with the interest of the collective because each must focus on the visible and tangible – if a waterman does not focus on the interests of the other rowers present, his own safety is in jeopardy. Ironically, this sort of logic is a tangible correlative to the more abstract argument Daniel Defoe makes in order to advocate for commitment earlier in the century (discussed in Chapter 2).

The break-up of the family and household becomes financially necessary for the survival of its component members. They are obliged to divide their shared property and dismantle their household economy. The narrator emphasizes the deep ambivalence in this process, for dividing property means dividing the community into separate individuals:

> The small Stock of Money *David* was now possessed of, he divided with his Friends, to enable them to defray any unlooked-for Expences; and this was the first time the Word DIVIDED could, with any Propriety, have been used, in relating the Transactions of our Society; for SHARING in common, without any Thought of Separate Property, had ever been their friendly Practice, from their first Connection.[39]

This division of property is the first moment when the family must adhere to the conventions of the world that they had sought to leave behind.

Another iteration of what takes place at the Royal Exchange has to do with the emergent public sphere within which the novel self-consciously positions itself. When David attends a play, he is taken aback by the chatter of the critics in the audience, who are unable to watch the play "owing to Envy and Anger at another's Superiority of Parts."[40] It is telling that Fielding here points out that the critics fail to watch the actors on the stage. David, trying to enjoy what the theater company presents, is distracted by whistles, catcalls, groans, hollowing, beating with sticks, and clapping with hands from members of the audience.[41] Critics are not there to enjoy the play but rather to use the occasion to compete with one another, another mode of 'bartering for interest' in a less obvious realm. Professional critics were more common by the middle of the century, but the novel's disdain for them hearkens to older conservative attitudes toward them such as observed in Jonathan Swift's writings. This turns into a larger attack on critics in general a few pages later, when the narrator weighs in on contemporary proliferation of criticism like many before her (such as Alexander Pope, Addison, and Swift).[42] In the case of criticism, the primary medium seems not to be the problem: David seeks to enjoy the actual performance at the theater, after all. Rather, the fact that the medium allows people to come together to once again barter for their interests (this time through the less systematic but nonetheless rule-governed terrain of criticism) ruins the experience David desires to have.

The use of the older forms of media beg the question of how the novel differentiates between 'good' and 'bad' media through its conservative stance. After all, it does not write off all media as being problematic in the end. Letters from loved ones, for example, are most welcome to David. How do the novel and its sequel *as media* exempt themselves from the very problems they pose? The answer lies, at least in part, in the sacrifice of David in the end of the second volume. The various new media – new systems predicated on abstraction that render communities virtual rather than actual – destroy David and his family, but in the end the reader does not find herself believing that seeking friendship is a matter of tilting at windmills (to use the idiom quite precisely). And David is not cured of his quixotism in the end, either, for he dies. This does not make for a particularly useful model of how to cope with the newer social reality.

Rethinking quixotism and sensibility through public credit

Several references to the quixotic figure pervade *David Simple*. The narrator even suggests that David's search to find a friend, in itself, is quixotic:

> [Finding friendship predicated on a union of minds] was the Fantom, the Idol of his Soul's Admiration. In the Worship of which he at length grew such an Enthusiast, that he was in this Point only as mad as Quixote himself could be with Knight Errantry.[43]

The reader also learns that David values people in a way analogous to the foundational text in the history of quixotism, "for his Man of Goodness and Virtue was, to him, what *Dulcinea* was to Don *Quixote*."[44] These explicit references to the quixote are followed by a statement that what one reads is a "moral romance." The way *David Simple* and *Volume the Last* foreground David's simplicity places his character in the tradition of the quixote, which reminds one that Miguel de Cervantes' *Don Quixote* (1605, 1615) had a formative influence on the development of the novel.

The quixote is not merely a simple or a mad character, but one who obeys a logic of his own, a set of beliefs that differs from what is seen by the mainstream as being rational. Unlike in other European countries, the quixote was "everywhere in eighteenth-century England."[45] Ronald Paulson writes:

> In England, *Don Quixote* was read, interpreted, and utilized in a way it was not and could not have been in its native Spain or (where it was also immensely popular) in France, both centralized, absolutist Roman Catholic governments. One reason was the rise, in England at the end of the seventeenth century, of empiricism, which accompanied the decentralizing power

in a wavering economy of Crown, Parliament, and the rights of the English people.[46]

The rise of empiricism and the accompanying political transformation is not the only mechanism that accounts for the quixote in the English novel, but also the rise of a particularly English form of aesthetics.[47] Through the creation of Sir Roger de Coverley in *The Spectator*, Paulson argues, Addison refines the English quixote by suggesting that the character need not be satirical or derisive.[48] The resurgence and redefinition of the quixote can be read next to the rise of empirical method, a mode of thinking based on experience. The quixote also triggers the novelistic question of belief because, contrary to modes that tend to persuade through empirical method or description, the quixote clings to his own empirical understanding.

The quixote's understanding comes from an alternate social logic, another type of reason that may not come from the same system but nonetheless derives from experiential knowledge. Wendy Motooka writes:

> The trope of the quixotic thus prompts serious questions about the uniqueness and universality of reason. For if reason is unique to individuals (such as Don Quixote or John Locke) or to specific communities of individuals (such as knights-errants or Whigs) rather than unique in nature, then by what standard and in what meaningful way can reason be called universal?[49]

Motooka's work also makes an important link between quixotism and sensibility – or rather its pejorative face of sentimentality, arguing that

> sentimentalism is a mode of representation, reading, and/or understanding that assumes – in the face of plausible alternatives – that the empirical existence of an empirically unverified moral truth that can be denied only by those willing to be excluded from the community that testifies to this moral truth. Sentimentalists translate private feeling into universal truth, urging moral uniformity to advance a new fiction of empirical, rational authority.[50]

She also reads *David Simple* in this way, posing David's experience against the increasingly standard ideology of self-interest.[51] Motooka's work on quixotism helps one to see what systems of knowledge have to do with the modes of representation employed by a novel such as *David Simple*. However, I would like to qualify an equation of self-interest and immorality by examining the novel in the context of other novels of sensibility as well as through some of the complicated ethical quandaries that can be tied to public credit in particular.

Theorists of the novel of sensibility have almost all connected sensibility to questions of economy. Janet Todd describes sensibility as "a surplus in the economy with no exchange value," and, in this definition, Todd offers readers an explanation linking early capitalism to the advent of sensibility.[52] The emotional outpourings – the excesses – presented in these works of fiction (typically novels published in the latter half of the eighteenth century) produce a surplus value that is not able to be brought back into the general economy of exchange that now governs the public, one that I have linked to public credit in particular. That is to say, sensibility finds a way of valuing emotional excesses brought about by tangible, interpersonal interactions even if (or perhaps because) the virtual world no longer registers the personal as a form of value. Given the way public credit restructures values and recodes social relationships, it is perhaps time to rethink sensibility in terms of public credit, as well, through the various types of quixotes that seem to feature in these texts. Sometimes the quixote succeeds – and is cured of his or her quixotism – and sometimes she fails. Those successes and failures are productive for a reading of what is at stake in the novel's incorporation of the logic of public credit. It is not merely a moral attack on self-interest. Rather, it is also a pragmatic one, but one that can be resolved through a variety of formal techniques that we have come to associate with the novel.

The quixote also drives the plot of Sarah's brother Henry Fielding's *The History of Joseph Andrews* (1742). The subtitle of the novel reads "In the Manner of Cervantes, Author of Don Quixote." Many figures in *Joseph Andrews* are quixotic, but Parson Adams stands out more than the others. In one scene, Parson Adams hopes that he will be able to sell his sermons for much-needed money, "being encouraged ... by an advertisement lately set forth by a society of booksellers, who proposed to purchase any copies offered to them, at a price to be settled by two persons."[53] But when the actual bookseller arrives, Adams' understanding is revealed to be very different from the bookseller's market-driven notion of the value of sermons. Assuming that the sermons are valued for the content, Adams unwittingly reveals his desperation:

> And to induce the bookseller to be as expeditious as possible, as likewise to offer him a better price for his commodity, he assured him their meeting was extremely lucky to himself; for that he had the most pressing occasion for money at that time.[54]

The bookseller tells them that "sermons are mere drugs" and that they are worth very little, making fun of Adams' belief that they are for conveying the good and instructing mankind.[55] Despite this bookseller's opinion, Adams insists on traveling to London. Comically, it turns out that Adams' wife has neglected to pack the sermons, assuming that his shirts would be more useful. Despite all the clues from others, Adams persists in his plan because of the sincerity of his belief. This pattern of behavior gets Adams into difficult situations, ones which drive the overall plot of the novel. But, importantly, the reader is possibly able to feel for Adams. His plight may be due to his quixotism, but the reader might also understand his belief in the "good for mankind," and, most importantly, might see how his seemingly naïve conduct results from the gap between his belief and the values of the burgeoning literary marketplace, a discourse that goes back to Swift and the Scriblerians.

The novel as a whole, however, is not sentimental, for it is not Adams' perspective that is used to 'read' the story-world. Adams is not cured – he remains a comical, though lovable, figure. This is where Mikhail Bakhtin's notion of heter-oglossia becomes especially relevant to the development of eighteenth-century fiction, insofar as "the novel can be defined as a diversity of social speech types … and a diversity of individual voices, artistically organized."[56] The narrative strategies we associate with realism contextualize the sensible, quixotic subject-ivity – the individual experience governed by feeling – in order to play this per-spective against others. By contrast, works given the more pejorative label of 'sentimental' fail to do this. It is as if the forms of novels that one associates with realism are the ones whose emotional energies have a built-in mechanism for saving face by aspiring to a higher viewpoint – for seeming disinterested – very much like other modes of representing public credit. One can see this in Henry Fielding's response to Samuel Richardson as well as in the critical dis-tinction between sentimentality and sensibility.

Henry Fielding is not the only novelist to find such a higher perch,[57] as there are many attempts in the latter half of the eighteenth century. One fictional tech-nique is to cure the protagonist's quixotic sensibility. Charlotte Lennox's *The Female Quixote* (1752) is a narrative about a young woman who is raised on chivalric romances. Her beliefs about courting, grounded in the romantic tradi-tions of the romances she reads, get her into trouble when she is confronted with the more modern money-grubbing fortune-seekers who actually court her.

> By [the romances] she was taught to believe, that Love was the ruling Prin-ciple of the World; that every other Passion was subordinated to this; and that it caused all the Happiness and Miseries of Life. Her Glass, which she often consulted, always shewed her a Form so extremely lovely, that, not finding herself engaged in such Adventures as were common to the Hero-ines in the Romances she read, she often complained of the Insensibility of Mankind, upon whom her Charms seemed to have so little Influence.[58]

In order for her to marry in the end of the novel, she must be cured of her quix-otism: A cleric is brought in to help her to distinguish between the real world and the chivalric world of her imagination. In this novel, reading romances – indulging in the wrong type of media – is what inculcates a problematic senti-mentality, as their promotion of feeling over economy fail to prepare her for the economic reality that has come into being. Romances keep her in an imaginary world whose traditional values and practices no longer serve the social reality she is called upon to engage with.

Another technique is what Henry Mackenzie's *The Man of Feeling* (1771) achieves through its protagonist, Harley, who – like David Simple – fails to pro-gress. William J. Burling and Gillian Skinner argue that Mackenzie attempts to differentiate between genuine human sentiment and those of high fashion tied to the economy.[59] Burling's and Skinner's readings deal with Mackenzie's response to increasing consumerism. What they point out is that even feeling comes to be exploited insofar as Harley is manipulated into helping others owing to his sensitivity to their plight. One of the techniques for not falling into the trap of sentimentality is to ensure that the character, another sort of quixote, does not live by the rules others are increasingly governed by, including rules about how to feel in excess. Harley must fail over the course of the story, which he does when the reader learns that he dies in the end. The character is sacrificed in order to ensure that the integrity of feeling is not appropriated by the general economy of affect that turns into its more pejorative version: sentimentality. Like Fielding's *Volume the Last, The Man of Feeling* attempts to get the reader to sympathize with protagonist Harley and his traditional values precisely because he does not progress. And with him is the idea of an old-fashioned world. He is a marginal figure in a society that has radically changed. One scene makes a direct connection to the world of finance. Harley visits Bedlam, where he encounters one of the inmates who had sold South Sea annuities and East India Company stock but had lost all of his money and subsequently gone mad.[60] The lack of progress made by Harley is mirrored by the fact that the manuscript the reader reads is purportedly a found one, having been put to practical use as wadding for a gun at the time of its discovery.[61] The 'found' nature of this manuscript distances the reader from the internal narrator, producing an aesthetic effect of creating another perch. The narrative seems disinterested.

This is not quite the way *David Simple* functions. David's desire to have friends without "separate interest" is simple and goes against the grain of what seems common to the time.[62] David obsesses quixotically over finding a friend (and then a true community when others around him pursue interests at the expense of the community). His desire, unlike those surrounding him, is for people who do not adhere merely to the pursuit of their own interests, for others, like him, who are willing to invest in the happiness of a tangible community. In the end, he dies. The alternate universe of reason from which David's empirical experience derives is not (or is no longer) pragmatically viable. There are two forms of reason here, and the novel develops a heteroglossic structure in order to deal with them both.[63]

The problem with *David Simple* and its sequel is that the narrator never leaves David's perspective in order to provide its critique, which means that it becomes sentimental (in the pejorative sense) for its lack of disinterestedness. It never finds a high enough perch. But, I would argue, its lack of disinterestedness is also part of its critique. The reader is meant to take on David's mode of reason, for it is through this mode that one sees the systematic reasoning that is, at the end of the day, unreasonable. The intention here is not to recuperate a nostalgic and sentimental work for the sake of implementing it as a relevant and productive countercultural force for today's readers,[64] but rather to note that when one reads for realism, one is also reading for a totalizing discourse that came into being through a series of contingencies. The exaltation of individual interest through the idea of disinterested systems as the core logic of society, as we have seen, is something that came into being in fits and starts. A key ideological component of public credit, economic interest too has its own mythologies, ones that are effaced when one relegates the aesthetic work of various fictions to the dustbin of Enlightenment progress. Focusing on the side of the losers by rethinking

David Simple allows one to de-naturalize the social worlds determined by abstraction, mediation, and virtualization that come into being at the same time as public credit.

Toward a social critique of credit

However *David Simple* fails aesthetically, however it too nostalgically adopts an ethos that reads as 'sentimental,' it undertakes epistemological work similar to that of the novels valued from the perspective of the present to which Richetti alludes. *David Simple* and *Volume the Last* engage a critique of public credit by incorporating a discussion of finance into the plot in order to reflect specifically on the nature of credit – one mode of social mediation in a sea of social mediation. It is credit, after all, that strikes the final blow to the community. The gap between the new values propagated by a system of public credit and those of the community is revealed when David approaches Nichols for a loan using Valentine's future job prospect as a security. Nichols is astounded that David and Valentine share property. He tells David that "you don't live together now; and if … Mr. *Valentine* is a wise Man, he may think it most prudent to keep separately what he hath separately gotten."[65] Nichols, dealing only in the credit system that imagines units of individual interest, cannot comprehend a friendship based on such a standard of trust grounded in social obligation, one that does not divide up property between individuals. Calculating that it is nonetheless in his own interest to lend David a small sum, however, Nichols acquiesces.[66]

Tellingly, taking out a loan from Nichols proves fatal to David's community, not because of an actual lack of its creditworthiness, but through a gross misperception of it. David takes in a poor man out of a traditional sense of charity. After doing so, he is accused by the Orgueils and Nichols of taking in a servant (and thus lying about his financial status).[67] David's generosity to others, combined with his complacence with regard to the precarious nature of private credit, ruins his creditworthiness. What is significant is that David's financial status is not calculated by the quantitative measuring tools of a creditor. Instead, fictional hearsay (of the type Defoe describes in *The Compleat English Tradesman*, as discussed in Chapter 2) creates a collapse in Nichols' trust that David deserves credit. Public opinion, and not the auditing of his accounts, is the driving force behind David's ruin. Nichols behaves irrationally, as do people in a run on the bank, a response that entails the terrible irony that although the new system dealing in virtual credit will not tolerate the traditional, positive values of community that David had sought to sustain, it is all too vulnerable to the irrationality of innuendo that negatively marked the fragility of trust in traditional credit cultures.

David's community fails, even though it had attempted to progress by using the new financial tools that had become available. This time, the failure marks the elephant in the room: the fact that, while the virtual system is predicated on nominal and abstract values that bespeak disinterested management, it too is subject to failures through the 'irrational' assumptions that come from the older model of trust from which David's own mode of reason derives. In this way, the novel interweaves two discourses in order to test them against one another. David's mode of reason may lead to personal demise, but Nichols' is vulnerable and volatile even despite the rational financial logic backing it.

Without the security created by looking after their individual interests, David and his family become problematically beholden to those who only have financial interests in mind. Besides representing the impossibility of returning to a traditional value system, *Volume the Last* undermines the pretense that a credit system can provide the possibility of fairly competing for one's interest by revealing its irrational basis, one that has been part and parcel of public credit since its inception.

When David dies, Fielding encourages readers to "use their own Imaginations, and fancy David Simple still bustling bout the Earth."[68] After all, David is no purportedly real figure but rather a product of fiction. This call for the reader to imagine characters, or even to help the author with the use of his or her imagination, gets reiterated in various places throughout the first novel and can therefore be seen as a sort of cognitive tool.[69] And, like many novels of sensibility, the novel calls on the reader to put himself or herself in the position of the main character to restore a sense of social belonging that is felt to be lost. The novel – this time defined as a work of fiction that weaves together modes of reason or discourse – is a new medium in a sea of new media, but one that has (as Thompson suggests) the capacity to restore value to the increasingly monetized, nominalized world. When one reads the emergence of the novel in light of the rise of public credit, sensibility and quixotism seem to have just as big of a place in the rise of the novel as the emergence of realism.

By reading *David Simple* as a quixotic novel, one is asked to question the gap between the logic of the rest of society and that of the protagonist and his community. As a novel of sensibility, readers are enticed to value, or to approve of, the attempt made by David and his household-family, even though it is not viable in the surrounding economy. Some readers will deem the attempt 'sentimental' and continue to marginalize its significance. Others, by seeing the way it incorporates abstraction and virtualization into its formal structure, might be tempted to see it as an important precursor for what is to come. Reading *David Simple* and *Volume the Last* together deepens our understanding of what is at stake in any definition of sensibility. Sensibility in Fielding's novel cannot be explained merely by the advent of capitalism but by the way tangible value becomes eroded by the virtual. The sacrifice of the main character leads to the critique of this. In terms of novelistic credibility, this sacrifice means that the characters are not 'realistic,' but are rather generalized types from competing value systems. And yet, despite *David Simple*'s 'sentimental' tendencies, this sacrifice remains rational, for it (like Richardson's *Pamela*) presents a 'higher truth' regarding the loss of the tangible that ensues when virtue gives way to the virtual.

Or, perhaps one does not read *David Simple* as a novel at all, but as a simple allegory. As one might expect from an allegory, there is a moral to the story of the rise of public credit. Public credit is a key mode of "universal encirclement"

to which Siskin and Warner refer. In a credit economy facilitated by City interests but increasingly implicating the everyday person, looking out for a friend
rather than for one's interest is risky and therefore not at all simple, even if one
is not 'of' the City. The tangible community cannot make itself into the kind of
collective individual that would allow it to function through its own values, separate from the State. The City, its anxious and atomized citizens doomed per-
petually to higgle and bargain for their competing and conflicting interests, has
been transformed from a geographical location into a way of life. That is to say,
the City has become the State. The economic model has finally arrived.

Critical discourses on public credit: luxury and consumerism

In quixotic fiction, formal strategies are employed to represent different and
often competing perspectives in order to try to resolve them. For this, it is useful
to skip ahead in time to see what happens to the logic of public credit as it con-
tinues to compete with and recode traditional value systems. Warner's *Licensing
Entertainment* (1998) discusses the gradual process by which the novel became
a respectable medium. Just as today some of us worry about the impact of social
media, eighteenth-century contemporaries worried about the effects of novels,
especially foreign ones.[70] One can see this in works such as *The Female Quixote*,
in which media – romances in particular – contribute to the protagonist's misery.
Critics worried that novels had the capacity to inflame the (usually female) reader's passions or to create expectations about life that could not be met in the real
world. (Indeed, one can see this very clearly in *Pamela* and the controversy that
ensued, which required a formal reshaping of the novel so that it became culturally viable.) But as the century progressed, Warner suggests, the novel came to
be seen as respectable, primarily through its becoming regarded as more mascu-
line, nationalist, and literary.[71] This coincides with a growing acceptance of other
new media, such as paper money, which enabled consumption.

The notion that using money became important for more and more people
later in the century is substantiated by the publication of texts that helped to
socialize people in using it, such as the it-narratives discussed in the previous
chapter. One such publication instructed the public on how to use the Bank of
England. *The Bank of England's Vade Mecum; Or Sure Guide* (1782) advertised
itself as being "extremely proper and useful for all Persons who have any Money
Matters to transact in the HALL of the BANK, &c. particularly to those who are
not practiced in that Business." Inside its pages,

> every Office, Place, and the Manner of procuring Notes of every Sort for
> Cash, or Cash for Notes, is so distinctly described, that the greatest Strangers
> to the Bank, may with Certainty and Propriety do all they want, without
> being obliged to ask any Questions of any Persons whatever.

Manuals such as this provide evidence that there was an increased need for
public literacy on how to use this new form of money. The advertisement

addresses people who are not used to engaging with finance. Historians often link the expansion of money and credit to luxury and consumerism.

Consumerism and luxury can be seen as a side effect – or, indeed, an enhancer – of a functioning public credit system. Julian Hoppit makes an explicit link between the expansion of the credit economy and the growing significance of luxury, which was often blamed for bankruptcy. He writes:

> Excessive use of credit, especially when linked to over-adventurous risk-taking ... was the main way in which onlookers at the time described and analysed bankruptcy. But a second way that failure was confronted was through the idea of luxury and extravagance. At several points credit and luxury overlapped as issues.... The accusation of "luxury" was used in two ways, one which cursed the extravagance of businessmen themselves, the other which cursed the indulgence of society more generally.[72]

Neil McKendrick describes a radical transformation in the way people thought about consumption from 1700 to 1800.

> The ideas that "consumption was the logical end of production," that the "latent consuming capacity of the public at large might become an engine for sustained growth," that "society was an aggregation of self-interested individuals tied together to one another by the tenuous bonds of envy, exploitation and competition" were new and, to many, alarming.[73]

With the expanding credit economy through public credit came the commercialization of fashion, advertising, and leisure. However, the expansion of credit also came with volatility, such as the crises of 1772, brought on by stock market speculation, and 1778, when 673 businesses went bankrupt. Margot C. Finn writes that, by the 1770s, "fiscal crises had become a commonplace feature of the English economic landscape, occurring roughly every six years."[74] That is to say, contemporaries found themselves within a changing economy, both volatile and luxury-producing. While after the Seven Years War one notes fewer explicit attacks on public credit, one nonetheless observes many attacks on luxury.

The expansion of credit-money and luxury can be felt in the fictional world of the later eighteenth century. Tobias Smollett's *The Expedition of Humphry Clinker* (1771), for example, registers both of these through Matthew Bramble's hypochondriac, misanthropic tirades on money, the mixing of social groups in London and Bath, the corruption of governments through commerce, the proliferation of luxury and consumption, and so on.[75] *The Man of Feeling*, published the same year, is also an attack on luxury, as is Oliver Goldsmith's *The Vicar of Wakefield* (1766).

A critique of luxury can be detected in other literary forms, such as pastoral poetry, as well. Goldsmith's *The Deserted Village* (1770) directly laments the expansion of trade at the cost of the decaying countryside. Specifically, changes in land ownership resulted in the depopulation of Auburn, a small village he had been fond of. He writes of a correlation, "where wealth accumulates, and men decay."[76] Later in the poem, the speaker even defines the sort of wealth he is describing as an abstraction: "This wealth is but a name/That leaves our useful still the same."[77] William Cowper's *The Task* (1785) similarly condemns the excesses of the City at the expense of rural life in the first book, "The Sofa." He writes:

> In London; where her implements exact/With which she calculates com-putes and scans/All distance, motion, magnitude, and now/Measures an atom, and now girds a world?/In London; where has commerce such a mart,/ So rich, so throng'd, so drain'd, and so supplied/As London, opulent, enlarged, and still/Increasing London?[78]

The Task deliberately points to London in a way similar to how *David Simple* emphasizes the City.

These poems emphasize the abstractions of wealth and simultaneously lament the emergence of its proliferation into new forms. Novels, however, have the capacity to do much more than describe what the authors feel to be cultural decay. In fiction of the later eighteenth century, there are not so many references to the credit economy as there are to its effects. These effects are often registered in later conservative novels as forms of impropriety and corruption, ones which the savvy protagonist, as the emergent financial subject, would have to negotiate in order to progress.

Cecilia and the rise of the financial subject

It is in this general context – of a conservative critique of luxury – that Burney's *Cecilia* comes into being. But, given the role of public credit in the increase of consumption, luxury is only the tip of the iceberg. *Cecilia*, like *David Simple*, does intellectual work on the new credit economy in addition to pointing to the same problems as other works of fiction. That is to say, it not only laments the loss of traditional values like, for example, pastoral poetry does, but it also uses its formal components to offer a solution for the poten-tially quixotic character who has found herself caught between radically dif-ferent modes of reason and social value systems. Even more so than *David Simple*, *Cecilia* will employ a heteroglossic technique for evaluating these competing systems.

As though Burney were telling a joke rather than orchestrating a 940-page story about the coming-of-age of an heiress, features the characters *Cecilia* with the entrance of a miser, a debtor, and an aristocrat – Briggs, Harrel, and Delvile respectively – all of whom have the shared responsibility of managing Cecilia's fortune until her majority. She leaves her country home for London and mixes with people of fashion in order to get acquainted with her three guardians.[79] In some ways, the first half of the novel reads like an elaborate joke, for Cecilia could not have a more contradictory set of custodians of her money. Briggs is frugal to the point of self-injury. Harrel's gregarious expenditures lead to his eventual suicide. Delvile's unabashed pride in the family name repulses the sensible protagonist, preventing her from marrying Mortimer as her heart desires (until the very end of the novel). In a period increasingly marked by the financialization of daily life as well as rapacious consumerism,[80] Burney's novel questions contemporary ideas about the nature of wealth through this trio of money managers.[81] Indeed, Cecilia must learn who she should trust, whose values to align herself with, in order to secure for herself the best possible future. In this way, the novel models a financial subject.

What is most striking about *Cecilia* is not its attack on consumerism and luxury – the easiest targets for conservative critics of public credit in the latter half of the century – but rather its ethical modeling of credit and debt. *Cecilia* offers readers interested in the history of the novel a fruitful place to observe "universal encirclement" insofar as its work on credit reflects a public credit system whose existence is no longer much of a question. Commitment no longer seems to be the problem, in other words. Further, while the novel nostalgically looks back on traditional, pre-public credit values, it employs realist techniques – most notably a disinterested narrator – to do such work. Unlike *David Simple*, therefore, *Cecilia* presents conflicting modes of reason without succumbing to the trap of sentimentality. Instead, in anticipation of Jane Austin's realist approach, it offers the reader a model of probabilistic thinking that accommodates its protagonist to a financialized world.[82]

Catherine Keohane, Cynthia Klekar, and Catherine Gallagher have all discussed the way social obligation and fiscal obligation operate together within *Cecilia*. Klekar shows how Cecilia's "acts of gift giving and charity are compelled acts in response to a paternal debt – a debt that, by its very nature, can never be repaid and always is experienced as an imposition."[83] Gallagher conceptualizes Cecilia's indebtedness explicitly in terms of her gender:

> Cecilia's inability to clear this debt, like the necessity of resorting to usurers, is obviously and insistently linked to her femaleness.… Cecilia may be eccentric in believing that she owes what she owns to the poor, but she concurs with her patriarchal custodians in imagining that she owes it to someone.[84]

The lesson Cecilia learns by the end of the novel is that she had erroneously presumed economic independence as if she were an economic individual. Keohane also discusses the novel in the context of eighteenth-century anxieties regarding charity and debt, the older 'moral economy' still very much at odds with the economic model. In her account, Burney puts pressure on contemporary conduct-book notions of charity in a period when charity was prevalent.[85] In so doing, she challenges a model of fiscal obligation increasingly accepted by contemporary writers of political economy. In place of fiscal obligation, which requires an abstraction such as 'the nation' or 'the commonwealth' of public credit in order to function virtually, Burney's novel will insist on maintaining social obligation. But the novel does this by combining the two systems: Money management (and not land) is now king, but it is revalued in terms of how it might benefit immediate social connections. This might seem familiar at this stage, for this is the move that *David Simple* makes, as well. Only this time, the strategy works and the hero progresses rather than succumbs to her demise. In other words, *Cecilia* accommodates an ethic of fiscal obligation to that of social obligation.

Briggs, Harrel, and Delvile provide three examples – three discourses – on how not to behave. Their outlooks – which conflict with one another profoundly – represent three problematic stances on credit, which Cecilia will need to sort through and evaluate in order to discover her way forward. Briggs, the miser, takes pleasure in the management of Cecilia's money, so much so that he is upset when he is discharged of the responsibility:

> [U]pon inspecting his accounts, they were all found clear and exact, and his desire to retain his power over her fortune, proved to have no other motive than a love of money so potent, that to manage it, even for another, gave him a satisfaction he knew not how to relinquish.[86]

At first glance, it may seem as if the passage resembles Defoe's virtuous gentleman tradesman. However, this is complicated by Briggs' household management style in other passages. Briggs' affective relationship to the double-entry accounting balance, a quantity that gets its value from a virtual system, means that he is so frugal that his home, despite his own financial security, is drab and unpleasant.[87] Briggs is so enamored with numbers that he does not seem to differentiate between his own property and that of his charge, and Cecilia cannot even bear to stay in Briggs' filthy, shabby home. Briggs, like the people of the Royal Exchange represented in *David Simple*, is obsessed with abstraction to the degree that his practices fail to function effectively. He is what would happen if public credit really were based purely on double-entry bookkeeping. And yet, as we have seen, mastery of double-entry bookkeeping is nonetheless an important virtue of the tradesman. Briggs' perspective is partly what wins in the end, but the extradiegetic narrator will offer the reader further models to assimilate.

One might read Briggs' affective state as a foundation for the problem of the character of Harrel. The contrast between Briggs and Harrel is one of "meanness" and "profusion."[88] Unlike Briggs, the Harrels love only what money can do for them in social terms, to the extent that they lose track of how deeply they are in debt. That is to say, they are victims of luxury products that dominated the eighteenth-century landscape. Here, it is important to reflect on the affective, fictional side of credit. The Harrels live beyond their means precisely because they make others feel that they are able to pay by buying luxury items that frame them as wealthy. In effect, their extravagance is one of manipulating the opinion – and the trust – of their immediate connections. When Cecilia confronts Harrel over the obsession with only appearing socially affluent by living on credit, he replies:

The unfortunate affair of this morning is very likely to spread presently all over the town; the only refutation that can be given to it, is by our appearing in public before any body knows whether to believe it or not.[89]

Harrel also uses Cecilia's status in order to maintain his extravagant lifestyle:

Mr. Harrel had contracted with Sir Robert Floyer a large debt of honour before the arrival in town of Cecilia; and having no power to discharge it, he promised that the prize he expected in his ward should fall to his share, upon condition that the debt was cancelled.[90]

Harrel tries to use Cecilia and her estate as a sort of collateral on a line of credit with Floyer. That is to say, he tries to capitalize on Cecilia's social value that originates from the traditional value system.

Harrel's pattern of seeming utterly undone and then "keeping up appearances" culminates in his suicide, in which he gathers the family together for one final lavish outing at Vauxhall before he 'remits' his debts through his death, an act that D. Grant Campbell attributes to the emergent consumer revolution that created a false appearance of prosperity.[91] Whereas Briggs loves *imaginary credit* that has no bearing on the way he lives his life, Harrel loves the fact that *credit is imaginary* and manipulates his social milieu by indulging in luxuries in order to continue living beyond his means. Whereas Briggs represents the purely abstract side of public credit, Harrel represents the virtual. Harrel is the one who embraces luxury without acknowledging the tether to the real, an unsustainable mode of being that subjects the investor to inevitable ruin.

What is more, Harrel's solution to the problem of fiscal indebtedness is shown to be unethical. Harrel's actions have cheated others out of property. His creditors make legitimate claims about the lack of justice in his actions. Mr. Hobson states:

A man has a right to his own life, you'll tell me; but what of that? that's no argument at all, for it does not give him a bit the more right to my property; and a man's running in debt, and spending other people's substances, for no reason in the world but just because he can blow out his own brains when he's done.[92]

The section presents a curious ethical dilemma: Mr. Hobson *deserves* to be paid for the amount Harrel owes him, but Harrel has, through his suicide, made it impossible to demand such repayment. Cynically embracing the virtuality of credit undermines the very ethic – the rule – that grounds its abstraction through the double-entry ledger. *Cecilia* acknowledges the ledger's ethical imperative even while critiquing Briggs.

Ultimately, Cecilia's best bet is neither to follow Briggs or Harrel, but rather the Delviles. However, despite his higher social status, Delvile is presented from early on as another example of how not to behave. While the narrator describes the Harrels as practicing "unjust extravagance," Delvile in particular has "unfeeling extravagance."[93] Delvile, unlike Harrel and Briggs, places little importance on money: He only values the family name that dates back to the Norman Conquest, affirming the social connection over every other virtue. This is a starting point for understanding the ethic of sensibility that Cecilia and the Delviles share, and thus what allows her to marry Mortimer in the end. But it is necessary to register Cecilia's own attitude toward money.

Cecilia ought to be sharply contrasted to Briggs and Harrel, insofar as she only places affective value on what money might do for her happiness or the happiness of others whom she values:

> Money, to her, had long appeared worthless and valueless; it had failed to procure her the establishment for which she once flattered herself it seemed purposely design; it had been disdained by the Delviles, for the sake of whose connection she had alone ever truly rejoiced in possessing it; and after such a conviction of its inefficiency to secure her happiness, she regarded it as of little importance to herself, and therefore thought it almost the due of those whose distresses gave it a consequence to which with her it was a stranger.[94]

Cecilia experiences money as a means for fulfilling her immediate desired social obligations and connections. Money is only significant in terms of the happiness it produces in the people around her, which also helps to explain her charity to Mrs. Hill and to Belfield. This idea of money as a means for fulfilling social obligations, however, is what paradoxically leads to her own fiscal indebtedness to Harrel. And this is the case because, as Klekar, Keohane, and Gallagher all suggest through their respective readings of the evolution of patriarchy at this stage of the Financial Revolution, she too readily imagines herself as the economic individual with rights to dispense with her own money as she sees fit.

But, at the same time, the novel suggests that a traditional value system also has its merits insofar as what gets lost in financialization is the tangible well-being of the local community eroded by the abstract and the virtual. Indeed, Sir Albany's feelings toward the allocation of resources (accompanied by his notably archaic English) reflect a time before the advent of economic individualism: "Is it but on the stage, humanity exists?... Oh thither hasten, then, ye monopolizers of plenty! ye selfish, unfeeling engrossers of wealth, which ye dissipate without enjoying, and of abundance, which ye waste while ye refuse to distribute!"[95] For Albany, the rich are fundamentally indebted to the poor – the rich are mere hoarders of money who do not use it for the purpose of bettering people around them. Unlike Cecilia's debt caused by Harrel, her debt from giving charity makes a difference in the lives of people around her, even though, as she finds out, her inheritance is really not hers to give in the end.

This attitude about traditional charity, though, is what aligns her with the value system of the Deviles and is one that, once she realizes her place in a patriarchal value system, allows her to secure her future. Toward the end of the novel, Cecilia finds herself in a precarious situation, which entails even a psychological crisis. By all appearances, it seems to Delvile that she is in love with Belfield, whom she has been helping out of her sense of charity. She goes mad when she realizes she has been understood this way. Cecilia's bout of madness results from a symbolic economy that requires an imagined (abstract) form of value from the outset: namely, the mysterious workings of credit.[96] Her madness, however, helps to get the elder Delvile to sympathize with Cecilia and believe that she is who she represents herself to be. In the end, Cecilia abnegates her fortune in order to become a Delvile, placing her financial interest below her social obligations. She acquiesces to patriarchy, in other words, and the Delviles place her within their own social milieu.

The conclusion of the novel is not a simple return to older values, however. After all, the language of the Delviles reads almost like a pamphlet on contemporary banking: "[H]ow much higher must we all rise, or how much lower you fall, ere any leveling principle will approximate us with you."[97] Gallagher writes of the end result of Cecilia's marriage into the Delvile family:

> It is as if Cecilia suddenly finds herself in debt to a brood of Harrels, who are themselves in debt to God-knows-who. Her estate, like her personal fortune, becomes an abstract debit, a link in a chain of debt with an unspecified origin and destination.[98]

The novel ends with the accommodation of the rules and ethics of the new financialized world to the social obligations still prevalent, meaning that Cecilia is put in her place through an emergent patriarchy that might be seen as traditional patriarchalism having found its way into the private sphere.[99]

In the end, even though Cecilia gives up the belief that she is an economic individual, the novel nonetheless integrates a model of finance into its storyworld, one to which Cecilia will find herself subject. Social obligation and fiscal obligation are both shown to be problematic insofar as they imply conflicting value systems. The financial subject is one that can integrate both into his or her overall ethical outlook. The novel mediates between two conflicting systems without succumbing to the mass suicide of the quixote (through failure, death, or the cure). But, in this period as in the two centuries to follow, becoming the financial subject will also entail a restriction of possibilities for women.

Public credit and the rise of the novel

By the end of the eighteenth century, it seems that the State can no longer be equated with the government. Rather, the State looks more like the application of City rules to the general public and not just the citizen-creditor who had already engaged in trade or commerce. In this public, it has become necessary for each individual – each creditor, each debtor, each investor, each reader – to internalize the ethics of finance and to take on the role of what I have called the financial subject. This is pertinent to the credible commitment thesis insofar as public credit requires commitment from the State, but this commitment is no longer the commitment of a government, but of an abstract entity comprised of individuals whose interests are conceptualized as an aggregate. For the reason that public credit has always been deeply intertwined with public opinion, this requires one to address the role of fiction – and especially the novel – in the feedback loop between the State and investors. Fiction is part of the process that allows a virtual public credit system to be just that insofar as it teaches the reader how to cope with competing value systems – the tangible, personal world and the abstract world we now call the economy.

By the time of the publication of *Cecilia* in 1782, public credit was no longer a temporary solution for the nation's financial problems but rather a State institution. A year earlier, in 1781, Lord North described the Bank of England as "the public exchequer," demonstrating post-Seven-Years-War stabilization of the relationship between the State and its creditors. This relative stability also entails the integration of the rules and practices of finance into the general public sphere. The protagonists of novels are emergent financial subjects insofar as their progress or plight comes to be determined by how well they have integrated older social rules into newer financial realities. As Finn's work shows, a permanent public credit system is not without crises. *Cecilia* seems to suggest that it now behooves individuals to behave in a way that best anticipates crisis from the outset: Individuals are required to manage their own personal risks. It is their responsibility to live – and to model themselves – after the new rules of finance.

By the end of the century, to be critical of public credit is to be critical of the social transformations it has facilitated. Tory opposition in the early part of the century, which was explicitly critical of public credit insofar as it was seen to empower those whose interests were tied to newer forms of property, gives way to conservative ideology at the end of the century. This ideology should not be read in the same vein as earlier opposition, for what is critiqued is not the existence of public credit as such but rather its effects. Even in light of these critiques – of abstraction and social mediation on the one hand, and of consumerism and luxury on the other – fiction that we now associate with the novel serves to accommodate readers to the complicated social tensions created by the Financial Revolution.

The novel is another medium that is circulated alongside the various media that make up the virtual public sphere. Like paper money or other credit instruments, it mediates between people who do not know each other. This in itself is at odds with traditional social connection. What this chapter has attempted to show is that the novel's role as a social mediator has the effect of accommodating readers to a new social milieu whose existence is, at least in part, owing to public credit. The work the novel does in this context should be added to the list of traits it takes on as it comes to be seen as being more respectable – and more realist – by the end of the century. The novel is an ambivalent genre, but its ambivalence is instrumentalized through its heteroglossic approach to the contradictions it seeks to resolve. Insofar as the novel can be seen as attempting to resolve some of these contradictions inherent to the uneasy transformation from a traditional hierarchy to the "economic model," one can also say that the rise of public credit and the rise of the novel have stronger ties than previously thought.

Notes

1 Michael F. Suarez, "Towards a Bibliometric Analysis of the Surviving Record, 1701–1800, 48.
2 Christopher Flint, "The Eighteenth-Century Novel and Print Culture: A Proposed Modesty," 343.
3 Ibid., 344.
4 John Richetti, *Popular Fiction Before Richardson*, 2.
5 Ibid.
6 Ibid., 4.
7 See Jürgen Habermas, *The Structural Transformation of the Public Sphere*, 27.
8 Clifford Siskin and William Warner, "This is Enlightenment," 10.
9 Ibid., 16.
10 David Hume, "Of Public Credit," 360–1.
11 Ibid., 358.
12 Niklas Luhmann, *Trust and Power*, 51.
13 Georg Simmel, *The Philosophy of Money*, 79.
14 Ibid., 470.
15 Jean-Joseph Goux, *Symbolic Economies*, 3.
16 James Thompson, *Models of Value*, 83.
17 Patrick Brantlinger, *Fictions of State, 1694–1994*, 40.
18 See Anthony Giddens, *The Consequences of Modernity*, 83–4.
19 Thompson, 21.
20 Between the two volumes Fielding herself suffered a personal financial crisis, to which critics have attributed the tragic conclusion to the story of David, Camilla, Valentine, and Cynthia. According to her personal correspondence, friends worried about Fielding's relative poverty and ill health during this period. See Linda Bree, *Sarah Fielding*, 24.
21 Gillian Skinner, *Sensibility and Economics in the Novel*, 31.
22 Richard Terry, "*David Simple* and the Fallacy of Friendship," 532.
23 Bree, 34.
24 Sarah Fielding, *The Adventures of David Simple and Volume the Last*, 11.
25 Ibid., 35.
26 Ibid., 46.
27 Ibid., 142.
28 Ibid., 130.
29 Ibid., 28.
30 Joseph Addison, *The Spectator*, 1:292–3.
31 The moralization of gambling has to do with distinguishing between acceptable and unacceptable forms of speculation. In Marieke de Goede's reading, the condemnation of gambling reflects a moral acceptance of finance: "Over time, the attack on gambling became a means through which finance distinguished itself as a morally responsible sphere of thought and action" (*Virtue, Fortune and Faith*, 50).
32 Sarah Fielding, 79.
33 Molesworth, *Chance and the Eighteenth-Century Novel*, 68.
34 Sarah Fielding, 318.
35 Ibid., 336.
36 Ibid., 372.
37 Ibid.
38 Ibid., 252.

39 Ibid., 338.
40 Ibid., 68.
41 Ibid., 69.
42 Ibid., 88.
43 Ibid., 26.
44 Ibid., 96.
45 Wendy Motooka, *The Age of Reasons*, 2.
46 Ronald Paulson, *Don Quixote in England*, xi.
47 Ibid., xiii.
48 Ibid.
49 Motooka, 5.
50 Ibid., 21.
51 Ibid., 110.
52 Janet Todd, *Sensibility*, 97.
53 Henry Fielding, *Joseph Andrews and Shamela*, 55.
54 Ibid., 65–6.
55 Ibid., 66.
56 Mikhail Bakhtin, *The Dialogic Imagination*, 262.
57 I am borrowing from Swift's *Tale of a Tub* (1704), which uses a similar metaphor to discuss the early literary marketplace. The introduction begins by defining the marketplace in terms of competition for attention in public, which requires "*a superior position of place*" (27): "Whoever hath an ambition to be heard in a crowd must press, and squeeze, and thrust, and climb, with indefatigable pains, till he has exalted himself to a certain degree of altitude above them" (25).
58 Charlotte Lennox, *The Female Quixote*, 7.
59 William J. Burling, "A 'Sickly sort of refinement,'" 136; Skinner, 2.
60 Henry Mackenzie, *The Man of Feeling*, 24.
61 Ibid., 5.
62 Sarah Fielding, 26.
63 Bakhtin, 278.
64 Indeed, like other works of fiction dealing with monied property, it also imagines otherness through anti-Semitic stereotypes, especially when David plans on marrying early on and a Jewish jeweler usurps his intended. See Sarah Fielding, 32–3.
65 Ibid., 368.
66 Ibid., 317.
67 Ibid., 398.
68 Ibid., 432.
69 Ibid., 303, 326.
70 William Warner, *Licensing Entertainment*, 21.
71 Ibid., 39.
72 Julian Hoppit, *Risk and Failure in English Business, 1700–1800*, 168.
73 Neil McKendrick, "The Consumer Revolution," 18–19.
74 Margot C. Finn, *The Character of Credit*, 152.
75 See Tobias Smollett, *The Expedition of Humphry Clinker*, 88.
76 Oliver Goldsmith, "The Deserted Village," 461.
77 Ibid., 18.
78 William Cowper, "The Task," 544.
79 Frances Burney, *Cecilia*, 9.
80 Examples of consumerism abound. For example, tickets for sale have replaced calling cards to social events. The obnoxiously fashionable Miss Larolles tells the astounded Cecilia: "Why, a ticket is only a visiting card with a name on it; but we call them tickets now" (ibid., 24). The transformation of fashionable culture from one predicated on social connection alone is wrapped up in the buying and selling of social privilege.

81 For an analysis of the way *Cecilia* engages with the sublimity of credit, see Joyce Goggin, "Learning Finance through Fiction: 'Cecilia' and the Perils of Credit."
82 See William H. Galperin, *The Historical Austen*, 215.
83 Cynthia Klekar, "'Her Gift was Compelled,'" 108.
84 Catherine Gallagher, *Nobody's Story*, 244.
85 Catherine Keohane, "'Too Neat for a Beggar,'" 380.
86 Burney, 766.
87 Ibid., 372.
88 Ibid., 119.
89 Ibid., 273.
90 Ibid., 433.
91 D. Grant Campbell, "Fashionable Suicide," 136.
92 Burney, 447.
93 Ibid., 99.
94 Ibid., 796.
95 Ibid., 749.
96 See Susan C. Greenfield, "Money or Mind?," 54.
97 Burney, 937.
98 Gallagher, 245.
99 See Michael McKeon, *The Secret History of Domesticity*, 112.

Works cited

Addison, Joseph. *The Spectator*, vol. 1, edited by Donald F. Bond. Oxford: Oxford at the Clarendon Press, 1965.

Bakhtin, M.M. *The Dialogic Imagination: Four Essays*, edited by Michael Holquist, translated by Caryl Emerson and Michael Holquist. Austin: University of Texas Press, 1981.

The Bank of England's Vade Mecum; Or, Sure Guide ... in which every office, place, and the manner of procuring notes of every sort for cash, or cash for notes is distinctly described. London: M. Becket, 1782.

Brantlinger, Patrick. *Fictions of State: Culture and Credit in Britain, 1694–1994*. Ithaca: Cornell University Press, 1996.

Bree, Linda. *Sarah Fielding*. Boston: Twayne Publishers, 1996.

Burling, William J. "A 'Sickly sort of refinement': The Problem of Sentimentalism in Mackenzie's *The Man of Feeling*." *Studies in Scottish Literature* 23 (1988): 136–49.

Burney, Frances. *Cecilia; or, Memoirs of an Heiress*. 1782. Oxford: Oxford University Press, 1999.

Campbell, D. Grant. "Fashionable Suicide: Conspicuous Consumption and the Collapse of Credit in Frances Burney's *Cecilia*," in *Studies in Eighteenth-Century Culture*, edited by Leslie Ellen Brown and Patricia B. Craddock, 131–46. East Lansing: Colleagues Press, 1990.

Cowper, William. "The Task," in *Eighteenth-Century Poetry: An Annotated Anthology*, 2nd edn, edited by David Fairer and Christine Gerrard, 527–45. Malden: Blackwell Publishing, 2004.

De Goede, Marieke. *Virtue, Fortune, and Faith: A Genealogy of Finance*. Minneapolis: University of Minnesota Press, 2005.

Fielding, Henry. *Joseph Andrews and Shamela*. 1742, 1741. Boston: Houghton Mifflin, 1961.

Fielding, Sarah. *The Adventures of David Simple and Volume the Last*. Oxford: Oxford University Press, 1969.

Finn, Margot C. *The Character of Credit: Personal Debt in English Culture, 1740–1914*. Cambridge: Cambridge University Press, 2003.

Flint, Christopher. "The Eighteenth-Century Novel and Print Culture: A Proposed Modesty," in *A Companion to the Eighteenth-Century English Novel and Culture*, edited by Paula R. Backscheider and Catherine Ingrassia, 346–64. Malden: Blackwell, 2009.

Gallagher, Catherine. *Nobody's Story: The Vanishing Acts of Women Writers in the Marketplace, 1670–1820*. Oxford: Clarendon Press, 1994.

Galperin, William H. *The Historical Austen*. Philadelphia: University of Pennsylvania Press, 2002.

Giddens, Anthony. *The Consequences of Modernity*. Stanford: Stanford University Press, 1990.

Goggin, Joyce. "Learning Finance through Fiction: 'Cecilia' and the Perils of Credit." *Finance and Society* 1.1 (2015): 61–74.

Goldsmith, Oliver. "The Deserted Village," in *Eighteenth-Century Poetry: An Annotated Anthology*, 2nd edn, edited by David Fairer and Christine Gerrard, 459–69. Malden: Blackwell Publishing, 2004.

Goux, Jean-Joseph. *Symbolic Economies: After Freud and Marx*. Translated by Jennifer Curtiss Gage. Cornell: Cornell University Press, 1990.

Greenfield, Susan C. "Money or Mind? *Cecilia*, the Novel, and the Real Madness of Self-hood," in *Studies in Eighteenth-Century Culture*, edited by Catherine Ingrassia and Jeffrey S. Ravel, 49–70. Baltimore: Johns Hopkins University Press, 2004.

Habermas, Jürgen. *The Structural Transformation of the Public Sphere: An Inquiry into a Category of Bourgeois Society*, translated by Thomas Burger. Cambridge: The MIT Press, 1991.

Hoppit, Julian. *Risk and Failure in English Business, 1700–1800*. Cambridge: Cambridge University Press, 1987.

Hume, David. "Of Public Credit," in *Essays Moral, Political, and Literary*, edited by Eugene F. Miller, 349–65. Indianapolis: Liberty Fund, 1985.

Keohane, Catherine. "'Too Neat for a Beggar': Charity and Debt in Burney's *Cecilia*." *SEL* 33.4 (2001): 379–401.

Klekar, Cynthia. "'Her Gift was Compelled': Gender and the Failure of the 'Gift' in *Cecilia*." *Eighteenth-Century Fiction* 18.1 (2005): 107–26.

Lennox, Charlotte. *The Female Quixote, or The Adventures of Arabella*. 1752. Oxford: Oxford University Press, 1989.

Luhmann, Niklas. *Trust and Power*, translated by Howard Davis, John Raffan, and Kathryn Rooney. Chichester: John Wiley & Sons, 1979.

McKendrick, Neil. "The Consumer Revolution," in *The Birth of a Consumer Society: The Commercialization of Eighteenth-Century England*, edited by Neil McKendrick, John Brewer, and J.H. Plumb, 9–33. Bloomington: Indiana University Press, 1982.

Mackenzie, Henry. *The Man of Feeling*. 1771. Oxford: Oxford University Press, 2001.

McKeon, Michael. *The Secret History of Domesticity: Public, Private, and the Division of Knowledge*. Baltimore: Johns Hopkins University Press, 2005.

Molesworth, Jesse. *Chance and the Eighteenth-Century Novel: Realism, Probability, Magic*. Cambridge: Cambridge University Press, 2010.

Motooka, Wendy. *The Age of Reasons: Quixotism, Sentimentalism and Political Economy in Eighteenth-Century Britain*. London: Routledge, 1998.

Paulson, Ronald. *Don Quixote in England: The Aesthetics of Laughter*. Baltimore: Johns Hopkins University Press, 1998.

Richetti, John. *Popular Fiction Before Richardson: Narrative Patterns, 1700–39*. Oxford: Clarendon Press, 1969.

Simmel, Georg. *The Philosophy of Money*, 2nd edn, translated by Tom Bottomore and David Frisby. London: Routledge, 1990.

Siskin, Clifford and William Warner, "This is Enlightenment: An Invitation in the Form of an Argument," in *This is Enlightenment*, edited by Clifford Siskin and William Warner, 1–33. Chicago: University of Chicago Press, 2010.

Skinner, Gillian. *Sensibility and Economics in the Novel: The Price of a Tear*. New York: Palgrave Macmillan, 1998.

Smollett, Tobias. *The Expedition of Humphry Clinker*. 1771. Oxford: Oxford University Press, 1966.

Suarez, Michael F., S.J. "Towards a Bibliometric Analysis of the Surviving Record, 1701–1800," in *The Cambridge History of the Book*, vol. 5, edited by Michael F. Suarez, S.J. and Michael L. Turner, 39–65. Cambridge: Cambridge University Press, 2009.

Swift, Jonathan. *A Tale of a Tub and Other Works*. 1702. Oxford: Oxford University Press, 1986.

Terry, Richard. "*David Simple* and the Fallacy of Friendship." *SEL* 44.3 (2004): 525–44.

Thompson, James. *Models of Value: Eighteenth-Century Political Economy and the Novel*. Durham, NC: Duke University Press, 1996.

Todd, Janet. *Sensibility: An Introduction*. London: Methuen, 1986.

Warner, William B. *Licensing Entertainment: The Elevation of Novel Reading in Britain, 1684–1750*. Berkeley: University of California Press, 1998.

Conclusion

According to many literary historians, the English novel came into being around the same period that many financial and economic historians say commitment issues regarding public credit began to resolve themselves. Although this book has not argued for a causal relationship between the rise of the novel and the rise of public credit, it has nonetheless suggested that the coincidence of these two events is more than an accident. The particular problems of commitment endemic to the radical transformation associated with the rise of public credit illuminate some of the formal decisions taken by writers of fiction in the eighteenth century. Public credit is, therefore, relevant to literary history. Literary history, which accounts for fictional texts circulating in the public sphere that also facilitated a virtual world of public opinion, adds to the discussion of how individuals transformed themselves into the types of individuals that make up the modern economy.

As I began working on this project in its dissertation form nearly a decade ago, I found myself asking questions that needed answers from scholars outside of literary studies, namely because as I dug deeper into the archive, I found that public credit was a complex site of negotiation and debate rather than a stable entity easily attributable to modern economic principles. Having come into the world in the heartland of the United States exactly two weeks prior to the election of Ronald Reagan, an event that came with a paradigm shift in understanding the relationship between politics and economics, my first exposure to the English eighteenth century was filled with many surprises. Throughout my early life, the economy was presented as something that functioned because of our natural tendency to use money, an inevitable outcome of a human need to barter and trade – it was seen as independent of historical development, and we discovered how to treat it more scientifically during the Enlightenment. This liberal understanding might be enriched by considering the struggles of the past in more depth. What seems radically different today from early eighteenth-century conceptual outlooks is the virtualization of trust through a shared concept of money that has forgotten what this transition was like. While some describe money as a reification of social relationships, this book suggests that it might also be conceptualized as a reification of commitment.

Douglass C. North and Barry R. Weingast's provocative thesis, and the rich discussion that has ensued since its publication, has provided a way of looking deeper into some of the issues that find their way into eighteenth-century aesthetics. Upon closer examination of eighteenth-century fiction using this context, one observes a variety of versions of commitment – from Daniel Defoe's own discussion of the Glorious Revolution in his *Compleat English Tradesman* (1726) to Clarissa's use of accounts to ensure that the readers of her letters believe she is virtuous. The difference between these two versions might be described in terms of the difference between the private and the public spheres. What seems to happen in commitment is the production of a feedback loop in which an actor, anticipating from the outset that he or she might be audited, produces the standard by which he or she is to be held to account. In effect, commitment becomes internalized in private sphere contexts. Just as Defoe "domesticates" public credit through the image of Lady Credit, novelists "domesticate" other aspects of commitment through the rules and values of finance so central for the management of a public credit system.[1] That is to say, what one finds in the private sphere is an outpost of public-sphere concerns, with similar stakes and modes of representation. While *Robinson Crusoe* (1719) posits an economic individual on an island, later novels have to deal with individuals who are enmeshed in their social surroundings, which feature characters who are not necessarily geared for the world of trade and finance like Crusoe is. Reading eighteenth-century fiction through the question of credible commitment reveals very different discourses that were accompanied by radically different understandings of society.

Rethinking the rise of the novel through debates about public credit sheds light on a key transformation in conceptualizing the relationship between the individual and the whole of society. Charles Taylor says that the modern economy requires a normative principle, "that the members of society serve each other's needs, help each other, in short, behave like rational and social creatures they are."[2] Reconciling an understanding of the individual as he or she who is driven to pursue his or her own interests with that of a socially sympathetic person is tantamount to resolving what German scholars in the twentieth century called "Das Adam Smith Problem," or bridging the gap between what Smith says about human nature in *The Wealth of Nations* (1776) with that of *The Theory of Moral Sentiments* (1759). *The Theory of Moral Sentiments* begins with the statement that there are "principles in [a person's] nature, which interest him in the fortune of others,"[3] and this is often seen to clash with how many have interpreted his statement in *Wealth of Nations* that "[i]t is not from the benevolence of the butcher, the brewer, or the baker, that we expect our dinner, but from their regard to their own interest."[4] Eighteenth-century fiction, understood through the problem of commitment, helps to bridge this gap. It works as a feedback loop. Individuals may be conceptualized as being self-interested insofar as the whole of society can be thought of as a network of individuals who, through natural tendencies to sympathize, already serve to benefit each other. We become interested in the fortunes of abstract others through reading about them as they calibrate their own propriety in a world of competing definitions of property. This, in turn, allows us to calibrate our own propriety in an equally abstract economy. Novels help to facilitate a disinterested imagination of the social other, with those from whom one is potentially benefitting.

The novel provides a space for rethinking propriety in a world where there are different versions of what is 'proper to' the individual, and this mirrors what eighteenth-century political economy achieves when it addresses manners in the same passage in which it addresses credit. Sir James Steuart, for example, discusses qualitative social attributes in the same breath as he analytically describes the workings of the economy:

> Credit, therefore, is no more than a well established confidence between men, in what relates to the fulfilling of their engagements. This confidence must be supported by laws, and established by manners. By laws, the execution of formal contracts may be enforced: manners, alone, can introduce that entire confidence which is requisite to form the spirit of a trading nation.[5]

The Financial Revolution required people to behave a certain way, to model themselves after the mechanistic form of State also found in seventeenth-century political discourse. The varieties of representation entailed by the rise of public credit helps to reconcile "Das Smith Problem" by positing individual interest as a motivator of society while also understanding society to be made up of sympathetic individuals who are invested in the way others perceive them: financial subjects who have internalized the feedback loop between the State and the investor, the State being the institution made up of individuals with common interests that constitute a horizontal model of society.

Very different concepts of society (one could say: the one tending toward Taylor's "economic model" and the one which sought to preserve a vertical hierarchy with traditional modes of social obligation) was something that the novel – as a fundamentally heteroglossic entity – developed in order to be able to handle, a theory supported by Marxian literary criticism of the twentieth century, the school most prone to accounting for economic factors. These critics point to the formal features that come into being which allow one to distinguish the novel from other genres. Mikhail Bakhtin, not a self-proclaimed Marxian but a thinker who influenced many critics through his work on ideology, argues that the general work of the novel is to promote a plurality of languages and discourses over a single and unitary one, calling the novel "an artistic system of languages."[6] Fredric Jameson argues that novels resolve what is socially irreconcilable (85). They dramatize "the imaginary resolution of a real contradiction" (77). Michael McKeon conceptualizes the novel in historical terms:

> "The novel" must be understood as what Marx calls a "simple abstraction," a deceptively monolithic category that encloses a complex historical process. It attains its modern, "institutional" stability and coherence at this time because of its unrivaled power both to formulate, and to explain, a set of problems that are central to early modern experience. These may be problems of categorial instability, which the novel, originating to resolve, also inevitably reflects.[7]

The Lukácsian hero of the novel, the "problematic individual" defined in terms of his or her "transcendental homelessness,"[8] can be imagined in terms of a need to believe in a gold standard in a world where competing voices produce competing standards by which people hold themselves to account:

> The novel is the epic of an age in which the extensive totality of life is no longer directly given, in which the immanence of meaning in life has become a problem, yet which still thinks in terms of totality.[9]

In each of these theories of the novel, what makes the novel just that is the fact that it puts together different values and perspectives – what many discuss as ideologies and discourses. And this is particularly modern. What this book has hopefully achieved is to further specify a significant cultural turn by shedding light on the "economic model," with its ascendancy of interest, at the same time as the concept of ideology itself becomes culturally relevant. Doing so, I hope, illuminates some of the epistemologies underlying various viewpoints, which combine in order to be resolved in a single aesthetic object that is still a beloved part of modern – and postmodern – culture: the novel.

While public credit as a concept would gradually drop out of public discourse as it became naturalized over the course of the eighteenth and nineteenth centuries, past debates and transformations bear resemblances to present ones. In the first chapter, I boldly stated that this book was about empire. This statement can be corroborated insofar as the British model, and the financialization of subjects it entailed, expanded outwards to other nations.[10] But this book's focus has been on the way empire works from the inside. The "financialization of daily life" to which Randy Martin refers was a long time coming, and it comes as a form of "encircle-ment" just as do other forms of Enlightenment.[11] Karl Marx would define the individual who holds money as one that cannot avoid being a capitalist. "As the conscious bearer of this movement," he writes, "the possessor of money becomes a capitalist. His person, or rather his pocket, is the point from which the money starts, and to which it returns."[12] Indeed, eighteenth-century fiction, and the social processes and feedback loops contained within it, can enliven our understanding of the present insofar as financial subjectivity has become an even more defining feature of the modern – and postmodern – experience.

Notes

1 Michael McKeon, *The Secret History of Domesticity*, 447.
2 Charles Taylor, *Modern Social Imaginaries*, 12.
3 Adam Smith, *The Theory of Moral Sentiments*, 9.
4 Adam Smith, *An Inquiry into the Nature and Causes of the Wealth of Nations*, 1:26–7.
5 James Steuart, *An Inquiry into the Principles of Political Oeconomy*, 3:121.
6 M.M. Bakhtin, *The Dialogic Imagination*, 416.
7 Michael McKeon, *The Origins of the English Novel*, 20.
8 Georg Lukács, *The Theory of the Novel*, 83, 41.
9 Ibid., 56.

10 See Geoffrey Ingham, *The Nature of Money*, 130.
11 See Clifford Siskin and William Warner, "This is Enlightenment," 16.
12 Karl Marx, *Capital*, 254.

Works cited

Bakhtin, M.M. *The Dialogic Imagination: Four Essays*, edited by Michael Holquist, translated by Caryl Emerson and Michael Holquist. Austin: University of Texas Press, 1981.

Ingham, Geoffrey. *The Nature of Money*. Cambridge: Polity, 2004.

Lukács, Georg. *The Theory of the Novel*, translated by Anna Bostock. London: Merlin Press, 1971.

McKeon, Michael. *The Origins of the English Novel, 1600–1740*. Baltimore: Johns Hopkins University Press, 1987.

McKeon, Michael. *The Secret History of Domesticity: Public, Private, and the Division of Knowledge*. Baltimore: Johns Hopkins University Press, 2005.

Marx, Karl. *Capital: A Critique of Political Economy*, 1867, vol. 1, translated by Ben Fowkes. London: Penguin, 1976.

Siskin, Clifford and William Warner. "This is Enlightenment: An Invitation in the Form of an Argument," in *This is Enlightenment*, edited by Clifford Siskin and William Warner, 1–33. Chicago: University of Chicago Press, 2010.

Smith, Adam. *An Inquiry into the Nature and Causes of the Wealth of Nations*, 1776, 2 vols. London: Oxford University Press, 1976.

Smith, Adam. *The Theory of Moral Sentiments*. 1759. Oxford: Clarendon Press, 1976.

Steuart, James. *An Inquiry into the Principles of Political Oeconomy*, 1767, edited by Andrew S. Skinner, Noboru Kobayashi, and Hiroshi Mizuta, 4 vols. London: Pickering & Chatto, 1998.

Taylor, Charles. *Modern Social Imaginaries*. Durham, NC: Duke University Press, 2004.

Bibliography

Abramson, Daniel M. *Building the Bank of England: Money, Architecture, Society, 1694–1942*. New Haven: Yale University Press, 2005.

The Accomplish'd Housewife. London: n.p., 1745.

Addison, Joseph. *The Spectator*, vol. 1, edited by Donald F. Bond. Oxford: Oxford at the Clarendon Press, 1965.

Althusius, Johannes. *Politica Methodice Digesta*. 1603. Cambridge, MA: Harvard University Press, 1932.

Anderson, Benedict. *Imagined Communities: Reflections on the Origin and Spread of Nationalism*. London: Verso, 1983.

Anderson, B.L. "Money and the Structure of Credit in the Eighteenth Century." *Business History* 12 (1970): 85–101.

Appleby, Joyce Oldham. *Economic Thought and Ideology in Seventeenth-Century England*. Princeton: Princeton University Press, 1978.

Armstrong, Nancy. *Desire and Domestic Fiction: A Political History of the Novel*. New York: Oxford University Press, 1987.

Bakhtin, M.M. *The Dialogic Imagination: Four Essays*, edited by Michael Holquist, translated by Caryl Emerson and Michael Holquist. Austin: University of Texas Press, 1981.

Bank of England Archive. General Courts. ADM 30/47.

Bank of England Archive. Minutes Committee of the Bank of England. 6A30/1. October 19, 1727.

The Bank of England's Vade Mecum; Or, Sure Guide ... in which every office, place, and the manner of procuring notes of every sort for cash, or cash for notes is distinctly described. London: M. Becket, 1782.

Behn, Aphra. *Love letters from a noble man to his sister: mixt with the history of their adventures*. London: A.B., 1685.

Bellamy, Liz. "Introduction," in *British It-Narratives, 1750–1830*, vol. 1, xli–lv. London: Pickering & Chatto, 2012.

Bellamy, Liz. "It-Narrators and Circulation: Defining a Subgenre." *The Secret Life of Things: Animals, Objects, and It-Narratives in Eighteenth-Century England*, edited by Mark Blackwell, 117–46. Lewisburg: Bucknell University Press, 2007.

Blackwell, Mark, editor. *British It-Narratives, 1750–1830*, 4 vols. London: Pickering & Chatto, 2012.

Botero, Giovanni. *The Reason of State*. 1589. London: Routledge and Kegan Paul, 1956.

Bourdieu, Pierre. "The Market of Symbolic Goods." *Poetics* 14 (1985): 13–44.

Bowen, H.V. "The Bank of England During the Long Eighteenth Century, 1694–1820," in *The Bank of England: Money, Power and Influence, 1694–1994*, edited by Richard Roberts and David Kynaston, 1–18. Oxford: Clarendon Press, 1995.

Braddick, Michael J. *The Nerves of State: Taxation and the Financing of the English State, 1558–1714*. Manchester: Manchester University Press, 1996.

Brantlinger, Patrick. *Fictions of State: Culture and Credit in Britain, 1694–1994*. Ithaca: Cornell University Press, 1996.

Bree, Linda. *Sarah Fielding*. Boston: Twayne Publishers, 1996.

Brenner, Robert. *Merchants and Revolution: Commercial Change, Political Conflict, and London's Overseas Traders, 1550–1653*. Cambridge: Cambridge University Press, 1993.

Brewer, John. *The Sinews of Power: War, Money and the English State, 1688–1783*. New York: Alfred A. Knopf, 1989.

Bridges, Thomas. *Adventures of a Bank-Note*, 4 vols. London: n.p., 1770, 1771.

Brown, Laura. *Ends of Empire: Women and Ideology in Early Eighteenth-Century English Literature*. Ithaca: Cornell University Press, 1993.

Broz, J. Lawrence and Richard S. Grossman. "Paying for Privilege: the Political Economy of Bank of England Charters, 1694–1844." *Explorations in Economic History* 41 (2004): 48–72.

Bryson, Anna. *From Courtesy to Civility: Changing Codes of Conduct in Early Modern England*. Oxford: Oxford University Press, 1998.

Burling, William J. "A 'Sickly sort of refinement': The Problem of Sentimentalism in Mackenzie's *The Man of Feeling*." *Studies in Scottish Literature* 23 (1988): 136–49.

Burney, Frances. *Cecilia; or, Memoirs of an Heiress*. 1782. Oxford: Oxford University Press, 1999.

Byatt, Derrick. *Promises to Pay: The First Three Hundred Years of Bank of England Notes*. London: Spink & Son, 1994.

Caffentzis, Constantine George. *Clipped Coins, Abused Words, and Civil Government: John Locke's Philosophy of Money*. Brooklyn: Autonomedia, 1989.

Campbell, D. Grant. "Fashionable Suicide: Conspicuous Consumption and the Collapse of Credit in Frances Burney's *Cecilia*," in *Studies in Eighteenth-Century Culture*, edited by Leslie Ellen Brown and Patricia B. Craddock, 131–46. East Lansing: Colleagues Press, 1990.

Carruthers, Bruce. *City of Capital: Politics and Markets in the English Financial Revolution*. Princeton: Princeton University Press, 1996.

Castle, Terry. *Clarissa's Ciphers: Meaning and Disruption in Richardson's Clarissa*. Ithaca: Cornell University Press, 1989.

Cervantes, Miguel. *Don Quixote*. 1605. Translated by John Rutherford. London: Penguin, 2003.

Clapham, J.H. *The Bank of England: A History*, vol. 1. Cambridge: Cambridge University Press, 1945.

Clark, Katherine. *Daniel Defoe: The Whole Frame of Nature, Time and Providence*. New York: Palgrave Macmillan, 2007.

Cleland, John. *Fanny Hill or Memoirs of a Woman of Pleasure*. 1748. Harmondsworth: Penguin, 1985.

Coffman, D'Maris. *Excise Taxation and the Origins of Public Debt*. Houndmills: Palgrave Macmillan, 2012.

Coffman, D'Maris. "Credibility, Transparency, Accountability, and the Public Credit under the Long Parliament and Commonwealth, 1643–1653," in *Questioning Credible Commitment: Perspectives on the Rise of Financial Capitalism*, edited by D'Maris

Coffman, Adrian Leonard, and Larry Neal, 76–103. Cambridge: Cambridge University Press, 2013.

Coffman, D'Maris and Larry Neal. "Introduction," in *Questioning Credible Commitment: Perspectives on the Rise of Financial Capitalism*, edited by D'Maris Coffman, Adrian Leonard, and Larry Neal, 11–20. Cambridge: Cambridge University Press, 2013.

Colley, Linda. *Britons: Forging the Nation, 1707–1837*. New Haven: Yale University Press, 1992.

Connor, Rebecca Elisabeth. *Women, Accounting, and Narrative: Keeping Books in Eighteenth-Century England*. London: Routledge, 2004.

Cowper, William. "The Task," in *Eighteenth-Century Poetry: An Annotated Anthology*, 2nd edn, edited by David Fairer and Christine Gerrard, 527–45. Malden: Blackwell Publishing, 2004.

Critical Remarks on Sir Charles Grandison, Clarissa and Pamela. London: J. Dowse, 1754.

Davenant, Charles. "Discourses on the Public Revenues, and on the Trade of England," in *The Political and Commercial Works of that Celebrated Writer Charles D'Avenant, LL.D.*, vol. 1, edited by Charles Whitworth, 125–459. London: n.p., 1771.

Davenant, Charles. "An Essay upon the Balance of Power," in *The Political and Commercial Works of that Celebrated Writer Charles D'Avenant, LL.D.*, vol. 3, edited by Charles Whitworth, 299–360. London: n.p., 1771.

Davenant, Charles. "A Memoriall Concerning Credit," in *Two Manuscripts*, 65–108. Baltimore: Johns Hopkins University Press, 1942.

De Bolla, Peter. *The Discourse of the Sublime: Readings in History, Aesthetics and the Subject*. Oxford: Basil Blackwell, 1989.

De Goede, Marieke. *Virtue, Fortune, and Faith: A Genealogy of Finance*. Minneapolis: University of Minnesota Press, 2005.

Defoe, Daniel. *The Villainy of Stock-Jobbers Detected, and the causes of the late run upon the Bank and bankers discovered and considered*. London: n.p., 1701.

Defoe, Daniel. *Essays upon Several Projects: or, effectual ways for advancing the interest of the nation*. London: n.p., 1702.

Defoe, Daniel. *Hymn to the Pillory*. London: n.p., 1703.

Defoe, Daniel. *A true relation of the apparition of one Mrs. Veal, the next day after her death, to one Mrs. Bargrave, at Canterbury, the eighth of September, 1705*. London: B. Bragg, 1706.

Defoe, Daniel. *An Essay upon Publick Credit*. London: n.p., 1710.

Defoe, Daniel. *A Brief Debate upon the Dissolving of the Late Parliament, and whether we ought not to chuse the same gentleman again*. London: n.p., 1722.

Defoe, Daniel. *The Fortunes and Misfortunes of the Famous Moll Flanders, &c. … Written from her own memorandums*. London: W. Chetwood, 1722.

Defoe, Daniel. *A Tour Through England and Wales: Divided into Circuits or Journeys*, vol. 1. London: J.M. Dent and E.P. Dutton, 1928.

Defoe, Daniel. *The Review*. 1704–13. New York: Columbia University Press, 1938.

Defoe, Daniel. *A Journal of the Plague Year*. 1722. London: The Folio Society, 1960.

Defoe, Daniel. *Roxana, or The Fortunate Mistress*. 1724. Oxford: Oxford University Press, 1964.

Defoe, Daniel. *The Compleat English Tradesman*. 1726. Gloucester: Alan Sutton Publishing, 1987.

Defoe, Daniel. *Robinson Crusoe*. 1719. Oxford: Oxford University Press, 2007.

Desan, Christine. *Making Money: Coin, Currency, and the Coming of Capitalism*. Oxford: Oxford University Press, 2014.

Dickson, P.G.M. *The Financial Revolution in England: A Study in the Development of Public Credit, 1688–1756*. London: Macmillan, 1967.

An Essay upon Public Credit in a letter a friend occasioned by the Fall of Stocks. London: Carpenter, 1748.

Ferguson, Frances. "Rape and the Rise of the Novel." *Representations* 20 (1987): 88–112.

Fielding, Henry. *Joseph Andrews and Shamela*. 1742, 1741. Boston: Houghton Mifflin, 1961.

Fielding, Sarah. *The Adventures of David Simple and Volume the Last*. Oxford: Oxford University Press, 1969.

Finkelstein, Andrea. *Harmony and the Balance: An Intellectual History of Seventeenth-Century English Economic Thought*. Ann Arbor: University of Michigan Press, 2000.

Finn, Margot C. *The Character of Credit: Personal Debt in English Culture, 1740–1914*. Cambridge: Cambridge University Press, 2003.

Flint, Christopher. "Speaking Objects: The Circulation of Stories in Eighteenth-Century Prose Fiction." *PMLA* 113.2 (1998): 212–26.

Flint, Christopher. "The Eighteenth-Century Novel and Print Culture: A Proposed Modesty," in *A Companion to the Eighteenth-Century English Novel and Culture*, edited by Paula R. Backscheider and Catherine Ingrassia, 346–64. Malden: Blackwell, 2009.

Gallagher, Catherine. *Nobody's Story: The Vanishing Acts of Women Writers in the Marketplace, 1670–1820*. Oxford: Clarendon Press, 1994.

Galperin, William H. *The Historical Austen*. Philadelphia: University of Pennsylvania Press, 2002.

Geddes, Philip. *Inside the Bank of England*. London: Boxtree Limited, 1987.

The Gentleman's Accomptant, or an essay to unfold the mystery of accompts, by way of Debtor and Creditor. London: E. Curle, 1721.

Gerrard, Christine, editor. *Samuel Richardson: Correspondence with Aaron Hill and the Hill Family*. Cambridge: Cambridge University Press, 2013.

Giddens, Anthony. *The Consequences of Modernity*. Stanford: Stanford University Press, 1990.

Giuseppi, John. *The Bank of England: A History from its Foundation in 1694*. London: Evans Brothers Limited, 1966.

Glaisyer, Natasha. *The Culture of Commerce in England, 1660–1720*. Bodmin: The Boydell Press, 2006.

Goggin, Joyce. "Learning Finance through Fiction: 'Cecilia' and the Perils of Credit." *Finance and Society* 1.1 (2015): 61–74.

Goldsmith, Oliver. *The Vicar of Wakefield*. 1766. London: Penguin, 1986.

Goldsmith, Oliver. "The Deserted Village," in *Eighteenth-Century Poetry: An Annotated Anthology*, 2nd edn, edited by David Fairer and Christine Gerrard, 459–69. Malden: Blackwell Publishing, 2004.

Goux, Jean-Joseph. *Symbolic Economies: After Freud and Marx*, translated by Jennifer Curtiss Gage. Cornell: Cornell University Press, 1990.

Graeber, David. *Debt: The First 5,000 Years*. Brooklyn: Melville House Publishing, 2011.

Greenfield, Susan C. "Money or Mind? *Cecilia*, the Novel, and the Real Madness of Selfhood," in *Studies in Eighteenth-Century Culture*, edited by Catherine Ingrassia and Jeffrey S. Ravel, 49–70. Baltimore: Johns Hopkins University Press, 2004.

Griffin, Dustin. *Authorship in the Long Eighteenth Century*. Newark: University of Delaware Press, 2014.

Gunn, J.A.W. *Politics and the Public Interest in the Seventeenth Century*. London: Routledge, 1969.

Habermas, Jürgen. *The Structural Transformation of the Public Sphere: An Inquiry into a Category of Bourgeois Society*, translated by Thomas Burger. Cambridge, MA: The MIT Press, 1991.

Häring, Norbert and Niall Douglas. *Economists and the Powerful: Convenient Theories, Distorted Facts, Ample Rewards*. London: Anthem Press, 2012.

Harrington, James. *The Commonwealth of Oceana and a System of Politics*. Cambridge: Cambridge University Press, 1992.

Haywood, Eliza. *Anti-Pamela*. London: n.p., 1741.

Hill, B.W. "The Change of Government and the 'Loss of the City,' 1710–1711." *The Economic History Review* 24 (1971): 395–413.

Hill, Christopher. "Clarissa Harlowe and Her Times," in *Essays on the Eighteenth-Century Novel*, edited by Robert Donald Spector, 32–63. Bloomington: Indiana University Press, 1965.

Hill, Christopher. *The Century of Revolution, 1603–1714*. London: Routledge, 1980.

Hirschman, Albert O. *The Passions and the Interests: Political Arguments for Capitalism before its Triumph*. Princeton: Princeton University Press, 1977.

Hobbes, Thomas. *Leviathan*. 1651. Cambridge: Cambridge University Press, 1991.

Holmes, Geoffrey. "The Sacheverell Riots: The Crowd and the Church in Early Eighteenth-Century London." *Past & Present* 72 (1976): 55–85.

Hoppit, Julian. "The Use and Abuse of Credit in Eighteenth-Century England," in *Business Life and Public Policy*, edited by Neil McKendrick and R.B. Outhwaite, 64–78. Cambridge: Cambridge University Press, 1986.

Hoppit, Julian. *Risk and Failure in English Business, 1700–1800*. Cambridge: Cambridge University Press, 1987.

Hoyle, Edmond. *A short treatise on the game of whist*. London: n.p., 1743.

Hume, David. "Of Public Credit," in *Essays Moral, Political, and Literary*, edited by Eugene F. Miller, 349–65. Indianapolis: Liberty Fund, 1985.

Hunt, Tristram. *The English Civil War: At First Hand*. London: Phoenix, 2002.

Hurt, Marjolein T. " 'The Devil or the Dutch': Holland's Impact on the Financial Revolution in England, 1643–1694." *Parliaments, Estates and Representation* 2.1 (1991): 39–52.

Ingham, Geoffrey. *The Nature of Money*. Cambridge: Polity, 2004.

Ingrassia, Catherine. *Authorship, Commerce, and Gender in Early Eighteenth-Century England: A Culture of Paper Credit*. Cambridge: Cambridge University Press, 1998.

Ingrassia, Catherine. " 'I am Become a Mere Usurer': Pamela and Domestic Stock-Jobbing." *Studies in the Novel* 30.3 (1998): 303–23.

Jameson, Frederic. *The Political Unconscious: Narrative as a Socially Symbolic Act*. Ithaca: Cornell University Press, 1981.

Johnstone, Charles. *Chrysal: or, The Adventures of a Guinea, Wherein are exhibited views of several striking scenes, with curious and interesting anecdotes of the most noted persons*, 2 vols. Dublin: n.p., 1760.

Johnstone, Charles. *Chrysal: or, The Adventures of a Guinea*, 3 vols. London: n.p., 1762.

Keohane, Catherine. " 'Too Neat for a Beggar': Charity and Debt in Burney's *Cecilia*." *SEL* 33.4 (2001): 379–401.

Keymer, Thomas and Peter Sabor. "General Introduction," in *The Pamela Controversy: Criticisms and Adaptations of Samuel Richardson's Pamela, 1740–1750*, vol. 1, edited by Thomas Keymer and Peter Sabor, xiii–xxix. London: Pickering & Chatto, 2001.

Keymer, Thomas and Peter Sabor. *Pamela in the Marketplace: Literary Controversy and Print Culture in Eighteenth-Century Britain and Ireland.* Cambridge: Cambridge University Press, 2005.

Kibbie, Ann Louise. "Circulating Anti-Semitism: Charles Johnstone's *Chrysal*," in *The Secret Life of Things: Animals, Objects, and It-Narratives in Eighteenth-Century England*, edited by Mark Blackwell, 242–64. Lewisburg: Bucknell University Press, 2007.

Klein, Lawrence E. "Politeness and the Interpretation of the British Eighteenth Century." *The Historical Journal* 45.4 (2002): 869–98.

Klekar, Cynthia. "'Her Gift Was Compelled': Gender and the Failure of the 'Gift' in *Cecilia*." *Eighteenth-Century Fiction* 18.1 (2005): 107–26.

Knights, Mark. *Representation and Misrepresentation in Later Stuart Britain: Partisanship and Political Culture.* Oxford: Oxford University Press, 2005.

Kreitner, Roy. *Calculating Promises: The Emergence of Modern American Contract Doctrine.* Stanford: Stanford University Press, 2006.

The Ladies compleat pocket-book for the year of our Lord, 1753. London: John Newbery, 1753.

The ladies' own memorandum-book. London: n.p., 1769.

Larkin, Charles James. "Monetary Policy and Central Banking: The Relevance of the Financial Revolution Today." *SSRN* (June 12, 2014). http://dx.doi.org/10.2139/ssrn.2588446. Accessed July 15, 2015.

Lennox, Charlotte. *The Female Quixote, or The Adventures of Arabella.* 1752. Oxford: Oxford University Press, 1989.

A Letter to a Friend, concerning the Credit of the Nation: and with relation to the present Bank of England, as now establish'd by Act of Parliament. London: E. Whitlock, 1697.

Locke, John. *Some Considerations of the Consequences of the Lowering of Interest, and Raising the Value of Money. In a letter to a Member of Parliament.* Awnscham & John Churchill, 1692.

Locke, John. *Several Papers Relating to Money, Interest and Trade.* London: A. and J. Churchill, 1695, 1696.

Locke, John. *Two Treatises of Government*, 2nd edn, edited by Peter Laslet. Cambridge: Cambridge University Press, 1967.

Locke, John. "Short Observations on a Printed Paper," in *Locke on Money*, vol. 2, edited by Patrick Hyde Kelly, 345–59. Oxford: Clarendon Press, 1991.

Locke, John. "Further Considerations Concerning Raising the Value of Money," in *Locke on Money*, vol. 2, edited by Patrick Hyde Kelly, 410–81. Oxford: Clarendon Press, 1991.

Lowndes, William. *A Report Containing an Essay for the Amendment of Silver Coins.* London: Charles Bill, 1695.

Luhmann, Niklas. *Trust and Power*, translated by Howard Davis, John Raffan, and Kathryn Rooney. Chichester: John Wiley & Sons, 1979.

Lukács, Georg. *The Theory of the Novel*, translated by Anna Bostock. London: Merlin Press, 1971.

Lupton, Christina. "The Knowing Book: Authors, It-Narratives, and Objectification in the Eighteenth Century." *Novel: A Forum on Fiction* 39.3 (2006): 402–20.

Lynch, Deirdre. *The Economy of Character: Novels, Market Culture, and the Business of Inner Meaning.* Chicago: University of Chicago Press, 1998.

Macdonald, James. *A Free Nation Deep in Debt: The Financial Roots of Democracy.* Princeton: Princeton University Press, 2003.

Macdonald, James. "The Importance of Not Defaulting: The Significance of the Election of 1710," in *Questioning Credible Commitment: Perspectives on the Rise of Financial Capitalism*, edited by D'Maris Coffman, Adrian Leonard, and Larry Neal, 125–46. Cambridge: Cambridge University Press, 2013.

McGowan, Randall. "From Pillory to Gallows: The Punishment of Forgery in the Age of the Financial Revolution." *Past and Present* 165 (1999): 107–40.

McKendrick, Neil. "The Consumer Revolution," in *The Birth of a Consumer Society: The Commercialization of Eighteenth-Century England*, edited by Neil McKendrick, John Brewer, and J.H. Plumb, 9–33. Bloomington: Indiana University Press, 1982.

Mackenzie, Henry. *The Man of Feeling*. 1771. Oxford: Oxford University Press, 2001.

McKeon, Michael. *The Origins of the English Novel, 1600–1740*. Baltimore: Johns Hopkins University Press, 1987.

McKeon, Michael. *The Secret History of Domesticity: Public, Private, and the Division of Knowledge*. Baltimore: Johns Hopkins University Press, 2005.

McKeon, Michael. "Civic Humanism and the Logic of Historical Interpretation," in *The Political Imagination in History: Essays Concerning J.G.A. Pocock*, edited by D.N. DeLuna, 59–99. Dexter: Owlworks, 2006.

Macpherson, C.B. *The Political Theory of Possessive Individualism: Hobbes to Locke*. 1962. Oxford: Oxford University Press, 2011.

Macpherson, Sandra. "Lovelace, Ltd." *ELH* 65.1 (1998): 99–121.

Macpherson, Sandra. *Harm's Way: Tragic Responsibility and the Novel Form*. Baltimore: Johns Hopkins University Press, 2010.

Mandeville, Bernard de. *The Fable of the Bees: or, Private Vices Publick Benefits*. London: J. Roberts, 1714.

Markley, Robert. *Fallen Languages: Crises of Representation in Newtonian England, 1660–1740*. Ithaca: Cornell University Press, 1993.

Martin, Randy. *Financialization of Daily Life*. Philadelphia: Temple University Press, 2002.

Marx, Karl. *Capital: A Critique of Political Economy*, 1867, vol. 1, translated by Ben Fowkes. London: Penguin, 1976.

Memoirs of the life of Lady H------ the celebrated Pamela. London: n.p., 1741.

The Moderator 28, August 21–28 (1710).

Molesworth, Jesse. *Chance and the Eighteenth-Century Novel: Realism, Probability, Magic*. Cambridge: Cambridge University Press, 2010.

The Monthly Review; or, Literary Journal, vol. XLIII. London: R. Griffiths, 1771.

Motooka, Wendy. *The Age of Reasons: Quixotism, Sentimentalism and Political Economy in Eighteenth-Century Britain*. London: Routledge, 1998.

Muldrew, Craig. *The Economy of Obligation: The Culture of Credit and Social Relations in Early Modern England*. Houndmills: Palgrave Macmillan, 1998.

Murphy, Anne L. *The Origins of the English Financial Markets*. Cambridge: Cambridge University Press, 2009.

Murphy, Anne L. "Learning the Business of Banking: The Management of the Bank of England's First Tellers." *Business History* 52.1 (2010): 150–68.

Murphy, Anne L. "Demanding 'Credible Commitment': Public Reactions to the Failures of the Early Financial Revolution." *The Economic History Review* 66.1 (2013): 178–97.

Nicholson, Colin. *Writing and the Rise of Finance*. Cambridge: Cambridge University Press, 1994.

North, Douglass C. and Barry R. Weingast. "Constitutions and Commitment: The Evolution of Institutions Governing Public Choice in Seventeenth-Century England." *The Journal of Economic History* 49.4 (1989): 803–32.

Novak, Maximillian E. *Economics and the Fiction of Daniel Defoe*. New York: Russell & Russell, 1962.

O'Brien, John. F. "The Character of Credit: Defoe's 'Lady Credit,' *The Fortunate Mistress*, and the Resources of Inconsistency in Early Eighteenth-Century Britain." *ELH* 63.3 (1996): 603–31.

Osteen, Mark and Martha Woodmansee, editors. "Taking Account of the New Economic Criticism: An Historical Introduction," in *The New Economic Criticism: Studies at the Intersection of Literature and Economics*, 3–50. London: Routledge, 1999.

Oxford English Dictionary Online.

Pamela Censured: in a letter to the editor: shewing that under the specious pretence of cultivating the principles of virtue in the minds of the youth of both sexes, the most artful and alluring amorous ideas are convey'd. London: J. Roberts, 1741.

Parry, James. *The true Anti-Pamela: or, Memoirs of Mr. J. Parry*. London: n.p., 1742.

Paterson, William. *A Brief Account of the Intended Bank of England*. London: Randal Tayler, 1694.

Paul, Helen Julia. *The South Sea Bubble: An Economic History of its Origins and Consequences*. Abingdon: Routledge, 2011.

Paulson, Ronald. *Don Quixote in England: The Aesthetics of Laughter*. Baltimore: Johns Hopkins University Press, 1998.

Peacham, Henry. *The Worth of a Peny, or, A Caution to Keep Money. With the causes of the scarcity and misery of the want hereof in these hard and mercilesse times, etc.* London: n.p., 1664.

Petty, William. *Sir William Petty's Quantulumcunque Concerning Money*. London: n.p., 1682.

Petty, William. *The Discourse made before the Royal Society 26 Nov. 1674, concerning the use of Duplicate Proportion ... Together with a new hypothesis of springing or elastique motions*. London: n.p., 1764.

Petty, William. "Political Arithmetic" in *Later Stuart Tracts*, edited by George A. Aitken, 1–66. Westminster: Archibald Constable and Co., 1903.

Pierce, John B. "Pamela's Textual Authority," in *Passion and Virtue: Essays on the Novels of Samuel Richardson*, edited by David Blewett, 8–26. Toronto: University of Toronto Press, 2001.

Pincus, Steve. *1688: The First Modern Revolution*. New Haven: Yale University Press, 2009.

Pocock, J.G.A. *The Machiavellian Moment: Florentine Political Thought and the Atlantic Republican Tradition*. Princeton: Princeton University Press, 1975.

Pocock, J.G.A. "Propriety, Liberty and Valour: Ideology, Rhetoric and Speech in the 1628 Debates in the House of Commons," in *The Political Imagination in History: Essays Concerning J.G.A. Pocock*, edited by D.N. DeLuna, 231–60. Dexter: Owlworks, 2006.

Pocock, J.G.A. *Virtue, Commerce, and History: Essays on Political Thought and History, Chiefly in the Eighteenth Century*. Cambridge: Cambridge University Press, 1985.

Pollexfen, John. *A Discourse of Trade, Coyn, and Paper Credit*. London: Brabazon Aylmer, 1697.

Poovey, Mary. *A History of the Modern Fact: Problems of Knowledge in the Sciences of Wealth and Society*. Chicago: University of Chicago Press, 1998.

Poovey, Mary. *Genres of the Credit Economy: Mediating Value in Eighteenth- and Nineteenth-Century Britain*. Chicago: University of Chicago Press, 2008.

Povey, Charles. *The Virgin in Eden: or, the state of innocency*. London: J. Roberts in Warwick-Lane, 1741.

Price, Richard. *Two Tracts on Civil Liberty*. 1778. Cambridge: Cambridge University Press, 1991.

A Proposal for the Restoration of Public Wealth and Credit, in a letter to a truely honorable member of the House of Commons. Dublin: n.p., 1760.

Richards, R.D. *The Early History of Banking in England*. London: Frank Cass and Company, 1958.

Richardson, Samuel. *The Apprentice's Vade Mecum, or Young Man's Pocket Companion*. London: J. Roberts, 1734.

Richardson, Samuel. *Letters written to and for particular friends*. London: n.p., 1741.

Richardson, Samuel. *Pamela; or, virtue rewarded. In a series of familiar letters from a beautiful young damsel to her parents: and afterwards, in her exalted condition, between her, and persons of figure and quality*. London: S. Richardson, 1742.

Richardson, Samuel. *The Correspondence of Samuel Richardson*, vol. 4. New York: AMS, 1966.

Richardson, Samuel. *Clarissa*. 1748. London: Penguin, 1985.

Richardson, Samuel. *Pamela: Or, Virtue Rewarded*. 1740. Oxford: Oxford University Press, 2001.

Richetti, John. *Popular Fiction Before Richardson: Narrative Patterns, 1700–39*. Oxford: Clarendon Press, 1969.

Richetti, John. *The English Novel in History, 1700–1780*. London: Routledge, 1999.

Richetti, John. *The Life of Daniel Defoe: A Critical Biography*. Malden: Blackwell, 2005.

Rogers, James E. Thorold. *The First Nine Years of the Bank of England*. Oxford: Clarendon Press, 1887.

Ross, Angus, editor. *Selections from The Tatler and The Spectator of Steele and Addison*. Harmondsworth: Penguin, 1982.

Rowlinson, Matthew. *Real Money and Romanticism*. Cambridge: Cambridge University Press, 2010.

Sahlins, Marshall. *The Western Illusion of Human Nature*. Chicago: Prickly Paradigm Press, 2008.

Schaffer, Simon. "Defoe's Natural Philosophy and the Worlds of Credit," in *Nature Transfigured: Science and Literature, 1700–1900*, edited by John Christie, 13–44. Manchester: Manchester University Press, 1989.

Schaffer, Simon and Steven Shapin. *Leviathan and the Air-Pump: Hobbes, Boyle, and the Experimental Life*. Princeton: Princeton University Press, 1985.

Sedlacek, Tomas. *Economics of Good and Evil: The Quest for Economic Meaning from Gilgamesh to Wall Street*. Oxford: Oxford University Press, 2011.

Shadwell, Thomas. *The Volunteers, or the Stock-Jobbers. A comedy, etc*. London: n.p., 1693.

Shakespeare, William. *The Merchant of Venice*. Oxford: Oxford University Press, 1993.

Sherman, Sandra. *Finance and Fictionality in the Early Eighteenth Century: Accounting for Defoe*. Cambridge: Cambridge University Press, 1996.

Sherman, Stuart. *Telling Time: Clocks, Diaries, and English Diurnal Form, 1660–1785*. Chicago: University of Chicago Press, 1996.

A Short View of the apparent dangers and mischiefs from the Bank of England. London: B. Bragg, 1707.

Siedentop, Larry. *Inventing the Individual: The Origins of Western Liberalism*. London: Allen Lane, 2014.

Simmel, Georg. *The Philosophy of Money*, 2nd edn, translated by Tom Bottomore and David Frisby. London: Routledge, 1990.

Siskin, Clifford and William Warner. "This is Enlightenment: An Invitation in the Form of an Argument," in *This is Enlightenment*, edited by Clifford Siskin and William Warner, 1–33. Chicago: University of Chicago Press, 2010.

Skinner, Gillian. *Sensibility and Economics in the Novel: The Price of a Tear*. New York: Palgrave Macmillan, 1998.

Smith, Adam. *An Inquiry into the Nature and Causes of the Wealth of Nations*, 1776, 2 vols. London: Oxford University Press, 1976.

Smith, Adam. *The Theory of Moral Sentiments*. 1759. Oxford: Clarendon Press, 1976.

Smollett, Tobias. *The Expedition of Humphry Clinker*. 1771. Oxford: Oxford University Press, 1966.

Smollett, Tobias. *The History and Adventures of an Atom*. 1769. Athens: University of Georgia Press, 1989.

Soll, Jacob. *The Reckoning: Financial Accountability and the Rise and Fall of Nations*. New York: Basic Books, 2014.

Sprat, Thomas. *The History of the Royal-Society of London, for the improving of natural knowledge*. London: n.p., 1702.

Starr, George A. "Why Defoe Probably Did Not Write *The Apparition of Mrs. Veal*." *Eighteenth-Century Fiction* 15.3–4 (2003): 421–50.

Sterne, Laurence. *The Life and Opinions of Tristram Shandy, Gentleman*. 1759. Oxford: Oxford University Press, 1983.

Steuart, James. *An Inquiry into the Principles of Political Oeconomy*, 1767, edited by Andrew S. Skinner, Noboru Kobayashi, and Hiroshi Mizuta, 4 vols. London: Pickering & Chatto, 1998.

Stewart, Larry. *The Rise of Public Science: Rhetoric, Technology and Natural Philosophy in Newtonian Britain, 1660–1750*. Cambridge: Cambridge University Press, 1992.

Suarez, Michael F., S.J. "Towards a Bibliometric Analysis of the Surviving Record, 1701–1800," in *The Cambridge History of the Book*, vol. 5, edited by Michael F. Suarez, S.J. and Michael L. Turner, 39–65. Cambridge: Cambridge University Press, 2009.

Swift, Jonathan. *The Examiner and Other Pieces Written in 1710–1711*, edited by Herbert John Davis. Oxford: Basil Blackwell, 1957.

Swift, Jonathan. *A Tale of a Tub and Other Works*. 1704. Oxford: Oxford University Press, 1986.

Tawney, R.H. *Religion and the Rise of Capitalism*. New York: Harcourt Brace Jovanovich, 1954.

Taylor, Charles. *Modern Social Imaginaries*. Durham, NC: Duke University Press, 2004.

Taylor, Charles. *A Secular Age*. Cambridge, MA: Harvard University Press, 2007.

Terry, Richard. "*David Simple* and the Fallacy of Friendship." *SEL* 44.3 (2004): 525–44.

Thompson, E.P. *Customs in Common*. London: The Merlin Press, 1991.

Thompson, James. *Models of Value: Eighteenth-Century Political Economy and the Novel*. Durham, NC: Duke University Press, 1996.

Thorne, Christian. "Thumbing Our Nose at the Public Sphere: Satire, the Market, and the Invention of Literature." *PMLA* 116.3 (2001): 531–44.

Todd, Janet. *Sensibility: An Introduction*. London: Methuen, 1986.

Trenchard, John and Thomas Gordon. *Cato's Letters: Essays on Liberty, Civil and Religious and other Important Subjects*. 1720–23. Indianapolis: Liberty Fund, 1995.

Valenze, Deborah. *The Social Life of Money in the English Past*. Cambridge: Cambridge University Press, 2006.

Vyse, Charles. *The Young Ladies Accountant, and Best Accomplisher*. London: n.p., 1771.

Wallace, R. *Characteristics of the Present Political State of Great Britain*. London: A. Millar, 1758.

Warner, Michael. *The Letters of the Republic: Publication and the Public Sphere in Eighteenth-Century America*. Cambridge, MA: Harvard University Press, 1992.

Warner, William B. *Licensing Entertainment: The Elevation of Novel Reading in Britain, 1684–1750*. Berkeley: University of California Press, 1998.

Watt, Ian. *The Rise of the Novel: Studies in Defoe, Richardson and Fielding*. London: Hogarth, 1957.

Weber, Max. *The Protestant Ethic and the Spirit of Capitalism*, translated by Talcott Parsons. London: Routledge, 1930.

Wennerlind, Carl. "Credit-Money as the Philosopher's Stone: Alchemy and the Coinage Problem in Seventeenth-Century England." *History of Political Economy Annual Supplement to Volume 35* (2003): 234–61.

Wennerlind, Carl. "The Death Penalty as Monetary Policy: The Practice and Punishment of Monetary Crime, 1690–1830." *History of Political Economy* 36.1 (2004): 131–61.

Wennerlind, Carl. *Casualties of Credit: The English Financial Revolution, 1620–1720*. Cambridge, MA: Harvard University Press, 2011.

Wilkinson, Henry. *The Debt Book, or a Treatise upon Rom*. London: R.B. and G.M. for R. Bird, 1625.

Wood, Ellen Meiksins. *The Origin of Capitalism*. New York: Monthly Review Press, 1999.

Woodhouse, A.S.P., editor. "The Putney Debates," in *Puritanism and Liberty: Being the Army Debates (1647–49)*, 1–124. London: Dent, 1938.

Woodmansee, Martha and Mark Osteen, editors. "Taking Account of the New Economic Criticism: An Historical Introduction," in *The New Economic Criticism: Studies at the Intersection of Literature and Economics*, 3–50. London: Routledge, 1999.

Yamamoto, Koji. "Reformation and the Distrust of the Projector in the Hartlib Circle." *The Historical Journal* 55.2 (2012): 375–97.

Index

Page numbers in **bold** denote figures. End of chapter notes are indicated by a letter n between page number and note number.

For Product Safety Concerns and Information please contact our EU
representative GPSR@taylorandfrancis.com
Taylor & Francis Verlag GmbH, Kaufingerstraße 24, 80331 München, Germany

www.ingramcontent.com/pod-product-compliance
Ingram Content Group UK Ltd.
Pitfield, Milton Keynes, MK11 3LW, UK
UKHW020955180425
457613UK00019B/692